"You Have Nothing to Fear from Me."

I don't intend to make love to you every second we're alone."

"I never supposed you did!"

"You're terrified that I'll touch you; you don't trust me or yourself. But right now you're yearning for me to make love to you, even though you won't admit it."

"That's absurd!" Laurel answered vehemently.

"Is it?" Stephen came to her and cupped her face in his work-roughened hands. A rippling shudder ran the length of her body, and Stephen felt it. A grim smile parted his lips. "Is it?" he repeated. He stepped back from her. "You're a liar, Laurel Patterson, and we both know it!"

SONDRA STANFORD
has written nine Silhouette Romances to date. One of Silhouette's best-selling authors, Sondra will continue to write Special Editions while she and her husband raise their two children in Corpus Christie, Texas.

Dear Reader,

Silhouette Special Editions are an exciting new line of contemporary romances from Silhouette Books. Special Editions are written specifically for our readers who want a story with heightened romantic tension.

Special Editions have all the elements you've enjoyed in Silhouette Romances and *more*. These stories concentrate on romance in a longer, more realistic and sophisticated way, and they feature greater sensual detail.

I hope you enjoy this book and all the wonderful romances from Silhouette. We welcome any suggestions or comments and invite you to write to us at the address below.

Karen Solem
Editor-in-Chief
Silhouette Books
P.O. Box 769
New York, N. Y. 10019

SONDRA STANFORD
Silver Mist

Silhouette Special Edition

Published by Silhouette Books New York

America's Publisher of Contemporary Romance

SILHOUETTE BOOKS, a Simon & Schuster Division of
GULF & WESTERN CORPORATION
1230 Avenue of the Americas, New York, N.Y. 10020

ISBN: 0-671-53507-2

First Silhouette Books printing March, 1982

10 9 8 7 6 5 4 3 2 1

Other Silhouette Books by Sondra Stanford

Golden Tide
Shadow of Love
Storm's End
No Trespassing
Long Winter's Night
And Then Came Dawn
Yesterday's Shadow
Whisper Wind
Tarnished Vows

Chapter One

Klunkety-klunk! Sputter-sput! The car gave another gasping cough and asthmatic wheeze as Laurel Patterson eased it over to the soft shoulder beside the road. When the vehicle expelled its last dying breath, she muttered something unladylike beneath hers. Her angry green eyes glared at the gas-gauge needle, which still pointed with mockery to almost a quarter of a tank. Ever since yesterday afternoon she had been growing increasingly suspicious of it. She supposed she had just been lucky to stop at service stations in plenty of time before running out of fuel. Now her luck, like the gas, had run out.

Sighing deeply, Laurel opened the door and climbed out of the car. Her head barely topped the roof as she stood uncertainly beside it. A cold north wind ruffled her curly mass of coppery hair and silvery beads of moisture coated it like fine stardust. Her beige corduroy jeans and lightweight white sweater were totally inadequate against the rawness of the January day. She shivered as the sharp, damp air sliced through her clothing and into her skin.

In a gesture of disgust, Laurel placed both hands on her hips, glanced at the small trailer hooked onto the back of the car, and then, with exasperation, swung around to gaze down the long stretch of road. Of course it was devoid of traffic. What else? Why

she had ever allowed Julia to talk her into coming to
this godforsaken part of Texas was beyond her.
Already she could tell it was going to be a big
mistake. Why else would she have such rotten luck
only thirteen miles short of her destination?

She crossed her arms over her breasts in an effort
to warm herself as her gaze left the road and scanned
the grazing pastures that bordered both sides. Even
cattle had better sense than to be out roaming
around on a dismal gray day like this. All that met
her eyes were gently rolling expanses of browned
winter grass and an occasional cottonwood tree.
There was no sign of life or movement anywhere
except for weeds bowing beneath the onslaught of
wind.

There was nothing else to do but to start walking.
She could hardly remain indefinitely out here in the
middle of nowhere. With another lingering sigh,
Laurel reached inside the car for her heavy jacket,
thrust her arms into it, and grabbed the keys from
the ignition and her purse from the seat. Then she
locked the doors and, without wasting another moment on regret or wishful thinking, she set off in the
direction of the town ahead.

Surely there would be a house along the way, she
comforted herself as she took long, determined
strides and tried to ignore the insistent presence of
the cold wind. Casting her mind back to six months
ago when she had been here, she tried to remember
if she had seen any houses along this road, but it was
useless. At the time such matters had been unimpor-
tant.

She was out of her mind, of course, she told
herself caustically as she pressed onward. Out of her
mind for ever listening to Julia in the first place, for
believing that a fresh start here for them both was
just what they needed. But then, last summer they
had both been a little mad, and when the idea had
come to Julia, Laurel had been just as excited as her
sister. The enthusiasm had been contagious, and

before either of them could think straight, sanely, or logically, they had set the wheels in motion. If either one had second thoughts later, each had been too embarrassed to admit to the other that they were behaving like fools.

But Becky had known. Trust a ten-year-old kid to have better sense than her elders, Laurel thought now as she flipped up the furry collar of her jacket. That was why she had kicked up such a ruckus about the move ever since the day they had told her.

Glancing around at the wide, endless countryside, Laurel felt lonelier than she had ever been in all her twenty-four years. This was a far cry from Boston, the only home she had ever known. She had given up a perfectly good job there, not to mention friends. And for what? A dusty little hick town in the heart of Texas where she knew no one, where they would be taking a huge gamble by opening their own business. Furious, she kicked a small rock and sent it skidding across the pavement. She ought to be clapped into a mental institution, that's what, she thought grimly, she and Julia both.

She had been walking for perhaps an hour with no sign of a house in view when she heard the sounds of a car from behind her. Without breaking her stride, Laurel turned her head to glance over her shoulder. A cream-colored Buick drew even with her, then slowed to a stop.

Laurel paused as a man leaned across the seat, rolled down the passenger window, and spoke. A large black dog seemed to fill up the entire back seat.

"Hello. That your car I passed a couple of miles back?"

She nodded.

"What seems to be the trouble?"

Laurel grimaced. "It won't run without gas."

His deep-throated laughter met her ears. "You picked a fine spot and a fine day, didn't you?" the man asked. "Well, climb in. I'll give you a lift to town."

Laurel hesitated. She desperately wanted a ride, but this man was a total stranger. Every horrid tale she had ever heard of or read in a newspaper about lone females being assaulted in similar circumstances flooded her mind. There was no way of knowing whether he was a Good Samaritan or something more sinister.

She chewed nervously at her lower lip and mustered a tiny smile as she made her decision. She gave her head a slight shake. "Thanks very much," she declined politely, "but I'll walk."

"Don't be an idiot!" the man snapped through clenched teeth. "It's freezing out there, and it's another ten or twelve miles to town." The dog behind him growled menacingly.

Laurel shook her head again, more firmly this time. "Thanks all the same," she said, "but I'll manage." To put emphasis on her statement, she turned from the car and started walking briskly.

From behind, a car door opened, then slammed shut. Heavy footsteps vibrated on the pavement. Panic zipped through her. God help her, the man was chasing her! He *was* going to attack her! Laurel broke into a run, but before she had even managed to dash two full yards, she was grabbed from behind. Steel arms clamped tightly around her waist. The force was so strong that it almost knocked the breath out of her.

"Let me go!" She clawed at the hands around her waist. Then she kicked backward into the man's shin with a satisfyingly resounding thump.

"Damn it, you little devil!" the man cursed. "Just for that I ought to leave and *let* you walk the whole way!" Somehow he retained a firm grip as he turned her to face him. His hands curled around her wrists, but he warily held her away at arm's length.

In cold silence they glared at each other. The black fury in the man's dark eyes sent new ripples of terror through Laurel's body. He was so huge! He towered a good twelve inches or more above her tiny five-foot-one stature. She had already felt a hint of his enormous strength. She still felt it; her wrists were imprisoned beneath the cruel pressure of his fingers. Her fearful gaze only vaguely took in his appearance, the faded denim Levi's and western boots, the denim jacket lined with tan fur, the Stetson hat that covered his hair. It was the dangerous, angry expression on his face that gripped her attention and sent tingles of alarm along her nerves. Never had she seen such suppressed violence as she did now in the narrowed, glittering eyes, the thinly pressed lips, and the fossilized hardness of his jaw.

"Now," he said at last, slicing the silence between them, "if you're ready to behave yourself, let's get in the car and I'll drive you to town. And"—now his mouth twisted into an ugly, mocking sneer—"allow me to put your mind at ease. I assure you that you're perfectly safe. I wouldn't *dream* of raping you!"

His white-hot gaze swept over her with contempt, leaving her with the impression that he didn't think her worth such a violent effort. Laurel's cheeks stung as embarrassment reddened them. Then, without another word, the man jerked on her arm and forced her toward the car.

When he opened the passenger door and roughly thrust her in, Laurel's mouth dried with renewed fear as the monster-sized dog in the back stood up on the seat and pressed his nose close to her face. Now she was as afraid of the enormous beast as she was of the man. Again the dog growled, this time from low in his throat, and it was a more intimidating sound than the louder one he had given earlier. Laurel inched toward the dashboard, not daring to take her eyes off the animal while the man went around the car to open his door.

As he slid inside he saw her fear and snapped impatiently, "Down, Vaquero. The lady's already as spooked as a doe during hunting season."

Obediently the dog backed off and sprawled in an ungainly fashion across the back seat, stretching his

fist-sized paws out in front of him. Laurel expelled a
long breath, unaware until that moment that she had
even been holding it.

"What . . ." She licked her parched lips and tried
to get a normal-sounding tone to her voice. "What
sort of dog is he?" she asked as the man started the
car.

He threw her a brief glance and laughed shortly as
the car slid smoothly onto the road. "He's a mon-
grel, a fellow of mixed blood like his master." When
he noticed the quizzical expression in her eyes, he
added, "I'm half Anglo, half Mexican. However, I'd
be willing to bet that Vaquero has more varieties of
blood flowing in his veins from his ancestors than I
do from mine."

Laurel gave a nervous smile at his little joke and
was glad when he turned his attention back to the
road. At least he had explained his looks, she
thought as she stole a sidelong glance at him. His
skin was a sun-bronzed color, like baked clay, but it
was not so brown as that of a full-blooded Mexican.
His height, on the other hand, must surely have
come from the other side of his family. Now that
they were enclosed together in the small space of the
car, she was acutely aware of things about him she
had not previously noticed. His profile was sharply
carved; his nose was straight and had an arrogant
strength to it; his lips, no longer drawn into an angry
line, were angular, yet with an aura of sensuality
about them; his cheekbones were lean and high, like
an Indian's; his jaw was of uncompromising firmness. There was an air of supreme self-confidence
about the man, as though he knew exactly what he
was doing at all times. There was a boldness about
him that bespoke command and a ruthless expecta-
tion of always getting what he wanted, no matter
what it was. He was hard through and through,
Laurel thought intuitively, like this vast land that
had for centuries challenged men to conquer it. But
though men might tame and control Texas, she was

not so sure anyone could ever conquer this man beside her.

"So you ran out of gas," he mused. There was condescension in his manner even before he shook his head and added, "Women! When will you ever learn to be more responsible when it comes to cars? I've never yet met one who could do more to a car than turn the ignition key, push the pedals, and steer."

Fire sizzled through Laurel's veins at his insulting tone and his sweeping condemnation of her sex. "I happen to be a very responsible driver," she said icily. "I can change tires and oil and do a few other things as well, but the gas gauge seems to have broken on my car. And you can keep your sarcastic remarks to yourself, thank you very much! I've had a lousy enough day already without having to put up with insults from a total stranger!"

The man laughed, which only intensified Laurel's anger. "I see you have a temper to match the color of your hair," he taunted in a maddening voice. "No wonder you fought so savagely back there on the road. Cat eyes and fiery hair! You must be the very dickens to live with! Tell me, do you possess a husband?"

"That," Laurel said sourly, "is none of your business!"

The hateful man merely shrugged his broad shoulders and laughed again, amused rather than put in his place as he should have been.

Laurel turned to stare out the window and saw that already they were entering the outskirts of Tierra Nueva.

"I suppose you want me to take you to a service station?"

"Please," she managed through stiff lips. Really, it was too bad the man was so obnoxious, she thought. She ought to be feeling more gratitude to him for the lift.

The Buick slowed as they entered Main Street

traffic, and a short time later it turned into a service-station drive.

"Thank you very much for the ride," Laurel muttered politely. "Goodbye." Eager to get away from the man, she opened the door and got out quickly, not waiting for any reply he might have made.

A moment later she entered the service station's chilly office. A heavyset Mexican-American man got up from behind a cluttered desk. "Afternoon," he said with a pleasant smile. "What can I do for you?"

Laurel outlined her problem quickly, and she was dismayed when the man's smile vanished and he shook his head.

"I'm sorry," he said regretfully. "My assistant is home sick today, and I can't leave the station unattended to drive you back to your car." He turned his head toward the door as a cold blast of air entered the room. "Hello, Stephen. *¿Qué tal?*"

Laurel looked in the same direction and saw that the man who had driven her here had not gone away as she had supposed.

"Fine," the man named Stephen said. "How's the family, Faustino? Has the *nieto* arrived yet?"

The station owner laughed and shook his head. "Not yet. If Alicia doesn't make us grandparents soon, my wife is going to have a nervous breakdown from the waiting!"

Stephen chuckled, then waved a hand toward Laurel. "Are you able to help this young lady?"

Faustino shook his head. "I already told her . . . Juan's home with the flu and I can't leave the station."

"What about another station?" Laurel asked.

Faustino rubbed his chin thoughtfully. "There's only Mr. Whittier, and he don't do road service no more. He's getting old and his eyesight's bad. And Bennett's station is closed right now because he and his wife are away on vacation."

"But . . . what am I supposed to *do?*" Laurel asked in desperation. Heaven deliver her from inefficient small-town living! Now she was more certain than ever that she and Julia had made a dreadful mistake in choosing to come to live here.

"Tell you what, Faustino," Stephen said. "Fill a gas can and I'll drive the lady back to her car."

"Sure thing," the Mexican man said cheerfully. "Should I put you on my payroll, too?"

Both men laughed, and then Faustino opened the door and went outside.

Five minutes later Laurel found herself back inside the Buick with Vaquero breathing down her collar while his owner stowed the can of gas in the trunk.

"Down, boy," she said and wished her voice sounded commanding instead of pleading. "Good boy."

Vaquero answered by baring his teeth. Laurel wasn't sure whether he was smiling or about to taste her, but just then the dog's master got into the car and the animal was distracted. Vaquero turned his head and nudged against Stephen's neck.

"Sit," Stephen ordered carelessly, and once again the beast obeyed.

Laurel was utterly chagrined to be forced to accept a second lift from this man. He was doing far more for her than most strangers would have done, and yet she could not feel happy about it. She hated accepting favors from others at any time. But accepting favors from a total stranger was even worse, and from one who was hateful and sarcastic almost unbearable—not to mention Vaquero's unpredictability.

"As soon as you get back to town," the man told her as they headed toward open countryside again, "you'd better take your car in and let Faustino work on that gauge. He's a good mechanic and has a garage there as well as the station."

"I intend to," Laurel said grimly. She had no intention of letting that faulty gauge put her into such an embarrassing predicament ever again.

"I noticed you had a small hauling trailer attached to your car. Are you in the process of moving?" His inquiring glance was friendly, just as though they had had no conflict between them at all.

"Yes, I am." But Laurel did not elaborate. She had no desire to get into a personal conversation with this man. She only wanted to get back to her car and be on her way. But it would be rude not to say something more. Regardless of whether she liked this man or not, the fact remained that he *was* helping her out, and so she deftly changed the subject. "I'm very grateful for all your help."

His thick, dark eyebrows lifted and he gave her a frankly skeptical look. "Are you really?" he drawled. "Somehow I got the distinct impression that you would have preferred to spend the night freezing on the side of the road before accepting any aid from me."

Laurel flushed and nibbled at her lower lip. "That isn't so," she denied. "But . . . well . . ." Her voice trailed off.

Stephen grinned mischievously. "Yes. You thought maybe you'd met up with the devil himself." His dark gaze traveled from her face past her thick jacket to her shapely thighs, which were emphasized by the snug-fitting corduroy jeans. "From what I can see, you've got a very alluring shape contained in that small time bomb of a body. But, even so, I doubt very much if it's worth facing criminal charges over. Besides, I'm the kind of man who would rather have a woman who melts in my arms and derives as much pleasure from the act of love as I do. So . . . unless you're definitely interested . . . ?" He left the impertinent question dangling in the air.

Laurel's skin burned. How she hated this man! He was deliberately baiting her, deliberately humiliating and embarrassing her as much as he possibly could,

and he was enjoying every second of it! Her hand
itched to slap that derisive grin from his face.

"You're disgusting," she told him flatly, "and I
find your conversation equally contemptible."

"Hmm," he said thoughtfully. "I would have
labeled it provocative rather than contemptible, but
of course I'll defer to your judgment. I'm sure you're
much better at English than I am."

Laurel was giddy with relief when she saw that
they were at last approaching her old Chevy.

In only a few minutes Stephen had poured the gas
from the can into her tank. When the job was done,
Laurel managed to thank him again. "May I pay you
for the time you've spent and the gas you've burned
driving me around?" she asked. She unhooked the
flap on her purse.

"Not a cent." He was curt and ungracious. "The
type of payment I like from women isn't money."
Again the mockery was back in his voice, the teasing
smile playing across his lips. "Since I gather you're
not interested in paying any other way, we'll just call
it an unsettled debt, shall we?" He gave her a jaunty
salute and moved back toward his car. Vaquero,
who had also tumbled out of the car with them when
they had stopped, still stood near Laurel.

Stephen opened his car door, then turned to
whistle. "Come on, boy," he called to the dog.

Vaquero wagged his tail and then, seeming to
realize they were saying goodbye to the girl they had
rescued, he moved closer to Laurel and licked her
hand. Before she could get over the shock of his
sudden friendliness, he bounded toward the Buick
and jumped onto the back seat.

An hour later, following Julia's directions and
hand-drawn map, Laurel parked in the driveway
behind the enormous old Victorian house that was to
be both her new home and the day-care center she
and Julia would run. It was a lovely, impressive
white building, with a veranda running around the

front and sides of the house and lacy gingerbread trim along the roofs and gables. Black shutters guarded the many windows.

Really tired now from the long drive, not to mention the long hike in the cold wind, Laurel unhooked the trailer that contained all her worldly possessions except for two suitcases. Those she took from the trunk of the car. The trailer could wait until morning to be unloaded.

Inside, the huge downstairs rooms were freezing cold, made to seem even colder because they were empty and dark. There was also a strong smell of fresh paint. Laurel did not linger to take a good look around but immediately mounted the stairs to the second floor.

Julia had said the upstairs had a comfortable furnished apartment that would be perfect for her, and Laurel was relieved to see that her sister had not misled her. There was a small living room with a cushioned sofa and several chairs, a trim little kitchen that would be adequate for her needs, an old-fashioned bathroom, and two bedrooms. Laurel opted for the larger one for her own use. The second one would be good for storage and could serve as a guest room for Becky anytime she chose to spend a night.

The utilities had been turned on as Julia had promised, and before reaching the house Laurel had stopped at a grocery store for a few supplies. She deposited her suitcases in the bedroom, went back to the car for the two grocery bags, and, as soon as she was upstairs once more, headed straight for the kitchen, where she made a pot of coffee.

When it was ready, she sat at the tiny kitchen table and sipped it while her eyes slowly scanned the kitchen and the living room beyond. It seemed strange to realize she was really here, that they were actually going through with it. She had indeed cut her ties with her old life and was about to embark on a new one.

Last summer, while Becky had spent a few weeks with her father, Laurel and Julia had taken a vacation trip to Mexico. Julia had been suffering a deep depression from her recent divorce and Bert's quick remarriage, while Laurel herself had also been licking the wounds inflicted by a broken romance.

On the trip Julia came up with the idea of opening a day-care center in Texas. She had been part owner of one in Boston a few years back, and Laurel had worked there even after Julia had later sold it. For the past year, since her separation from her husband, Julia had been working in another day-care center, and the two sisters had discussed using their inheritance from their father after his death three years ago to open up their own center together. The idea was sound; they were both well qualified to run such a service.

The madness of the scheme lay in coming to Texas to do it. But they had both grown excited by the idea of not only becoming independent but also of making a new start in life someplace different. When they had happened into Tierra Nueva on the return trip, simply because of a small roadside sign advertising antiques (a passion of Julia's), the idea first took on the beginnings of reality.

They had both been immediately enchanted by the small-town atmosphere, the wide, tree-shaded streets, and the large, gracious old homes that quietly bespoke another era. Shoppers strolled along the main street at an unhurried pace, pausing often to speak with acquaintances or to give a pleasant nod to a stranger. In the center of the town was an enormous square, with huge pecan trees shielding park benches and sidewalks below. Old people rested on benches here and there in the cool shadows while small children darted up and down the sidewalks, playing chase. At one end of the square was a yellowed limestone courthouse that was over a hundred years old. Across the street from it was a large Catholic church, and on the opposite side of the square was a tall-spired Methodist church. It was all serene and peaceful, light-years away from the bustling pace of Boston. That was when Julia had said, "Oh, Laurel, I'd like to live here!" And Laurel had replied, "So would I."

When they found the antique shop, the owner, a friendly, middle-aged lady, was happy to chat with them. During the course of the conversation, Julia casually asked about day-care centers in Tierra Neuva. The lady said there were none, which made it extremely difficult for young mothers like her daughter to find reliable child care while they worked. One thing led to another, and before Laurel realized it, Julia had told the lady they might be interested in opening a day-care center in town. The lady telephoned the mayor, a good friend of hers, who stopped by to add his encouraging comments about such a needed enterprise. He, in turn, put them in touch with a real-estate agent. The whole thing had just seemed to mushroom right out of thin air.

During the next few months Julia made several flying trips to Texas while Laurel stayed in Boston at her job and looked after Becky. Julia checked out locations and finally leased this house. She had been enthusiastic when she had told Laurel about it. The huge downstairs was amply large for their business, and it also boasted an enormous backyard that could easily be converted into a playground for the children. The apartment upstairs had been an added bonus; it was perfect for a single person. For herself and Becky, Julia had leased a two-bedroom house near the outskirts of town. She had told Laurel that both houses belonged to the same owner, a man who had been most cooperative and helpful concerning necessary renovations and changes. So now all that remained was to settle in, set up operations, and begin.

Laurel drained the rest of her cup of coffee and stood up. She was hungry now that she had time to think about it. But first, above all else, she wanted to enjoy a long, relaxing hot bath. Afterward she would heat a can of soup for her supper.

She soon had the bathroom warm and cozy with its heater going and went to the bedroom and pulled out her nightgown from one of the suitcases. But when she walked into the living room again, she realized that though the kitchen, because of the stove burners, and the bath, with its heater, were both warm, the remainder of the apartment was freezing. Her teeth chattered as she tossed the gown across the back of the sofa.

There was a wall heater on one of the living-room walls, but when she turned the ON dial, nothing happened. Laurel knelt on the floor and removed the front panel, then peered inside. No tiny telltale blue flame was visible. The pilot light had not been lit. With a sigh of disappointment, she rocked back on her heels and began to study the printed directions glued inside the panel door she had removed.

Twenty minutes later, with about ten or twelve burnt kitchen matches littering a saucer beside her knee, the pilot remained unlit. A knock on the door that led to the outside stairs startled Laurel. She got to her feet, wondering who it could possibly be. Julia and Becky weren't due to arrive until sometime tomorrow.

She opened the door. Frigid outside air stole into the already icy room, but Laurel didn't notice it. She was speechless as she stared at the man she had encountered earlier in the day. Beside him stood Vaquero.

The man seemed just as surprised to see her. His dark eyes narrowed. "Are *you* Miss Patterson?"

Laurel nodded. "What are you doing here?" she asked with swift suspicion.

"I'm the owner of this house," he answered. A sudden twitch of amusement tugged at his lips.

"Mr. Tanner?" He got no answering smile from Laurel as she stared incredulously at him. This *couldn't* be the kind, helpful man Julia had described.

Stephen Tanner nodded. "The same. You don't look much like your sister, you know. Or act like her, either, come to think of it," he mused, obviously referring to their earlier meeting today. "I would never have guessed you were related."

Laurel was beginning to get chilled again with the door standing wide open. Impatient, she ignored his comments and said, "Do you mind telling me why you came? It's very cold with the door open."

"Then how about inviting me in?" he suggested blandly. "I sent one of my men over earlier to check the heaters and stove. He said he lit the pilot on the kitchen stove and the hot-water heater but thought maybe he had forgotten to do the wall heater. Since it's hard to light sometimes, I came to do it for you . . . unless you'd prefer to be cold all night?"

Laurel wavered for only a fraction of an instant, then gave her head a shake. "There's no need for you to trouble yourself, Mr. Tanner. I can easily do it myself."

The man did not bother to respond. Before Laurel realized what was happening, he had thrust her aside and entered the apartment. Vaquero, naturally, trotted at his heels, and his large size made the comfortably sized room suddenly seem small and crowded.

Stephen Tanner knelt in front of the wall furnace, noted the stack of burnt matches in the saucer, and grinned up at her.

"Easily?" he taunted.

Laurel cringed inwardly. It wasn't fair that she, who above all wanted to be free and independent of the entire male sex, should be continually forced to endure this man's aid and his mocking, superior attitude. Everything about him—his virile, rugged good looks, his supreme confidence in himself, his supercilious behavior toward her—screamed of the much overworked macho image. Now she understood the term with razor-sharp clarity, and a premonition quivered through her.

Today's encounters with Stephen Tanner were only the first of many conflicts ahead. Laurel was as certain of it as anything in life. Coming here *had* been a dreadful mistake! But now she was committed. It was too late to back out.

Chapter Two

$\mathcal{T}$ he next morning Laurel was up early. She had a busy day ahead, and there was no time to waste lolling in the exquisitely warm bed, no matter how strong the inclination. She went into the kitchen, put a kettle of water on to boil, then shuttled back to the bedroom to dress in jeans and an old blue sweater. She paid scant attention this morning to her appearance beyond running a brush through her thick crop of tangled curls and applying a coat of lipstick to her mouth.

Back in the kitchen, she fixed herself a couple of slices of toast while the coffee dripped, and then sat down to eat. While she buttered the toast her mind clicked off what needed to be done today in order of priority. First she would begin unloading the trailer, which was going to be a huge job in itself. She little relished all the trips up and down the stairs she would have to make. Then, sometime this morning their day-care furniture would be arriving from San Antonio, and she would need to tell the men where to place everything.

Laurel ate hurriedly and cast a longing glance at the coffeepot. Not allowing herself the luxury of a second cup now, she went through to the living room, picked up her jacket, and slipped into it.

An hour later she had hauled every box up the

stairs and piled them in the living room to be unpacked whenever she could spare the time. The only thing she had not carried was her portable television set, because it was too heavy. But when the furniture delivery men arrived and she hesitantly asked, they cheerfully took it upstairs for her.

By the time the men had left, several of the downstairs rooms had taken on an air of purpose. The large main room now boasted low shelves along two walls, which would house learning materials; the center of the room had a number of child-sized tables and chairs. Other rooms contained beds, the sizes ranging from cribs to junior-sized beds. Monday the kitchen equipment and office furniture would be delivered from another firm.

Laurel returned upstairs and heated herself a well-deserved second cup of coffee. After drinking it, she took from the refrigerator lunch meat and cheese she had bought the previous afternoon. With efficient motions she put together several sandwiches, wrapped them, and put them inside a paper bag along with a package of chips, several chilled cans of soft drinks, and a thermos of fresh coffee.

When she was ready, she carried the bag down the stairs, got into the car, and backed out of the drive. A small brown dog dashed across the street and vanished behind a bush, and the sight reminded Laurel of the huge dog yesterday. And his owner.

Her delicately feathered eyebrows puckered into a frown of distaste, and she wished she had not remembered Stephen Tanner today. There was something about him that grated on her nerves and brought out the worst in her, even though, contrarily, her senses were sharply attuned to the magnetic appeal of him. No one could ever accuse him of being a classically handsome man; indeed, the notion was absurd. But, all the same, there was some earthy quality about him that clamored to be acknowledged by her wayward feminine consciousness, and she very much resented that. At this point in her life she was unwilling to be attracted to any man . . . and most certainly not to one she did not even like!

Laurel's face scalded as she remembered him last evening when he had pushed his way into the apartment and arrogantly taken over the chore of lighting the wall heater. It had taken him scarcely a minute to do it. When he had finished and stood up, amusement had lurked in his coffee-colored eyes as they swept from her filmy blue nightgown, which was draped across the back of the sofa like a bold banner, to her face.

"Now," he had said, with a hint of laughter thickening his voice, "you can slip into that piece of nothing there and still be warm enough to sleep alone in your bed tonight. Or do passionate dreams warm you instead?"

With great effort, Laurel thrust away all thoughts of him. He was the most disturbing and exasperating man she had ever met. If she let her mind dwell upon him, she would soon be suffering from high blood pressure!

She had no trouble finding the house that was to become Julia and Becky's new home. Julia had drawn her an explicit map for that, too. As she turned onto a pleasant, tree-lined street, she saw that they had indeed arrived and that the moving van was also there.

Laurel parked her car in the driveway behind Julia's blue Volkswagen and a moment later crossed the lawn toward the house. Julia came out along with two men, and she smiled wearily when she spotted Laurel.

"Thank you for everything," she said to the men.

"Sure thing," one of them replied as the other tipped his hat. Both men strode toward the van and climbed into the cab.

"Are they all finished?" Laurel asked.

Julia nodded. "Just this minute. Becky and I arrived at eight, and it's a good thing we got such an early start. They were here before nine, and I hadn't expected them until this afternoon. Did the nursery furniture come?"

Laurel answered even as she noted how tired her sister appeared. At thirty, Julia was still as lovely as she had been on her wedding day twelve years ago. But today fatigue filmed her hazel eyes, and fine tiny lines radiated across her skin outward from the edge of her eyelids. Her short, wavy brown hair was mussed, as though she had not even found time to comb it. Although she was at least three inches taller and twenty pounds heavier than Laurel, somehow she always conveyed an impression of delicacy, at times even a sense of helplessness that Laurel had always lacked. Now, as they stepped into the house and stood amid mountains of stacked boxes, Julia's slender hands fluttered as she indicated all the disorder around them.

"It's total chaos," she said, grimacing. "I doubt if I'll ever find a place to put everything."

Laurel laughed. "The apartment looks just as bad. But let's forget work for a while. I brought some sandwiches for lunch. Where's Becky?"

"Here I am." A pretty ten-year-old girl came out of one of the bedrooms. She wore faded jeans and a brown plaid long-sleeved shirt with the tail flapping loosely below her waist. Her long, silky golden hair swung free and unrestricted against her shoulders, and on her face was a fierce scowl. "What am I supposed to do about my stereo?" she demanded of her mother. "There aren't any shelves in my room, and I don't have anyplace to put it or the speakers."

"We'll put some up later," a harried Julia assured her. "Come on, Becky, let's eat. Laurel brought some sandwiches."

Becky tripped over a small box on the floor that she hadn't noticed. As she picked herself up and gingerly rubbed a thigh she grumbled, "I hate this place! I don't *want* to live here!"

Julia pressed her lips together into a tight line.

"Let's not go into that again, please!" she said, with just an edge of sharpness in her voice. She removed the grocery bag from Laurel's arms and went into the kitchen.

Laurel waited until Becky reached her, then lightly draped her arm across her niece's shoulders. "Hey, pal," she said in a low voice. "It's not so bad. This seems like a nice house, and once you and your mom get it fixed up to suit yourselves, you'll enjoy it. And you'll soon make new friends at school. In no time at all we'll probably like small-town living so much we won't even miss Boston."

"I will," Becky stated uncompromisingly. "I *do* miss it!" She jerked herself away from Laurel's touch. "This is a dumb place, and I *hate* it!"

Lunch was not a pleasant affair. Becky sulked and merely nibbled at her food. Laurel sympathized with her unhappiness, but, all the same, she couldn't help being a little irritated with her, too. Life was difficult enough for Julia these days without her daughter's making things even harder for her.

With lunch over, Becky found a sweater, shoved her arms into it, and went outside, to no one's objection. When the door was firmly closed behind her, Julia gave a shuddering sigh.

"She's been like that ever since we left Boston. She was miserable enough about making this move, as you know. But, to make things worse, Bert had promised to spend our last evening there with her, and he didn't come. He didn't," she added bitterly, "even call her to say goodbye."

At that moment Laurel felt she could cheerfully have murdered her ex-brother-in-law. "How could he do that to her?" she asked indignantly. "How could he hurt his own daughter like that?"

Julia managed a wan smile. "It's been a long time," she reminded her sister, "since either of us came first in his life."

As if Laurel could forget! But it was something she would never forget . . . Bert, the handsome, charming husband of her sister, the adoring father of Becky, abruptly smashing their lives to bits. Even now Laurel still felt the shock of disbelief that Bert Adams could actually leave a loving wife for another woman, and his own daughter for someone else's children.

"She'll be better off here," she said now. "Here she won't expect to see her father and then have to suffer from his broken promises."

"I hope you're right," Julia said, but doubt and anxiety clouded her eyes. "Maybe she'll be okay once she gets settled in school."

"Sure." Laurel smiled encouragingly. "You know kids. They always adjust to changes better than adults do."

Julia got up from the table and dumped their empty sandwich wrappers into the trash. "Oh, I almost forgot to tell you," she said casually. "Ken called the last night I was there."

Laurel's neck tensed and her entire body went rigid. "Yes? And what newsworthy conversation did he have to discuss? All his latest girl friends?"

Julia gave her a reproving look. "Don't be like that," she said. "I hate it when you're trying to be flippant and sarcastic. It isn't you."

Laurel ignored the lecture and got back to the point. "Well, what did he want?"

"He asked for your new address here," her sister said mildly. She began to wipe crumbs from the table.

"You didn't give it to him, did you?" Laurel asked sharply.

Julia was careful to avoid her eyes. "Yes, I did. I couldn't see any harm in it."

"No harm?" Laurel got to her feet, her breasts heaving beneath the sweater she wore as she glared at her sister. "You know I'm done with him, Julia! That's what this move is all about, isn't it? To get away from the men who hurt us both?"

Julia shrugged. "For me it is, but I have no

choice," she said in a quiet, accepting voice. "Bert wanted the divorce, and now he's remarried. That part of my life is over for good. But for you it's different. Ever since you broke your engagement Ken has been trying to apologize, to make things up. He really loves you, Laurel, and I believe you should think long and hard before you turn your back on that."

Laurel sniffed. *"Love!* Ken's good at that game and he likes to spread it out far and wide. He was cheating on me while we were engaged, so how can you believe we could ever have had a successful marriage? Look at you! You thought that was what you had all along. But after almost eleven years you found out how wrong you were! As far as I'm concerned, no man can be trusted! They're all unfaithful, and I want no part of them!"

"You know, Laurel," Julia said, "these last few months you've become . . ."

Whatever she had been about to say was drowned out by the sound of the front door opening and Becky shouting, "Mom? We've got company!"

Julia's startled gaze flew to Laurel's, and then both of them hurried into the cluttered living room.

"Oh, Mr. Tanner," Julia sang out cheerfully when she saw the tall figure blocking the doorway. "How nice to see you again."

"It's nice to see you again, too, Mrs. Adams," Stephen Tanner said with an easy smile as they shook hands. He inclined his head toward Becky, who stood beside him. "I recognized your daughter at once. She's as pretty as her mother."

A slight flush stained Julia's cheeks, and Becky was glowing at the compliment as well. "Thank you very much," Julia said demurely. Turning toward Laurel, she beckoned her to come forward, and Laurel did so most reluctantly while her sister performed the introductions.

"We've met," Stephen Tanner said as his amused brown eyes acknowledged Laurel.

Coolly, Laurel gave an almost imperceptible nod to him, but she said nothing. She resented the laughing way he was regarding her, as though they shared some intimate joke together.

"You've met?" Julia asked with obvious puzzlement.

Stephen grinned broadly. "I believe she thinks I'm the devil of Texas and that Vaquero is my first assistant."

"Devil?" Julia repeated in thorough bewilderment. "And who is Vaquero?"

"That's his dog," Becky volunteered. "He's outside. Is it okay if I play with him, Stephen?"

"Becky!" Her mother's voice was scandalized. "His name is Mr. Tanner."

"I told her to call me by my first name," he intervened with a flashing smile at Julia. "You must do so, too. You'll find we don't stand on a lot of ceremony here." Then he answered Becky's question. "Sure, you can play with Vaquero. He *likes* girls." A teasing glint lit his eyes as he glanced deliberately at Laurel.

Becky went out, and, like a bee persistently returning to a flower garden, Julia quizzed, "Where did you two meet, and what did you mean about the devil?"

"I'll tell you later," Laurel promised through tight lips. She was furious with the man for coming here and bringing up the whole embarrassing episode. Yet it was hard, desperately hard, to keep on ignoring the teasing, friendly gleam in his eyes. She always had liked men with a sense of humor, but, really, this Stephen Tanner seemed to have more than his share.

With a tiny, helpless shrug of her shoulders, Julia decided to drop her questioning about how they had met. She turned back to Stephen and asked pleasantly, "Did you just drop in for a visit, or was there something particular you needed to see me about?"

His smile was effortless. "I just stopped to see

whether you had arrived yet and to find out if there's anything you need, anything I can do for you."

"Nothing at the moment, but I appreciate your offer. I think we'll be fine once we can get everything unpacked and *find* everything." She gave a little laugh as her gaze traveled around the cluttered room, then back to her visitor. "Do you have time for a cup of coffee?"

To Laurel's dismay, he accepted, and soon the three of them sat around the kitchen table facing one another.

"Sorry I can't entertain you in the living room," Julia apologized, referring to the sofa and chairs stacked haphazardly with boxes and a miscellaneous assortment of lamps, wall hangings, and the like. "You'll have to come back again when we're settled in properly."

"I will," Stephen promised. "We'll give you time to get organized, and then we'll have a party so you can meet some of our local citizens and make some new friends."

Julia's eyes sparkled. "That sounds lovely, doesn't it, Laurel?"

"Yes," Laurel conceded grudgingly. "It does." Darn the man, anyway, she thought. Why must he thrust himself continually into their affairs? Here he was, winning over both Julia and Becky by his charm just as easily as most men breathed. He was being helpful and kind, which was going to make it most difficult to avoid him in the future if he was thoroughly entrenched as a family friend.

She hoped her face showed none of her feelings, though, and she struggled to appear both calm and interested as the other two carried on their conversation. But when Stephen stood up to take his leave at last, Laurel was relieved.

The three of them walked outside together to see Becky throwing a stick for Vaquero to fetch. Obligingly, he bounded toward the stick, picked it up between his huge jaws, and turned to trot back to

SILVER MIST 33

Becky. But at that moment he spotted the adults, dropped the stick to the ground, and loped toward them.

He skidded to a halt directly in front of Laurel and nosed his face against her hand. His tail wagged furiously, just as though he had met a wonderful old friend.

Laurel laughed, no longer afraid of the gigantic beast. Cupping both her hands behind his ears, she began to scratch. "Hi, boy," she greeted him. "You remember me, do you?"

"Here, Vaquero," a disgruntled Becky called. "Come back and fetch the stick."

Stephen laughed, and his teeth gleamed against his golden-brown skin. "I'm afraid you've got competition, Becky," he told her. "Vaquero fell in love with Laurel yesterday."

Becky abandoned her attempts at luring the dog from Laurel's side and came to join them. She lightly stroked his dark, silky back while he continued to nuzzle against Laurel. "Why is his name Vaquero?" she asked Stephen. "It sounds like a funny name for a dog."

"It means 'cowboy' in Spanish," Stephen told her. "In the early days of Texas, many of the ranch hands came here from Mexico and they were called *vaqueros*. When I first got him as a pup, he took to my ranch and chasing cows with such a vengeance that we just naturally named him that."

"You have a ranch," Becky asked, wide-eyed, "with horses and cows and everything?"

"I sure do," Stephen replied. He turned toward Julia and Laurel then. "Well, I must go. Thanks for the coffee, and remember, if there's anything I can do for you, just let me know."

"Isn't he the *nicest* man?" Julia asked after he had driven off.

"Personally," Laurel replied, "I could do without ever seeing him again."

"What is it with you two?" Julia demanded. "He

said you thought he was the devil, and I must say you acted like he was, too. What did he do to you?"

"Do?" Laurel's laugh was short. "He helped me." She outlined what had happened about the car and how he had come by the apartment later to light the wall heater.

"But you should be grateful to him," Julia pointed out.

"I am grateful for what he did," Laurel admitted. "At least, I am when I'm not being angry with him. It was just his attitude, his macho, superior-to-a-woman attitude. I'll bet he thinks he's God's gift to women, to boot!"

"He didn't strike me that way," Julia said thoughtfully. "It's true he's a very good-looking man, and a woman would have to be blind not to recognize that fact. But he didn't give me the impression that he might have a swelled ego. All he seemed interested in was being neighborly and helpful. You know what, Laurel? I think that thing with Ken has made you become a little paranoid where men are concerned. You don't want to see the good traits in any of them."

Maybe so, Laurel thought that night as she soaked in a hot bath and tried to relax her aching muscles from all the work she had done during the long day. Maybe she *had* developed a blind spot where men were concerned; but, if so, that was fine with her. She had learned her lesson well. She was wary of men now, and so long as she remembered that no matter how nice or kind or charming one might seem he could never be trusted, she would be safe. As long as she kept up her guard, she could never be hurt again.

Being ruthlessly honest with herself now, she analyzed her current feelings about Ken Waters, the man she had once planned to marry. She was pleasantly surprised to realize that now all she felt was indifference. The hurt had gone; time had closed the wound, even if it had left a scar. She had

always been aware that Ken, with his blond good
looks, had been appealing to other women and that
he enjoyed lighthearted flirtations with them all,
young or old. But she had honestly believed he was
completely open and aboveboard until one evening
when she had actually seen him with another girl. He
had told her that he was working late that night, and
she had believed him. She had decided to go to a
movie, and just as she was arriving she had spotted
Ken and the other girl. And that, as far as she had
been concerned, was that.

True, as Julia had pointed out, Ken had been
trying to make up with her ever since. He called, he
came by, he sent flowers and other gifts. Though
Laurel recognized that he *must* truly feel something
for her or he wouldn't keep on trying in the face of
absolute rejection, the love she had believed she had
felt for him was gone. It wasn't, as her sister
believed, a matter of being unforgiving. She simply
wasn't interested anymore.

On Sunday morning Laurel was up early again,
and she spent most of the morning unpacking her
personal belongings. The apartment slowly began to
take on the air of a home, with her needlepoint
throw pillows on the sofa, her handmade macramé
wall hangings, and her own books in the bookcase.
By ten-thirty she had stored away all her kitchen-
ware, pots and pans, and dishes, and she decided to
take a break. She would go over to Julia's and keep
her company for a while.

Julia's house, too, was beginning to look more
livable. Many of the boxes from the previous day
were gone from the living room. Laurel pitched in to
help by storing away linens and bath towels, while
Becky unpacked a box of summer clothes and stored
them in bureau drawers.

At eleven they were all surprised when Stephen
Tanner arrived again. Today he looked more commanding than ever in dark blue slacks and a white

shirt topped by a pale blue sweater. Though he did not wear his Stetson, the pointed toes of his shiny leather western boots peeped out from below his pants.

"I came to invite you all to my house for lunch," he announced. "And I won't take no for an answer. I'm sure you need a break from your work, and my housekeeper has cooked a nice meal for you."

"We'd love it," Julia said. "Just give me time to change into something else," she added, indicating her faded jeans.

"Where's Vaquero?" Becky asked.

Stephen smiled. "He's at home. There wouldn't be room in the car for all of us plus him, but he'll be there to greet you."

"Come wash up, Becky," Julia called to her daughter from the hallway.

As soon as the two were out of hearing, Laurel said, "Thank you all the same, but I think I'll pass. I'm not dressed properly and . . ."

"Nonsense." Stephen Tanner frowned, and his dark gaze swept over her beige slacks and chocolate-brown sweater. "You look fine to me. Besides, if you back out, you'll spoil it for Becky and Julia. You'll come," he ended emphatically.

Laurel glared at him, knowing the truth of what he said. If she made a scene and flatly refused to go, it would make Julia feel uncomfortable about accepting. Drat the man, anyway, for thinking of it!

When they all went out to the car, Stephen ushered Laurel into the front seat beside him with a no-nonsense set to his jaw, while Julia and Becky got into the back. Just his touch on her arm sent odd tingles racing through her veins. When she happened to glance up at him as he opened the door for her, Laurel felt something akin to shock. He had felt it, too. This was no time, however, to analyze it, and, with an effort, Laurel thrust the incident to the back of her mind.

Stephen's ranch was a few miles out of town. On

the drive they crossed a rock-strewn, rushing river that he told them was called Rio de Piedras, which meant "stony river." "It skirts the western edge of my property."

"Can you swim in it?" Becky asked.

Stephen nodded. "Yes. It's very small as rivers go and it's not very deep. However, its bottom is quite rocky. You need to wear tennis shoes when you go in or else you'll hurt your feet."

The car swept through a large wrought-iron gate, across a cattle guard, and down a private road. After rounding a couple of bends, they arrived at the house, a large, impressive two-story building of pristine white brick. Large columns fronted the house, giving it quiet, understated elegance. Several large live oak trees surrounding it gave an aura of steadfastness, of permanence in an impermanent world. In the distance, behind the house, could be seen numerous outbuildings, obviously used for the actual business of running the ranch.

A Mexican lady named Ana Marie, whom Stephen introduced as his housekeeper, served them a wonderful meal of roast and steaming vegetables, topped by a spice cake for dessert.

Afterward Stephen took them on a tour of the ranch headquarters. There was a large barn stocked with bales of hay and bags of grain, winter food for the cattle. In an adjacent building were tractors and other machinery. Two horse trailers and a pickup truck were stored in another building. Near the buildings was a corral, part wood, part metal.

Stephen explained, "I'm in the process of building a new corral before spring roundup. The old wooden part has been here since my father's day; besides needing constant repairs, it was inefficient."

In a fenced pasture beyond the main ranch headquarters a number of cattle were grazing, and Laurel asked curiously, "What sort of cattle do you raise?"

"Santa Gertrudis and Herefords," Stephen replied.

"Where are your horses?" Becky wanted to know.

He laughed at her. "Off in a pasture somewhere," he replied. "My own is a quarter horse named Jet, but I have a nice filly named Daisy that would be perfect for a girl like you. She's gentle and good-tempered, and I'll bet the two of you will get along fine. Sometime when you come, I'll take you riding if you like."

"Will you really teach me to ride?" Becky asked with shining eyes.

"I promise," Stephen told her.

As they walked slowly back to the house he spoke again to Julia about various people in the town, assuring her that in no time both she and Becky would have an entire army of new friends. He did not assure Laurel of such delights in store, and she vaguely resented it, even while she appreciated his kindness to her sister and niece. It was almost as though he were deliberately leaving her out of his attention, which seemed strange considering that he was the one who had insisted that she come today.

When they reentered the house, it was to discover a beautiful young woman sitting in the living room, looking very much at home with a drink in one hand and a cigarette in the other. She had short, wavy platinum-blond hair and blue eyes fringed with incredibly dark lashes. As soon as she saw the others, she got languidly to her feet.

"Annette!" Stephen exclaimed with obvious warmth. "Why didn't you let me know you were coming today?" He moved forward, wrapped his arms around her, and kissed her upturned cheek.

"I didn't know myself that I could get away until the last moment, so"—the woman shrugged daintily—"I just decided to come."

"That's wonderful!" Stephen said. "That must mean your dad is better?" There was concern in the question.

Again she shrugged. "Only a little. Actually, it

was he who shoved me out and made me go off for a while, but I can't stay long."

With his arm around her waist, he led her forward to the rest of the group and introduced them. "Annette Pharr, I'd like you to meet some new friends of mine who have only just this week moved here to Tierra Nueva."

Introductions over, everyone sat down, and Stephen explained that Annette was a friend of many years' standing, that she lived in San Antonio, and that her father, who was recuperating from a severe heart attack, was also a close friend of his. "For the past couple of months Annette's scarcely left his side. Tell me you can stay for dinner tonight," he added to the girl, who sat beside him on the sofa.

Annette Pharr smiled but shook her head even as she patted his hand with a fond gesture. "I'd really love it, Stephen, you know that, but I just can't stay away that long."

For the remainder of their visit Laurel felt like an outsider. Although Annette Pharr was charming and polite toward them, Laurel had an instinctive feeling that the other woman wished them anywhere except here. And Stephen himself, she thought sourly, must also be wishing the same thing. He smoothly continued his role as a hospitable host to them all, but surely he would have preferred to be alone with her.

Observing the two, the easy way they smiled and the affectionate way they had greeted each other, Laurel was certain that they were having an affair. It was none of her business, of course, and it certainly didn't matter to her. But, all the same, an unaccountable depression washed over her, and she longed for the afternoon to end.

Chapter Three

*N*ew office furniture now occupied a small room near the back of the ground floor of the house. Gleaming new appliances were in place in the kitchen. As soon as the delivery truck left, Laurel crossed the vast central hall, passed through the spacious glassed-in garden room across the back of the house, and went outside, where several men who worked for Stephen Tanner were busy setting up playground equipment.

The work was coming along nicely, and with pleasure Laurel watched the progress being made. There were swings, but instead of regular seats hanging from the top, there were tires secured by sturdy ropes. There was also a large red, white, and blue wooden climber and, of course, a large sandbox. In a sunny spot at one end of the yard, two men were digging a garden area for the children to use.

Seeing her standing there watching, one of the men came forward to speak to her. "Ma'am, we've still got an extra tire and piece of rope left from the swings. Would you like me to hang it from one of those big branches on the pecan tree?"

Laurel gave him a delighted grin. "You're obviously a family man," she told him.

The man gave her an answering grin and nodded. "I've got five kids," he answered, "and there ain't nothin' kids like better than to swing on a rope or a tire from a tree branch in the summertime."

"You're right," she answered. "I'm glad you have one left over and that you thought of it. Please do put it up for us."

He went away, and Laurel's thoughts went naturally to the man who was providing all this help—Stephen Tanner. Yesterday, when Julia had happened to mention that they would need to hire some men for the job and had asked Stephen if he could tell her where they could get such help, he had immediately offered some of his own employees, with an arrogant and firm rider that there would be no charge. Julia and Laurel had both argued about that, but he had refused even to discuss a fee. Sure enough, first thing this morning the men had arrived and set to work.

Julia came around midmorning, and she was excited to see everything that had been accomplished. The two sisters stood in the center of the large room with tables and chairs and learning-center materials, and Julia nodded with satisfaction. "As soon as we get some bright-colored curtains on the windows and some cozy rugs on the floor, it's going to look wonderful, Laurel!"

Laurel agreed, then asked, "Did you get Becky enrolled in school all right?"

"Yes. Mr. Baskin, the principal, was most kind. He showed Becky and me around the school personally and then took us to her classroom and introduced us to her teacher, who also seemed very nice." She expelled a tiny sigh. "I just hope Becky fits in and makes some friends right away. She's so unhappy over this move."

"I'm sure she will," Laurel said optimistically.

"Oh, and guess what, Laurel!" Julia exclaimed. "Mr. Baskin, the principal, is a widower with a four-year-old son. When he learned we're going to open a day care-center, he said he would like to be one of our first customers. It seems the lady who is presently caring for his child is about to move away

and he was already desperately searching for someone else to watch him."

Laurel laughed. "How about that? We've already
got our first client, and we haven't even done any
advertising yet!" She glanced at her wristwatch.
"Which reminds me, I need to visit the newspaper
office today and turn in our advertisement for help.
Now that you're here, I'll go on to town. I also need
to stop at the post office and the office-supply store.
By the time I get done with everything, it'll probably
be around noon. Want me to pick us up a couple of
hamburgers to bring back here for lunch?"

"Please," Julia said. "As soon as I change out of
these clothes, I'm going to measure all the windows
and then start setting up the learning-center equipment. This afternoon I'll go shopping for fabric, and
tonight I'll start sewing the curtains."

"Good luck to you." Laurel grimaced. "I'd give
you a hand, but you know I'm all thumbs when it
comes to sewing."

"I don't mind," Julia stated. "I love it. Mean-
while, you'll just be the general flunky and gofer."

Laurel stuck out her tongue at her sister, then,
laughing, left the room.

The morning errands took longer than Laurel had
anticipated, and it was a little after twelve before she
finally arrived at a small café on Main Street. She
groaned inwardly when she walked inside its dim
interior and saw that the place was packed. Even
though she only wanted a takeout order, she had a
feeling she would be waiting for a considerable time
before it would be filled.

She went to the counter and placed her order, then
stood aside as other customers crowded around.
While she waited, she idly glanced at one of the men
placing his order. He appeared vaguely familiar to
her, yet she could not place him. Since she had as yet
met few of the inhabitants of Tierra Nueva, the
sense of knowing him plagued her. He seemed to be
in his late twenties, a few years younger than Ste-

phen Tanner, and his looks were the complete opposite of the other man. He was of medium height, probably not quite six feet, and he had dark blond hair. He wore neat gray dress slacks and a soft blue shirt with a gray-and-blue tie.

When he finished ordering, he stood back as Laurel had done, to make room for other customers. When he did, he backed into Laurel. Instantly he turned to apologize.

"Hello." An easy smile came to his lips as he peered quite openly at her. "Haven't we met before?" he asked.

Laurel smiled back. "I've been thinking the same thing," she replied, "only I can't remember where."

The man extended his hand. "I'm Dan Silsby, a Realtor," he told her.

The light dawned, and Laurel offered her hand. "That's it!" she exclaimed. "You're Davis-Silsby Realty Company. I'm Laurel Patterson. My sister and I visited your office last summer when we were here together, and since then you've met with her quite often—she's Julia Adams. You found us the house we've leased for our day-care center."

"Of course!" Dan Silsby's smile stretched with warm friendliness. "How are you? Are you all set up for business yet?"

"We're getting there, slowly but surely," she replied. For the next fifteen minutes they chatted casually about the problems of setting up a new business, about the town itself, and a little about their personal lives.

At last Laurel's order was ready, and she moved forward to the counter to pay for it. When she picked up the bags and turned to leave, Dan Silsby stopped her. "Say, I hope you won't think it too forward of me, but it *isn't* as though we just met, you know. So I was wondering if you'd care to have dinner with me tonight? We could go to the country club."

Laurel hesitated. She liked Dan Silsby from their

brief encounter. But, on the other hand, she could hardly claim to know him well. Besides, she had no desire to get involved with any man just now.

Dan Silsby seemed able to read her mind because he said quickly, "It's only dinner. I'll take you straight home afterward. It's just that I would enjoy getting to know you better, and I figured, after all the work involved with moving the past few days, you could use a break yourself."

"You're right," she answered finally, with a friendly smile. "Thanks, Dan. I think I would indeed enjoy it."

"That's fine," he said heartily. "How about if I pick you up around seven-thirty?"

"It's a date," she told him. "See you later, then." Laurel said goodbye, left the café, and walked down the street to her car.

At three-thirty that afternoon Laurel drove to the elementary school a few blocks away. It was near enough that ordinarily Becky would be able to walk to the day-care center after school most days as long as the weather was nice. But this was her first day, and Laurel was anxious to find out how she had fared. Julia was still out shopping for curtain fabric.

The grammar school, probably built back in the thirties or forties, was of weathered yellow brick. Laurel parked the Chevy along the front curb that bordered the wide expanse of lawn. Near the entrance to the building the Stars and Stripes fluttered in a gentle breeze from the top of a flagpole.

A couple of minutes later, children began spilling from the building. They raced down the front steps and from side doors, and in no time the lawn was swarming with energetic young bodies in an array of colorful clothing.

It took some time before Laurel spotted Becky's shining hair and tomato-red Windbreaker jacket. When she did, Laurel got out of the car and called to her. Becky lifted her head, looked around in her direction, and then strode with brisk purpose toward Laurel and the car.

As soon as they were inside the car and pulled out into the street, Laurel asked, "How'd it go, honey?"

To her dismay, Becky burst into tears. "It was horrible!" she cried.

Laurel shot her a worried glance before turning her gaze back to the traffic.

"What happened?"

"Nobody wanted to be friends with me!" Becky sniffed hard and wiped her tear-filled eyes with the back of her hand.

"Nobody at all?" Laurel asked incredulously.

Becky sniffed again. "Only a boy and girl in my class who are twins. They were both nice to me in class. They shared their books and map pencils with me, but at recess they had other friends."

"Well, of course they do," Laurel pointed out reasonably, "but surely they were kind to you then, too."

"Well," Becky conceded, "the girl, Pat, was, but the other girls who came up to us kept talking to her and ignoring me, so I couldn't really make friends with her. And I didn't like *them!*" she stated emphatically. "They're all silly and stupid, and I hate it here! I want to go home!" she ended in a wail.

When they arrived at the Victorian house, Laurel was vastly relieved to see Julia's car in the drive. She thought that her mother would be able to offer Becky the comfort she needed. But when they went inside and Becky had recited again all of her unhappiness of the day, she refused to accept any sympathy from her mother when Julia tried to offer it.

"It's all your fault!" Becky accused hotly. "If you hadn't made me come here, I wouldn't be all alone in a school where everybody's mean and hateful and stupid! I want to go home! I want to go home to Daddy!"

Julia attempted to put her arms around Becky.

"You know that's not possible, sweetheart," she said gently.

"Yes! Yes, it is! I want to live with Daddy!"

Julia's face paled at that. "You don't mean that," she said urgently. "Daddy has a new family now. You told me yourself you didn't like them when you stayed with them those weeks last summer. It just wouldn't work out, Becky, and besides, even if it did, don't you know I'd miss you dreadfully?"

"But why can't we go back home to live?" Becky insisted. "Why did we ever have to come here?"

There was no answer to that, and Julia looked up helplessly at Laurel even as Becky jerked herself away from her mother's embrace.

"Come on, Becky," Laurel said with sudden firmness. "Let's go outside to talk while your mom fixes you a snack." She grabbed Becky's hand in a tight grip and pulled her toward the door.

They sat down on the back steps together, Becky's face pinched and sullen, Laurel's thoughtful. For a time neither spoke.

Finally Laurel said, "You know your mother loves you very much, don't you, Becky?"

Becky stared mutinously toward the garage and she nodded curtly.

"And you love her, too?"

There was a longer hesitation this time, but at last the child bobbed her head up and down again. "Yes," she admitted, "but why did she have to make us come here? It was already bad enough at home without having Daddy anymore, but this is even worse! Laurel, *nobody* likes me here!" Although she fought it, a lone tear slithered down her face and chin to finally fall onto her hand.

"You just need to give it a little time, honey," Laurel said soothingly. "First days at school or a new job are always hard, but it gets better soon. All you have to do is be your normal sweet self, and I'm sure that in no time you'll have as many friends as you ever had back home."

"Do you really think so?" Becky asked in a hopeful voice.

"I'm certain of it," Laurel said positively. "Now, how about us going inside? I'm sure your mother has some nice snack for you to eat. And after that, would you help me set up the learning-center equipment?"

"I guess," Becky agreed, with only a slight tinge of reluctance in her voice. She stood up and tucked her hand inside Laurel's.

That evening Laurel dressed in a simple but very becoming black dress for her dinner date with Dan Silsby. It had a V neck and long, slender sleeves. The skirt was slightly flared but snug enough at the hips to be flattering. To relieve the severity of it, she wore a cream-colored belt with matching accessories. She piled her thick waves of hair atop her head, giving it a curly, yet sophisticated and controlled, appearance. She put makeup on with a light hand, so that there was only the vaguest hint of blue eye shadow behind the deep brown eyelashes. A bright russet-red lipstick offset the possibly overwhelming effect of the black dress.

When she stood back at last, she felt satisfied. Dan Silsby, she thought, would not be ashamed to be seen with her.

Dan was far from ashamed of her appearance. In fact, he was so effusive with his compliments that Laurel began to be a little embarrassed.

The Tierra Nueva Country Club was not a large one by the standards of a big city. It was built along Spanish-Mexican lines, with an adobe look and large beams extending outward from the top. The grounds boasted rock gardens with a wide variety of cacti, century plants, and yuccas.

Dan pulled open the massive Spanish door for her and they went inside. A waiter soon seated them in a quiet spot overlooking the rolling greens of the golf course, which could be seen dimly in the darkness by the outdoor spotlights.

Dan chose a wine, they ordered dinner, and then they sat back to relax and get acquainted.

"Tell me about yourself," he insisted as his blue-gray eyes openly admired her.

Laura laughed. "That's a tall order," she said, "especially since there isn't much to tell. I used to work in a day-care center in Boston, Julia used to own it, and now here we are."

Dan shook his blond head and gave her a mock fierce scowl. "That isn't what I want to know at all," he told her frankly. "What about the men in your life? I want to assess the competition. Are there slews of them, or, far worse, one in particular?"

Laurel shook her head and there was a smile on her lips. "None at the moment, nor are there likely to be. I have to warn you, Dan: though I may enjoy having dinner with a man like you for one evening, I'm definitely not in the market for anything long-term."

Dan gave her an easy grin. "Thanks for the warning. Though, to be perfectly honest, neither am I. I've been divorced only a couple of months."

Laurel glanced down at her hand to avoid the momentary flash of pain she had seen in his eyes. "I'm sorry," she said simply. "There seems to be a lot of that going around these days."

"That's a fact," Dan agreed soberly. Then his voice brightened. "Meantime, let's get off that subject. Tell me about your hobbies instead. Do you like to golf, play tennis, swim, sky dive, mountain climb, big-game hunt, what?"

Laurel laughed at his nonsense. Soon they were launched into a friendly discussion of a multitude of things, none of them important but all of which new acquaintances must say in order to give each other a bit of background.

Their dinner came, delectable, juicy steaks with asparagus and parsley potatoes, and for a while little conversation ensued. As though a compulsive force made her do it, Laurel looked up to see a group of men crossing the room. One of them was Stephen Tanner. She swallowed hard when she realized that he had also seen her and was parting from the others in order to come over to speak to them.

"Hello, Dan. Laurel. How are you?" he asked pleasantly.

Dan stood up briefly to shake his hand. "Fine, fine. And you, Stephen?"

"The same."

"I tried to call you today," Dan said. "The lease is almost up on that house on Haber Street, and I need to know whether you want me to lease it for another year. The tenants are willing and they seem a good sort."

Stephen Tanner shrugged. "Sure, Dan. Whatever you think best. I . . ."

He was interrupted by a white-jacketed waiter who came to Dan's side. "Excuse me, Mr. Silsby, but you have a telephone call and they said it was urgent."

Dan lifted his eyebrows in faint surprise, then tossed Laurel a look of apology. "I can't imagine what it can be about," he said. "Excuse me, Laurel. I'll be right back."

"Certainly." She smiled at him.

With Dan gone, Laurel was left alone with Stephen Tanner. He showed no inclination whatever to leave her to go and join his own friends at his table.

"How are you settling in at the center?" he asked pleasantly as he gazed down at her.

"Very well." A genuine smile parted her lips. "Thanks for sending some of your employees over. They put the playground equipment up in no time and they were very kind and helpful. Julia and I both appreciate your thoughtfulness very much."

Stephen flashed her a teasing grin, and Laurel was struck by his extraordinary masculine appeal this evening. He wore a conservative dark business suit and a white shirt with a wine-colored tie. The formality of his attire emphasized the midnight darkness of his thick hair and the laughing lights that danced in his eyes. "You almost sound as though you really meant that," he said in an amazed voice.

"But of course I did!" Laurel stiffened with indignation.

Stephen Tanner shook his head, and there was only the tiniest hint of a smile on his lips. "I find that hard to believe," he said. "Until now you seem to have resented any efforts I've made to help you."

Laurel flushed with embarrassment and resentment. "It isn't that I'm ungrateful," she replied. "It's only that I prefer to be independent and do things for myself rather than rely on others."

There was a knowing glint in his eyes as Stephen grinned down at her. "Ah," he drawled, "you're one of those true-blue women's libbers, hmm?"

"Perhaps." Laurel sat up as straight as she could and unconsciously squared her shoulders.

"Didn't anybody ever tell you that no man is an island?" he taunted. "That also applies to beautiful women with copper-gold hair."

Relief surged through Laurel when she saw Dan returning. But it was short-lived when she noted the whiteness of his face, the somber expression darkening his eyes.

"Bad news?" she asked anxiously as he reached her side.

Dan nodded. "I'm afraid it is. My brother has been involved in a car accident in Waco. He's been taken to a hospital, but I can't get a clear picture at this point about whether he's hurt very badly or not. Anyway, I must leave immediately and drive my parents there tonight. I'll have to take you home right now, Laurel. I'm sorry to spoil your evening like this."

"Don't give me another thought," she told him

quickly. "And you mustn't waste time driving me home. I'll call a taxi."

"That won't be necessary, either," Stephen Tanner said. "I'll see that she gets home all right, Dan." He clasped the other man on the shoulder in a gesture of sympathy and friendship. "I hope Bob isn't badly injured and that he'll soon be all right."

"Thanks, Stephen," Dan said. "And I appreciate your offering to see Laurel home."

"No problem," Stephen assured him. "It's my pleasure. You just get going now and see to your folks and to Bob."

As soon as Dan was gone, Stephen told Laurel, "If you'll excuse me for just a moment, I'll go tell my friends that I won't be dining with them, after all."

"Oh, really," Laurel protested, "it's not at all necessary for you to change your plans for the evening." But she discovered that she was talking to thin air, because Stephen Tanner had already turned and begun to walk across the dining room.

When he returned, he summoned a waiter to remove Dan's plate, then placed an order for his own dinner. Thereafter, much to Laurel's total astonishment, they spent an enjoyable hour together. Stephen was a wonderful dinner companion, keeping up a lighthearted stream of interesting conversation and drawing her out in spite of her initial wariness. He gave her a colorful account of some of his exploits as a boy and soon had her laughing and matching stories about her own childhood.

Laurel was surprised to realize she felt a keen sense of disappointment when the dinner came to an end at last and there was no longer any reason to postpone going home.

Although it had been a mild day, the night temperature was chilling, and Laurel was glad to have her coat as they walked from the car and up the outside stairs leading to her apartment.

When they paused on the landing and Stephen

took her key and unlocked the door, Laurel said truthfully, "I really enjoyed the evening."

Stephen handed her back her key, and his face, so near hers, was easily readable even in the dark shadows. "So did I," he said softly. "Very much."

For a time neither spoke. They gazed at each other in something akin to awe as a current of electricity vibrated between them. Laurel's mouth felt like cotton, and she was unable to tear her gaze from him as those dark eyes searched hers so deeply.

At last she found her voice. "Would . . ." she said hesitantly, "would you like to come in for a while? I could make coffee or maybe offer you a drink. I believe there's a little vodka and brandy."

"I'd love to," Stephen murmured. He opened the door and followed her into the living room.

Laurel started to remove her coat, but instantly Stephen was behind her, lifting it from her shoulders and tossing it across a chair. Then his hands went to her shoulders as though to warm them in place of the coat and his lips brushed against the back of her neck.

The electricity that had vibrated between them before now jolted through Laurel's system in a strong current as his lips continued their sensual trip across the tingling skin of her neck.

"You smell so good," he murmured. "Like roses. I remember that scent from the day I found you on the road and I had to wrestle with you to get you to the car. You smelled of roses then, and you looked like a lovely Texas rose blooming out of season, with silver mist glittering in your hair." Now a hint of familiar amusement crept into his voice. "Though at the time I would have sworn it was more thorns than fragrant blossoms." Gently his hands slid down from her shoulders to her forearms, and he turned her to face him. A fiery light sparkled in his eyes. "You're even more beautiful tonight," he said huskily. "A rose in full bloom and your lips ripe to be kissed."

Bemused, Laurel was helpless to do anything but

gaze at him with wide, wonder-filled eyes as he bent his head and his mouth touched hers.

At first it was the gentlest of kisses, a newborn, fragile, and delicate thing for them both, like the unopened bud of a rose. Laurel closed her eyes and savored the warm sensations that filled her, sensations she had blocked from her memory and her life for such a long time.

But then the pressure of Stephen's lips changed. With gentle forcefulness he parted her lips, and an intensity of passion that had not been there before suddenly engulfed them both. His arms slid around her waist, drawing her close against the lean hardness of his body, and Laurel's breasts were pressed against the warmth of his firm chest.

For an instant Laurel's hand fluttered uncertainly against the roughly textured sleeve of his jacket, and then it slid upward to touch the curve of his neck. Stephen's lips now seemed to be devouring hers. His tongue probed the dark, warm recesses of her mouth, and their bodies molded together as one.

Wave after wave of violent emotions surged through Laurel, rendering her senseless as she gave kiss for kiss, touch for touch. Even had she been willing, she was unable to stop this glorious sensation that was pulsating fire through her veins.

Stephen's hand at her back groped for and found the zipper of her dress, and a moment later it was being slipped from her shoulders and arms to slither unheeded to the floor. Next went her bra, and her eyes opened at last when Stephen's lips left hers. She saw the admiration and the passion smoldering in his eyes as he gazed at her pale white skin.

"You're exquisite," he said thickly as one hand gently caressed a breast. Then his dark head lowered so that his lips could kiss the pink-tipped mound.

Unaware that she was doing so, Laurel groaned softly with unfulfilled desire. Her fingers laced through the rich darkness of his hair as he buried his face against the creamy thrusts of her breasts.

At length Stephen lifted his head again to look at her with soft, warm eyes before his lips claimed her mouth once more. When he did, Laurel's fingers went unerringly to the buttons on his shirt. After fumbling for a moment or two, she was able to slip her hand inside, to revel in the touch of his warm bare skin, to thrill to the feel of his crispy chest hair. She could even detect the beating of his heart.

Finally Stephen pulled back from her slightly and, with a tiny smile playing across his lips, put an arm around her waist and led her toward her bedroom.

It was only when they were there, when she saw the massive old-fashioned bed, that Laurel began to think rationally. She stopped abruptly several feet from the bed and turned to face Stephen, who was in the process of removing his jacket.

He went perfectly still when he saw her face. "What's the matter?" he asked anxiously.

Laurel's face went pasty-white. "I can't go through with it," she said in a low voice.

Stephen's face darkened like a black sky during a sudden spring storm. "What do you mean, you can't go through with it? What the hell are you, anyway?" he demanded furiously. "A tease? A little come-on?"

His words cut to the quick, even though Laurel could admit to herself that his anger was justified.

"No," she said in a quavering voice as she crossed her arms over her nude breasts in an ineffective effort to shield herself from his burning gaze. "I'm not that . . . though I know I can't expect you to believe me."

"You're damned right, I don't," Stephen interjected hotly.

Unable to meet his hostile eyes any longer, Laurel stared at the floor. "It's just . . . I just suddenly realized what madness this is. We scarcely know each other, for one thing. What happened . . . it was just a momentary weakness on both our parts . . . an unexpected attraction, but it means nothing." Now she braved herself to look directly at him. "I'm not out for any cheap one-time encounter, Stephen. Nor am I in the mood to get romantically involved with any man. So it's best if we call a halt to this insanity right now before it goes any further. I . . . I'm truly sorry."

There was a long, stinging silence, and then Stephen angrily thrust his arms back into his jacket sleeves and rebuttoned his shirt.

"You're a very selfish person, you know that?" he asked in such an icy voice that Laurel flinched. "You resent anyone's help, even when their motives are completely innocent. Now we see that you want your independence to such an extent that you'll even deny your own physical needs to get it. A moment ago you wanted me to make love to you just as much as I wanted it. There was a spontaneous combustion between us that admittedly took us both by surprise. But the fact remains that we *both* wanted each other! Now you are coldly turning your back on what was, after all, a perfectly natural thing between a man and a woman. That makes you as dishonest as you are selfish, Laurel Patterson. Frankly, I'm glad this happened. At least I learned at the outset what sort of person you are . . . and, to tell the truth, I don't like your sort at all!"

Without another word or glance, Stephen pivoted and swiftly walked out of the bedroom. In a matter of seconds Laurel heard the front door slam and knew that he was gone. Forlornly she gazed down at her half-naked body and struggled to hold back the tears that scalded her eyes.

Chapter Four

Although it was early February, it was a warm day, with a hint of spring in the air. Julia and Laurel, both clad in working attire of old jeans and shirts, stood in the center of the backyard of Tiny Tots' Palace Day-Care Center watching workmen putting up a sturdy new fence around the yard. The men had worked on it the previous day as well, and sometime that afternoon it would be finished. Both of the sisters were grubby from their own work. They had dug up the rosebushes and moved them to a new location, on the other side of the garage, that would be out of the fenced area, and out of harm's way.

It had been a frantically busy two weeks. They had hired several women to assist in the care of the children in the center and had also hired a cook, who had been recommended by Stephen Tanner. Carmen Garcia was a bright and efficient woman in her middle thirties, the daughter of Stephen's own housekeeper and cook; married and the mother of three, she had been seeking part-time work. Both Julia and Laurel believed she would work out perfectly, since she could arrive each morning after she saw her own children off to school, prepare the necessary midmorning snacks, a hot lunch, and an afternoon snack, and still be home again before her children returned. They had already tasted samples of her excellent cooking, an ability she had obviously learned from her mother.

Stephen had recommended Carmen to Julia a week ago at a dinner party he had given in his home. Julia had commented upon Ana Marie's excellent meal and mentioned that she and Laurel were looking for a cook for the center.

Laurel cringed whenever she thought of that evening. It had been a disaster as far as she had been concerned. She would not have gone in the first place if it hadn't been for Julia's excitement about it. Since it had been in their honor, planned by Stephen to present them to some of the local townsfolk, Laurel hadn't been able to think of a graceful way out, short of a sudden, dire illness, a delightful prospect that had not occurred.

There had been several married couples of various ages and a few singles as well at the party, and everyone had been friendly and welcoming to the newcomers. Julia was invited to join a Thursday evening bridge club, and a girl about Laurel's own age promised to call her soon for a movie or a shopping trip. Julia had enjoyed the evening and the opportunity to make new friends. But as friendly as their new acquaintances had been, Laurel had only longed for the evening to end.

When they had first arrived, Stephen had greeted her in a general way and introduced her to the other guests, just as he did for Julia. But thereafter he had left her strictly alone, while to Julia he had been warmly friendly. Laurel had been sharply aware that Stephen was obviously still angry with her over the way they had parted the last time they had seen each other. She felt certain that he would not even have thrown this party for them if he hadn't already committed himself before the incident in her apartment. Though he had not mentioned it to Laurel at the time, he had been in touch with Julia earlier that day and had extended the invitation to them both.

"I don't know about you," Julia said, breaking

into Laurel's reveries, "but I'm hot and thirsty, not to mention dirty." Ruefully, she glanced down at the soil beneath her fingernails.

The workmen, too, were pausing for a break, going to their pickup truck for water or soft drinks from a cooler.

"Let's go upstairs to my apartment," Laurel suggested. "We can wash up a little, and I'll make some iced tea."

A little later they both lounged in Laurel's living room, sipping their drinks. "Well, I'd say we've made real progress," Julia commented. "We've hired the help we need and signed up a respectable number of clients. Now that the fence is almost done, it won't be long before we can open for business." She gave Laurel a weary smile. "It's all been exhausting, but I feel it's worth it. I really think we're going to be successful here, Laurel."

"I sincerely hope so," Laurel said dryly as she brushed a tendril of hair away from her face. "I'd sure hate to see our investment go down the drain."

Julia gave a little laugh. "Bite your tongue!" she ordered. "Don't even *think* it! I'm broke enough as it is!" Now she grimaced. "Bert's child-support check is late, and I'm really feeling the pinch."

"I can lend you some money to tide you over until it comes," Laurel said quickly.

Julia shook her head. "Thanks, but no. At least, not yet. Until we get this thing really going and making a profit I know you're just as strapped for money as I am." She sighed. "I suppose he'll send it soon, but it's really aggravating. Every month he gets later and later about sending it."

By the time they went downstairs again, Becky was coming up the sidewalk, bedraggled like any normal ten-year-old after a day at school. As soon as she entered the house, she asked, "Do you have anything upstairs to eat, Laurel? I'm starved!" She dumped her books on one of the small tables.

"There are some cookies in the cupboard and

grape juice in the refrigerator," Laurel replied. "Just help yourself, honey."

"How did school go today?" Julia asked.

Becky frowned. "The same. Everybody hates me, and I hate them!"

"That can't be true!" Julia exclaimed. "Sweetheart, sometimes it just takes a little time to make new friends, that's all."

"I'll *never* make friends here!" Becky declared. "I don't even want to." She fished inside a notebook she had dropped on a table, extracted a paper, and handed it to her mother. "The teacher says you have to sign this."

Julia took the paper, glanced at it, and then gazed in horror at her daughter. "A forty on your math test? Becky! That's one of your strongest subjects! What happened?"

Becky shrugged carelessly but didn't answer.

"You had a spelling test today," Julia remembered. "How did you do on it?"

Becky avoided her mother's eyes and mumbled, "A sixty-eight." Without another word she rushed toward the stairs, dashed up them, and she vanished out of sight into Laurel's living room.

Julia gave Laurel a stricken look. "I can't believe this! You know what sorts of grades she always used to make! Her teachers said she was one of the smartest children in her grade!"

"Go easy on her," Laurel advised softly. "It's bound to be hard on her, moving to a new town and starting off in a different school. She'll soon settle in, make some friends, and then she'll concentrate on her schoolwork again and bring her grades up. You'll see. Just try to be patient. She's going through a rough time just now, you know."

Julia's smile was wan. "I know. But she sure is making it rough on me, too."

"Right now she resents you for this move," Laurel said, "and blames you for all her unhappiness. Maybe you need to have a little time apart. Tell you

what—on Saturday I'll take her to a movie. It'll give
you both a little breathing space from each other as
well as from school and work."

"Thanks," Julia said gratefully. "I know exactly
what I'll do with that time . . . rest!"

Becky was ready and waiting for her when Laurel
arrived early Saturday afternoon to pick her up. She
was dressed in a juvenile's standard attire, blue jeans
and a T-shirt with her name on it, and she carried
her red Windbreaker. Her hair was brushed neatly
and shone a golden yellow.

"Must it be the horror movie?" Laurel asked,
grinning, as Becky climbed into the car with her.
There were two movie theaters in Tierra Nueva from
which to choose.

"Yes," Becky said firmly. "Who wants to go see a
dumb, soppy romantic comedy?"

"I guess you're right," Laurel agreed with a laugh.
"Okay, kid, you're the boss, but I warn you, if I
have nightmares in the middle of the night, I'm
going to call you up and make you share my misery."

"You're not a scaredy-cat, are you, Auntie Laurel?"

Laurel stuck her tongue out at her niece. "Call me
'auntie' again and the deal's off!"

Becky giggled, enjoying the results of her teasing,
since it was an old, standing joke between them.
Laurel had never wanted to be called "aunt," so
Becky used the term only when she wanted to needle
her.

The town was packed with Saturday shoppers, and
traffic on the narrow streets was dense. Secretly
Laurel wished she could visit the shops along the
Main Street herself instead of enduring two hours of
a movie she knew she would not enjoy. But today
was for Becky, so she thrust the thought from her
mind.

When they reached the movie theater and got in
line for their tickets, a girl about Becky's age who

stood just in front of them turned around and smiled.

"Hi, Becky." The girl nudged the boy beside her and added, "Matt, look, Becky's right behind us."

The boy, the same age as the girls, turned to greet her, too. Both children looked so much alike, with their dark brown hair and clear blue eyes, that Laurel was sure they must be twins. A moment later her assumption was confirmed when Becky introduced her to them. "This is Pat and Matt Sinclair, Laurel. They're twins, and they're in my class at school."

Laurel smiled. "It's nice to meet you both."

"You like monster shows, too, Becky?" Matt asked.

Becky nodded. "I love 'em, don't you?"

"Yeah!" Pat shivered and grinned. "They give me goose bumps all over."

The line moved forward. They all bought their tickets, and once they were inside the lobby Pat suggested, "Why don't we all sit together, Becky?"

Becky was clearly pleased at the invitation, and she glanced up hopefully at Laurel. "Is it okay with you?"

Laurel nodded. "Fine."

A few minutes later, all four armed with boxes of popcorn and paper cups of Coke, they went into the theater and found their seats.

It was a rather juvenile monster picture, made to appeal to the ghoulish delights of the young rather than the more discriminating tastes of adults. But Laurel endured it in good grace because Becky was clearly having such a good time. She and the twins alternately giggled and whispered and squealed along with much of the rest of the audience.

When it was finally over and they left the theater, Laurel offered to treat all three youngsters to ice cream at a shop just down the street. Matt and Pat accepted enthusiastically.

While the children ate banana splits and ice-cream

sundaes, Laurel sipped at a cup of coffee and listened to their chatter.

"Do you like to skate, Becky?" Pat asked.

"I love it," Becky admitted. "But our driveway is made of gravel and I don't have anyplace to use my skates here."

"We've got a really big concrete driveway," Matt said. "It even curves around and slopes. It's neat for skating."

"Why don't you come over to our house tomorrow afternoon and skate with us, Becky?" Pat invited. "We could have a lot of fun."

Becky's face glowed with happiness. "I'd love it," she answered, "and I'm sure my mom will let me." She turned to Laurel for confirmation. "She will, don't you think?"

Laurel nodded. "I imagine so."

Matt was in the process of explaining to Becky exactly how to locate their house when Laurel happened to glance toward the counter. Her heart lurched and fluttered—there stood Stephen Tanner. Exactly at that moment, he turned, a Styrofoam cup in his hand, and his eyes met hers.

For an endless time they only gazed at each other, as though mesmerized. Then, slowly, he came toward their table. He was wearing Levi's and a tan western-style shirt that stretched across his shoulders and chest like a second skin. On his head was his Stetson. Although his attire was casual, it in no way suggested the urban-cowboy type. He looked exactly like what he was, a genuine rancher. Before he reached them Laurel had time to think that the clothes fitted his personality—tough and durable, but with a touch of class.

"Afternoon," he said with a pleasant smile, but whether it was for her alone or for everyone at the table Laurel couldn't tell. "Looks like you're all having a good time."

Becky smiled up at him. "Hi, Stephen. These are my friends, Pat and Matt."

Stephen's smile stretched. "It's nice to meet you." Now his gaze returned to Laurel, and he suggested, "Why don't you join me at that table over there?" He waved a hand in the direction of an empty table across the room. "I'm sure Becky and her friends won't mind, would you, kids?"

All three children agreed they wouldn't mind being deprived of Laurel's company. So Laurel was left with no choice but to stand up, carry her coffee cup, and go with him. Her heart hammered against her breast as she went, because she had no idea how Stephen would speak to her once they were alone.

But she worried needlessly. Today Stephen was in a friendly mood and not once did he mention what had happened between them. Instead, they talked about the center's progress toward opening and about Becky and her friends.

"Looks like she's fitting right in here," he observed.

Laurel shrugged. "It's a beginning, anyway," she answered. "Until now she's been telling Julia and me that she had made no friends at school at all, and it's really had us worried."

Stephen smiled lazily. "Pretty soon Becky'll have more friends than you can shake a stick at, as nice a kid as she is. What have you two been up to—shopping?"

Laurel shook her head and made a face. "No, we saw a monster movie."

Stephen's smile stretched into a taunting grin. "Now, the way I had it figured, you wouldn't need to see a movie for that. I thought that's what you considered me."

Laurel flushed. "That's not true, and you know it," she said in a low voice. "Stephen, about the other night, I'm sorry, really sorry."

He made a negative motion with his hand. "Think no more about it," he told her. "I suppose a lady is entitled to change her mind, even when she does do it at the last moment."

The conversation was necessarily dropped. Just then Becky joined them, saying her two friends had left since their mother expected them home soon. For the remaining few minutes that they were there, Stephen spoke only of general things—and, to Becky, of his horses.

For Laurel, the rest of the afternoon had a brighter glint to it simply because she had seen Stephen and he had not, as she had expected, harbored a grudge against her. For some reason, that thought was extremely cheering, though she did not analyze it. She merely allowed herself to be pleased about it.

On Sunday morning Julia telephoned and invited Laurel to eat with them at noon. "I bought a pot roast," she said, "and it's far too much for just Becky and myself. Come visit, okay?"

Laurel was glad enough to go, because she was at loose ends and felt strangely restless today. If Becky had no friends at school, her aunt was equally lonely. Since the short time she had been in Tierra Nueva, she had not had much free time to meet people. If it hadn't been for Julia's company the loneliness would have been unbearable.

Julia was a good cook, and her dinner, topped off by a lemon meringue pie, was delicious. When they had finished the meal, Becky was impatient to be driven to Pat and Matt Sinclair's house for her afternoon of skating.

"Go ahead and take her now," Laurel told Julia. "I'll do the dishes while you're gone. Besides, it should be my job. After all, you cooked the meal."

"Okay." Julia laughed. "You won't need to twist my arm to get out of doing dishes." To Becky she said, "Go get my purse from my bedroom, honey." As soon as she had finished speaking, the telephone rang.

"I'll get it," Becky said, rushing toward the wall phone. She picked up the receiver, said, "Hello," and a moment later squealed in delight. "Daddy! Oh, I'm so glad you called! I've made some friends, and I'm going to their house this afternoon to skate. And this nice man that Mom knows is going to teach me to ride horses at his ranch and . . ." Her conversation with her father went on for some little time, her own speech interspersed with silences as he spoke, then with little giggles from Becky and, finally, an "I love you, too, Daddy. Okay, 'bye." She held out the receiver toward Julia. "Daddy wants to talk to you, Mom."

For a fraction of an instant Julia hesitated. Laurel said quickly, "I'll drive Becky to her friends' house while you talk." A moment later she had hustled Becky from the house, realizing that it would be better for Julia to speak with her ex-husband without eavesdroppers.

She was gone perhaps a half hour. When she returned and entered the kitchen, she found Julia seated at the still-cluttered table, white-faced, almost as though she were in a daze.

"What's wrong?" Laurel demanded bluntly. "Did Bert say something to upset you?"

Julia looked up in surprise, as though she were only just realizing that she was no longer alone. Her lower lip quivered with bottled-up emotion.

"Wrong?" She gave a short, bitter laugh. "You name it and it's wrong! Bert said he lost his job and that he won't be able to send me any more child-support checks for a while. So there goes my budget!"

Laurel brushed that aside. "You know we'll work something out. One thing's for sure, you and Becky aren't going to starve. But there's something else, too. What is it?"

To Laurel's amazement, tears welled in Julia's eyes and one of them slid unheeded down her cheek. "Oh, he was so ugly, so hateful!" she exclaimed. "Remember Becky telling him about Stephen promising to let her ride his horses? Well, Bert accused me of having an affair with him! Can you imagine anything more ridiculous? All the man's ever done is be kind and polite to me and especially nice to Becky, but Bert was so horrible about it. He made me sound like a slut!"

Laurel put a comforting arm around her sister's shoulders. "Don't let it bother you," she told her. "Bert was just trying to make you look bad to hide his own guilt at having an affair with someone else while he was still married to you!"

Julia gave her a watery smile. "That's exactly what I told him," she said. "I also told him that if I *was* having an affair with any man, it was none of his business, anyway!"

"Good for you!"

"Yes," Julia agreed, "but it hurt all the same. I loved Bert so much, Laurel, and he's hurt me a lot, and now for him to say things like this . . . it's just hard to take, I guess." She gave a shaky laugh. "Stephen Tanner probably wouldn't come within a mile of us again if he knew what Bert had said, and that would be a shame. Becky really likes him."

"Are you interested in Stephen?" Laurel asked. Somehow she had been unable to stop herself from asking the question, because for some reason the answer was of vital importance to her.

"Don't be silly!" Julia snapped with spirit. "I think he's a nice man, but he isn't my type at all." She stood up and lifted a plate from the table. "I'd better get this kitchen cleaned."

"No," Laurel said firmly. "I promised I'd do it. You just sit there and rest. A little later I'll help you set out those gladiolus bulbs you wanted by the back door."

When Laurel arrived home at dusk and walked inside the apartment, the telephone was ringing. She dropped her purse and jacket onto a chair and went to answer it.

"Hello, Laurel. This is Stephen."

She felt suddenly breathless with surprise at hearing from him, but she hoped it was not evident in her voice. "Yes?"

"Yesterday after I saw you, I got back home and looked over my mail, and your check for this month's lease of the house was there."

"Yes?" she repeated.

A low chuckle came across the wire. "I'm afraid I won't be able to cash it as it is."

"Why not?"

"It was unsigned."

Laurel gnawed at her lower lip in irritation and chagrin. She remembered that the day she was paying the bills she had been in a hurry. Too much of a hurry, apparently, but why did it have to be Stephen's check she had neglected to sign instead of someone else's? It seemed she was forever doomed to deal with him in awkward situations.

"I'm sorry," she said as evenly as she could. "It was a stupid oversight. If you want, I'll drive out to your place this evening and sign it, or I can just mail you another check."

"I'm not busy tonight," Stephen replied in a languid tone. "Why don't you come over? Have you eaten yet?"

"Not since noon."

"My housekeeper cooked up a huge batch of fried chicken earlier today. If you don't mind eating a cold meal, we can share a buffet-style supper together."

"That sounds nice," she answered, hoping he could not detect her astonished pleasure at the invitation. "I'll be there in about an hour, then."

"Fine," Stephen said, then rang off.

When she arrived, Stephen, dressed in dark charcoal-gray slacks and an oyster-pearl silk shirt that was opened at the neck, ushered her into the enormous living room, where she sat down on a long white sofa while he mixed her a drink. Tonight, unlike the one previous time she had been here, Laurel was in a mood to admire the understated elegance of the room. A stone fireplace centered one wall, built-in bookshelves flanking both sides of it. The thick, pale gold carpet complemented the glass and chrome odd tables. A large stone indoor planter occupied a prominent position just inside the main entrance, next to a large window. Above the planter wound a carpeted curving staircase.

"You have a beautiful home," she murmured as Stephen handed her a vodka and tonic.

"Thanks," he said carelessly. "If you like, I'll show you over the whole house later." He lowered himself onto the cushion beside her. Though the sofa was large, only a scant few inches separated her from Stephen.

Laurel took a sip of her drink for courage and then, unable to think of anything more brilliant to say, asked, "Where is the check? I'll be happy to sign it now."

"It's in the library. We'll get to it later," he said easily.

"But what if we forget?"

Stephen grinned mischievously. "Meaning we might get involved in other matters that would cause us to forget?"

His insinuation was clear, and, angry with herself for laying herself open to such a comment, Laurel could feel her cheeks growing warm. "I only meant it *was* the reason I came here tonight, after all, and it seems to me we should attend to it now, before we eat."

"Very well." He got to his feet, held out a hand to help her up, and, keeping it in his grasp, led her across a hall and into a book-lined room. He went straight to a desk near a window, picked up a pen and held it out to her. "The check's right there," he told her, pointing to the center of the desk.

Laurel quickly scribbled her signature on the check, and then they walked into the dining room, where the table was already set for two and several cold dishes awaited them.

"Where is your housekeeper?" Laurel asked as she sat down.

"At her house," Stephen replied. "She's mainly here only on weekdays, but she usually comes and cooks a Sunday dinner for me after she attends mass."

The chicken, potato salad, and fruit compote were delicious. Afterward, Stephen reminded Laurel that he had promised to show her over the house. They carried their dishes into the beautiful kitchen, took a peek at the outside patio and swimming pool, and then he led her upstairs.

Laurel was dubious about seeing that part of the house, but she hated to appear foolish by her reluctance. So she forced herself to precede Stephen up the stairs, all the while feeling his gaze burning into her back.

She duly admired several guest bedrooms and a large game room, which contained a wet bar and a pool table. Then they entered a large room that could only be the master bedroom. A massive king-sized bed took up one wall. Even with a bureau and tables, there was still room for a small sofa against another wall, which was perfect for lounging on with a book or a magazine.

"This is my bedroom," Stephen said unnecessarily.

"I assumed it was," she replied, since a man's shirt was thrown carelessly across the arm of the sofa and a clutter of cuff links littered the dresser. "It's very lovely," she murmured, "but I really think I'd better be going now."

"What's your hurry?" he asked, with a throaty huskiness in his voice. He reached out a hand to rub a finger gently, sensuously, up and down her cheek. "Are you afraid of me? Of us both?"

Laurel was thrown into confusion, and her mind was not being cleared by the liquid warmth in his eyes or the tender little smile on his lips. "No," she said. Then: "Yes, yes, I am." She put out a hand against his chest, as though to ward him off, to ward off her own conflicting emotions. But when she did he covered her hand with his, then slowly drew her closer until his head bent and his lips took possession of hers.

Like the other time he had kissed her, the sensations it created in them both were like a powerful drug, rendering them senseless to everything except each other. Stephen's hands went around her, then slid down to her hips, pressing her closer to the hardness of his body. Exquisite pain flooded Laurel's being, the pain of consuming desire and unsatisfied need.

With a little moan of surrender, her hands went up to caress his face, the warmth of his neck, and the breadth of his shoulders. She snuggled even closer to him as Stephen's mouth parted hers with insistent, demanding pressure.

At last they drew apart enough to catch their breath, and he asked thickly, "Will you love me tonight, Laurel? Will you let me love you?"

And, unable to stop herself, Laurel nodded.

Chapter Five

Stephen flipped a switch on the wall, which instantly dimmed the bedroom lights to a soft, gentle illumination. Then he returned to Laurel, who still stood where he had momentarily left her. The smile on his lips was so tender, the glow in his eyes so adoring, that it almost brought tears to hers.

His head came down and his lips brushed fleetingly hers again, like the flutter of a butterfly's wings. Slowly, with no show of impatient haste, he began to undress her, his fingers sure, efficient, yet gentle.

Laurel closed her eyes and tipped back her head as his mouth burned a tantalizing trail from her throat to the pink tips of her breasts. Desire, an exquisite ache that raced through her veins, rendered her limp and vulnerable. Never had she felt so totally feminine, so beautiful or desirable, as she did now. Every touch, every caress, every kiss Stephen gave her told her so without any need for words. Her bemused mind blocked out everything except her awareness of him, his musky, male scent, and the wondrous sensations he was sending through her body.

At last he had her completely undressed. He groaned from deep in his throat, buried his face in the curling mass of her thick hair, and murmured huskily, "You're perfect, you know that? Absolutely perfect. You're as lovely as a rare porcelain figurine, and yet you're real . . . warm and wonderfully real." His hands slid down from her hair to stroke her silky-smooth back, sending thrilling tingles up and down her spine.

"Now it's my turn," she whispered. Slowly Laurel began working the buttons through the buttonholes of his shirt. After she slid it from his shoulders and it had fallen to the floor, she leaned toward him, raining kisses over his bare, dark golden skin. The crisp texture of his chest hair teased her fingertips, and her hands roamed daringly over the breadth and length of his torso, down and over his ribs, on to the point where his belt crossed his flat stomach.

For the first time Stephen displayed his eagerness. With another little groan, he scooped her up into his arms. Their eyes were level, their faces only a scant inch apart, as they gazed deeply at each other. "I ache for you," he whispered raggedly before he nuzzled her slender throat.

At last he carried her to the bed and gently placed her there. He finished undressing and joined her, and Laurel opened her arms in welcome. Their coming together was wildly frenzied, as though they had been waiting a lifetime for this one night. Stephen teased her taut, sensitive breasts with his tongue while his hands stroked her soft, creamy body until Laurel cried out with unfulfilled desperation. She kissed his face, his neck, his rock-hard shoulders, his broad expanse of chest, and raked her fingernails across his back in a furor of desire until he, in turn, could bear no more agony.

Finally, when the fire that had raged through their bodies was quenched, they drew slightly apart, sated, both needing a moment to catch their breath, to still their racing hearts. Moist perspiration beaded their skin and trickled between Laurel's breasts.

Stephen turned on his side, draped an arm across her rib cage, just below her breasts, and smiled.

"You're some woman, you know that?" he said in a low voice.

Drained of the fierce hunger that had gnawed at her, contented and drowsy, Laurel smiled and mumbled sleepily, "You're some man, you know that?"

Stephen laughed, lifted his thumb, and rubbed it between her creamy, rounded breasts, drying the dampness there. "I told you the first day we met that your body was a time bomb. Now I have certain proof. That was some explosion between us!"

"Yes," she said softly, acknowledging the truth of it. Her fingers again entwined themselves in the dark mat of hair. There was a dreamy expression on her face, on her slightly parted lips.

Propping himself up on an elbow, Stephen leaned over her and gave her a brief kiss. When he drew back, he was smiling once more. It was the smile of a man at peace with himself, a happy, satisfied man. "You look as though you're nearly asleep." His voice was tender as he reached down toward the foot of the bed and pulled the covers up over her, tucking them carefully around her. "Good night, little love."

His actions and words caused Laurel to sit bolt upright. The covers slid down, leaving the upper part of her body again exposed to Stephen's gaze, but she wasn't even aware of it.

"I must go," she said. She twisted toward the side of the bed, about to get to her feet.

Stephen gripped her wrist, holding her back as he, too, sat up. When she turned back toward him in surprise, she saw that the smile that had been on his lips was gone.

"Go?" he demanded. "What do you mean, go? Surely you're going to stay the night with me, aren't you?" His dark gaze held hers as his voice went deeper, with a vibrant, throbbing intensity. "I want you to stay, Laurel. I want to wake up in the morning with you at my side."

She shook her head agitatedly. Her tangled hair

swished against her bare shoulders. "I can't do that," she answered as she pulled her arm free of his restraining fingers.

"But why?" Stephen was clearly puzzled, and his somber eyes reflected his question. "You live alone. There's no one you must answer to."

"Yes," she said, nodding, "there is. You know our center opens tomorrow morning. I can't risk arriving after some of the parents are already there. They would be scandalized!"

Unexpectedly, Stephen roared with laughter. Then he lightly teased, "Such scruples! Honestly, Laurel, what the hell business is it of theirs where you spent the night? And how could they possibly know where you were coming from, anyway? You're making a big thing out of nothing, darling, believe me!" He tugged at her arm gently as he tried to make her lie down again. "Forget about them and stay with me. If you're really all that concerned about getting home early, I promise I'll set the alarm so that you'll have plenty of time to get there before anyone else does."

When he called her "darling," a warm thrill of joy raced through Laurel's veins. It sounded so natural, as though she belonged to him, really were important in his life. Laurel savored the feeling. Even so, she shook her head again. "I can't, Stephen. I just really can't. Someone might see me leaving here in the morning and put two and two together. I'm determined that nobody in this town is going to start pairing my name with any man's. Not yet, anyway. And surely," she added earnestly, "you can't want that any more than I do."

Stephen heaved a great sigh and capitulated. "Maybe you're right, at that," he said. "All right, then, go on home. We won't quarrel about it if it's that important to you."

His words disappointed her beyond all measure. The joy of a moment ago drained away, leaving Laurel with an empty, chilled sensation. Deep down she had hoped that he would go on protesting, that he would tell her other people's opinions didn't matter and he wouldn't mind in the least if his name was paired with hers in public. But he hadn't said it, showing her quite forcefully that he agreed with what she had said.

Laurel crawled out of the bed, grabbed her clothes, and then went into the bathroom to dress away from Stephen's knowing gaze. When she was ready and walked back into the bedroom, he was sitting on the edge of the bed, wearing a large bathrobe and smoking a cigarette.

When he saw her, he deposited the cigarette in an ashtray, stood up, and came to her. "I'll see you tomorrow night," he told her.

"No," Laurel answered dully, avoiding the inviting warmth that still lit his eyes. "No, Stephen, please don't do that. Things . . . well, things are just moving too fast between us."

There was a long silence. At last she braced herself to look at him. A frown carved deep furrows between his brows. "Do you regret what happened between us tonight?" he asked bluntly.

Laurel lowered her head and studied the complex pattern of the Persian carpeting beneath her feet. "I'm not sure," she answered after a long silence. "All I know for certain is that I need some space, some time to think."

Stephen stepped back from her with an abrupt movement, as though he had been slapped. The action lifted her gaze swiftly. His face was harsh and drawn, all angles and planes, with no warmth any longer to soften it.

"I'll give you all the space you need," he said in the most bitter tone of voice Laurel had ever heard. "You mustn't think that I would presume a relationship where none actually exists. Good night, Laurel." He turned his back on her with slow deliberation and picked up his smoldering cigarette.

Laurel wavered for an instant, one part of her

wanting to go to him, to erase the bitterness, to make things as they had been between them earlier. But another part of her, with its instinctive need for self-preservation, held back. If she went to him, somehow she knew she would be utterly lost. A part of her would be his forever and she would no longer belong completely to herself.

In the end, she left quietly, feeling thoroughly confused. In some way she had hurt Stephen as well as angered him, but there was nothing she could do to alter the situation. She had her own emotional wounds to deal with.

The opening day of Tiny Tots' Palace had begun. Already they had a good-sized group of children. An older woman had been hired to take care of the crib babies, another to handle the one- and two-year-olds, and Julia dealt with the three- and four-year-olds. They had purchased a new van for the center; there were several kindergarten five-year-olds Laurel would pick up from school at noon, and then at three-thirty she would make a second trip to the grammar school for a few first and second graders. In the mornings Laurel would help out where she was needed most. Her afternoons would be spent with the kindergarteners and older children. In addition, all the office work was hers, while Julia directed their assistants in the day-to-day operations.

So far, by midmorning, the daily plan Laurel had worked out was working smoothly. Various age groups took turns with their learning-center activities, which might vary from playing in the housekeeping area to finger painting or building with large blocks. While one group was busy there, another would be listening to records, singing, hearing a story, or playing outside on the playground. Luckily, for their first day the weather was sunny and mild, and the children enjoyed their time spent outdoors.

At eleven-thirty, just as Laurel was about to leave

the office to help with serving the children's lunch, the telephone rang. She scooped it up and answered.

"Hello," a man's voice said. "This is Clark Baskin, the principal at Tierra Nueva Grammar School. May I speak with Mrs. Adams, please?"

"Certainly," Laurel replied. "I'll get her." She placed the receiver on the desk and went into the main room, where the children were settling down at the tables for their noon meal.

"Julia," she spoke in an undertone as her sister assisted a small child into a chair and pushed it toward the table, "the school principal wants to speak to you on the phone."

"Oh, my!" Julia declared. "Something must be wrong. You don't suppose Becky's sick, do you?"

Laurel shrugged. "Go speak to him and find out. I'll take over here."

By the time Julia returned to the room, Laurel and the other ladies had all the children seated and served with their hot lunch of fried chicken legs, macaroni and cheese, green beans, and chocolate pudding. Laurel happened to glance up from her position behind one table and, seeing the worried look on her sister's face, she went quickly to her side.

"What is it?"

Julia shook her head. "I wish I knew. Becky isn't ill or anything, but he wants me to come in for a conference with him this afternoon. I set it for one-thirty. The children will be napping then, so I won't be needed here so badly."

Laurel nodded and glanced at her watch. "I'd better leave now to go pick up the kinders."

During the quiet period of the early afternoon, while all the children were napping and Julia was gone to the school for her conference, Laurel received a telephone call from Dan Silsby.

"I'm sorry it's been so long since I was able to call you," he told her. "I really felt badly about going off and leaving you that night at dinner."

"Don't think any more about it," Laurel told him. "How's your brother?"

"Doing fine now, but for a while there he had us really worried. I've spent most of my time lately trying to keep the business going here and taking my parents back and forth to see him. I simply didn't have any spare time to call you. But things are settling down now, and I was wondering if you'd give me another chance to take you out to dinner and make up for the one I spoiled. How about tomorrow night?"

Despite the fact that Dan seemed like a nice person and was so apologetic about something that had been beyond his control, Laurel still had little desire to see him. After last night, for her, everything had changed. And for that very reason, she quickly decided, she *should* see Dan, should prove to herself that she was indeed the free agent she wanted to be. For some reason it seemed important to prove that to herself.

"I'd love it," she answered firmly. "Only, instead of going out, why don't you let me cook you a meal here? It'll be more relaxing that way. Besides, until now I haven't had the opportunity to entertain anyone in my new home."

Dan laughed, sounding pleased. "Great. I'd much prefer your offer. I'll bring the wine."

"Fine. See you around seven."

Julia returned from her conference, white-faced and upset. Luckily, the children were still napping, because she didn't appear to be in any condition to attend to her job at the moment. She entered the office where Laurel was working on their expenses ledger and fell wearily into a chair.

"Becky has been misbehaving badly at school," she said outright. "Not only is she not doing her work, but she's belligerent to the teacher and she sulks most of the time. Laurel, I'm just about at my wits' end with that child. What am I going to do with her? It's reached the point where she simply tunes me out when I try to talk to her. I can't seem to get through to her anymore."

"Did the principal offer a suggestion?"

Julia sighed. "Just the usual assurance that he's sure she'll straighten up once I give her a good talking-to. Or at least her teacher said that before she had to return to the classroom. They both seem like wonderfully concerned people. After the teacher left I told Mr. Baskin how our difficulties seem to have started since the move. Coming on top of the divorce, it's made Becky resent and blame me for everything. He seemed really understanding and sympathetic, and he suggested perhaps someone else could get through to her, someone she cares about and trusts. Will *you* talk to her, Laurel?"

Laurel winced and spread her hands out in a gesture of uncertainty. "I can try, but, Julia, I can't promise any results."

"I know." Julia gave her a wan smile. "Just try . . . that's all I ask."

"All right." Laurel nibbled on a fingernail, lost in thought. "Tell you what—if you think you can do without me here this afternoon after I've picked up the schoolchildren and Becky arrives, I'll take her off somewhere so that we can be alone."

Julia stood up. "Thanks, sis," she said simply. "You're the best."

Laurel laughed. "Not so fast," she cautioned. "All I can do is talk to her. There's no guarantee she'll listen to me any more than she does to you."

"You know," Laurel said earnestly as the two of them strolled along the banks of the Rio de Piedras, "when you act up at school, the only person you're really hurting is yourself. You may annoy your teacher and your classmates and hurt your mother's feelings. But, ultimately, the one being hurt is Becky Adams and nobody else. It's *your* grades that are suffering, and *you* who are unhappy. You know, honey, the only way a person can ever be happy is from deep within herself. Maybe outside things do seem awful and you want to hit back at the world for hurting you, but that just doesn't solve a thing. It only makes everything worse than it would have been otherwise."

Becky frowned and poked a stick into the damp earth of the riverbank. "You mean *I'm* making my teacher hate me—and all the kids, too?"

"Nobody hates you," Laurel answered, "but they would certainly like you better if you acted like the nice girl you really are. Let me put it like this," she went on as she skirted a fallen tree branch and then hurried to keep close pace behind her niece. "Do you like old grouches and sourpusses?"

Becky giggled and shook her head. "Of course not. Who does?"

Laurel grinned at her. "I rest my case."

Becky stopped and stared at her for a long moment, and then, abruptly, she nodded. "Maybe you're right," she conceded. "I'll try to be nicer at school and see what happens."

"Good girl!" Laurel said with approval. She gave Becky a quick hug. "And you'll start boning up on the books, too?"

The child nodded. "Okay." Then, in a different voice, she exclaimed, "Hey, the river is really shallow here. And look at those big rocks! I'm going to cross over!" With no delay, Becky was suddenly hopping across the large stones in the swift currents of the water and was soon on the opposite bank.

"Come back over here," Laurel called in a stern voice. "That's private property. See the fence?" But she might as well have been talking to the river itself. At least it would have gurgled a response. Becky scrambled beneath the barbed-wire fence and disappeared through the underbrush.

"Little brat!" Laurel muttered beneath her breath. But she wasn't really angry, only annoyed. She hadn't forgotten the lure of unexplored terrain in her own youth. She sighed, eyed the distance between the stones with a measuring gaze, and began jumping from one rock to another herself.

Becky apparently knew that Laurel would follow her, because as soon as Laurel had slithered between the wires of the fence and pushed free of the thickets, she called out, "Laurel, come see what I found."

Laurel turned to the right in the direction of Becky's voice. About twenty yards away was a building. It was too small to call a house, but it looked too well kept to be some abandoned building.

"Do you suppose someone lives here?" Becky asked when Laurel reached her, and they both gazed toward the rough-hewn timber structure. Near the steps was a small live oak tree, but otherwise the area was cleared.

"Could be," Laurel guessed.

"Maybe it's a witch or a hermit that lives there," Becky fantasized.

Laurel laughed at her. "Maybe it's none of our business, nosy," she said. "Come on, Becky, we're trespassing on private property. We don't belong here at all. What if someone caught us?"

No sooner had she uttered the words than there came the sound of horse's hooves and the ground beneath their feet vibrated. They both turned. Emerging from a thick stand of pin oaks was a horseman astride a silky black stallion. Man and animal appeared as one in their graceful, easy movements. The man wore faded Levi's and boots, and a western hat shaded his face. But Laurel's throat went dry as she recognized him all the same, and her heart sank as he came straight toward them. A familiar ungainly dog loped behind him, seemingly unaffected by the dust curtain raised by the swiftly moving hooves.

"Stephen!" Becky yelped enthusiastically. "Vaquero!"

Stephen reined the horse and looked down at

them. "What you you doing here?" he asked
bluntly.

Becky waved in the direction of the river. "We
were taking a walk and decided to cross a shallow
place and see what was over here. Is this your land?"

He nodded and tipped back the brim of his hat.
"It is. Are you sure you two aren't cattle rustlers?"

Becky giggled as Stephen slid from the saddle.
While Vaquero thrust his damp nose into Laurel's
palm Becky went to the magnificent stallion and,
patting its long, slender neck, asked innocently, "Is
this the horse you're going to let me ride on Saturday?"

Stephen chuckled and shook his head. "Not a
chance. Jet's far too spirited for you." At Becky's
disgruntled expression, he laughed again. "Don't
look so unhappy. You'll still have fun with Daisy,
even if she is much more tame. I'm only thinking of
your safety, little one."

"All right," Becky said agreeably at last. She
smiled at him, then asked, "What is that building
over there? Does someone live there?"

Stephen shook his head. "No, it's a cabin that I let
friends stay in during hunting season."

"Can I go inside and look at it?"

He nodded. "Sure. The door's unlocked."

"Come on, Vaquero!" Becky called. "Come with
me, boy!" She darted off in the direction of the
cabin, with Vaquero close at her heels.

For the first time Stephen looked directly at Laurel. She could feel the heat rising in her cheeks
beneath his penetrating gaze, and her heart began
thundering against her breast.

Stephen Tanner was proving to be a difficult man
to either avoid or forget. Laurel wished fervently
that he had not happened upon them and that she
didn't look as disheveled as she did in faded jeans,
with her hair all windblown. She felt at a terrible
disadvantage, and most of all she wished he would

stop looking at her the way he was doing, as though he could see straight through to her soul.

At last he broke the strained silence that stretched between them like a taut rubber band. "After last night, somehow I didn't expect you'd be willing to set foot on my property again . . . at least, not this soon." There was no softness in his eyes or in his words; rather, they contained an unspoken accusation.

Laurel flushed more deeply. "I'm sorry. I didn't realize it was your property. Becky crossed the river against my orders and I came to get her."

Stephen lifted his left arm, slid back the cuff of his blue denim shirt, and glanced at his watch. "It seems an odd time of day for you to be out taking a walk. I thought your day-care center opened today."

"It did, but I came out with Becky to have a little private talk with her."

Stephen's brows knitted together. "Problems?"

Laurel nodded. "The school principal told Julia she's misbehaving in class. She's also making poor marks. She's still upset over the move and her parents' divorce. At the moment she won't listen to Julia, so"—she gave an expressive shrug—"the job fell to me."

"I see." There was another awkward silence as they gazed at each other, and Laurel wished she could read Stephen's thoughts. But his features were hard and implacable, as though he had put last night away from him and today she meant no more to him than any casual stranger he might happen to meet.

She was vastly relieved when Becky and Vaquero came racing back to them. As soon as she had joined them, Laurel said firmly, "It's time for us to go, Becky. We've got a good distance to walk back to the car. If we don't get home soon, your mother will start to worry."

They both said goodbye to Stephen, Becky with warmth, Laurel with a stilted reserve to match his own toward her. But as they parted Laurel could not stop herself from being unreasonably disappointed because Stephen had not mentioned seeing her again. It was a stupid way to feel, since she had refused to allow him to see her tonight and that had been what had established this coldness between them in the first place. But it *did* hurt, all the same. Stephen seemed to have done a complete about-face. Last night he had begged her to stay with him; today it was plain that he no longer wanted to see her at all.

The following evening Laurel saw Stephen again. If she had felt awkward and uncomfortable seeing him so unexpectedly by the river, it was nothing compared to her turbulent emotions when he showed up at her apartment while Dan was there.

They had just finished dinner and were having coffee in the living room when Stephen arrived. When she opened the door, Stephen gave her a slow, approving smile as his eyes drank in the sight of her oatmeal-colored knit dress that hugged her figure in all the right places.

"Good evening, Time Bomb," he said softly as his gaze slid down her body, then back up, until finally his eyes came to rest on her face once more. "You're *very* glamorous tonight. It's true, you know," he added, with an air of deep thought.

"What is?"

"That good things come in small packages. You're living proof of it." His grin was light and teasing.

"Er, th-thank you," she stammered nervously. She stepped back from him. His nearness was almost overpowering. It caused her heart to hammer erratically and brought a strange weakness to her limbs. "Won't you come in?" she added politely.

Stephen entered the room with a languid, fluid movement, but he seemed to freeze the moment he saw Dan seated on the sofa with his legs stretched comfortably out before him. Then he smiled and spoke politely to the other man, asking after his brother, before he turned back to Laurel again. She was near enough to him to see that the smile was forced and utterly devoid of warmth.

"I'm sorry to have interrupted your evening," he said stiffly. His eyes hardened into flint. "I only stopped by to say a friend of mine has some puppies he's trying to give away. Becky likes Vaquero so much I thought maybe she'd like to have a dog of her own. Do you suppose Julia would allow it?"

Suddenly Laurel was as angry as she knew Stephen was. He had absolutely no right to come here without notice, she thought resentfully, then to treat her as though she were doing something wrong by entertaining another man in her own apartment. Stephen Tanner had a hell of a lot of nerve when you got right down to it, she decided, and her green eyes glinted as she answered him, her own voice as frosty as his had been.

"I really have no idea," she said in a brittle tone. "You'd do better to consult Julia herself."

Stephen inclined his head in the briefest of nods. "You're right, of course. I apologize again for intruding. Good night."

For the remainder of the evening Laurel was alternately furious and miserably unhappy, though she masked it and tried to behave as though she were enjoying Dan's unassuming company. But she was hard put to keep her attention centered on him. Her mind kept straying instead to a large, overbearing, dark-headed man who meant nothing, absolutely nothing, to her.

Chapter Six

Laurel applied her makeup carefully, using a whitener to conceal the faint blue smudges beneath her eyes. Two sleepless nights had taken their toll. Her usually sparkling green eyes and glowing skin looked dull, and her body ached from lack of proper rest.

She could not erase the picture in her mind of Stephen's icy gaze upon her after he had seen Dan in her apartment last night. In a way, she couldn't blame him for being angry that she had refused to see him the evening before, especially after what had happened between them. On the other hand, she *did* need time to clarify in her own mind what she felt toward Stephen before she got more deeply involved with him. She simply couldn't make a second mistake in her life about men; she couldn't handle being hurt and disillusioned again.

She was still reeling from the blow Ken's deception had landed on her. Her problem, of course, was a basic insecurity. She had read enough books on psychology to recognize the problem, at least, even if she couldn't figure out a way to solve it. As a child she had been painfully shy, and in her teen years, though she had struggled and agonized over it, she had been unable to break out of her shell and attract boys the way other girls did. She had never known what to say or do whenever boys were around, and she had envied her girl friends' free and easy banter with the opposite sex. She was in her senior year in high school when she had her first date, with a boy who had been quiet and serious and almost as painfully shy as herself.

Once she had left school there had been a few dates and she had gradually begun to learn the art of conversation, but there had been no one serious until she had met Ken.

She had met him at a party of Julia and Bert's, and when the handsome, outgoing young man paid her exclusive attention, she had been overwhelmed with the wonder of it. Ken was popular, as she soon discovered, with both men and women, and she had been awed and felt privileged that he should fall in love with her—quiet, shy Laurel Patterson. It was like a dream come true, and she could no more have stopped herself from tumbling into love with him than she could have stopped breathing.

Only now she realized it hadn't been real love . . . on either side. If Ken had truly loved her, he would never have cheated on her, and her own lack of emotion now whenever she thought of him proved that she really hadn't been in love, either. Perhaps she had only been in love with love. She had been so thrilled by his attraction to her that she had been thrown off balance and had mistaken simple infatuation for the real thing.

It didn't matter now. What did matter was that he had hurt her badly, and since she had been severely burned once, she was wary of the same thing happening all over again. If it happened twice, Laurel wasn't sure she would ever recover. But of course Stephen couldn't understand all that. All he understood was that he had asked to see her again and she had refused and that when he had dropped by, she was entertaining another man.

It was an impossible situation, and there was no solution to it at all as far as she could see. With a sigh of despair, she went downstairs to face the day ahead.

Julia arrived before any of the assistants, and Laurel asked her if Stephen had phoned her or stopped by the previous evening.

Julia gave her a puzzled look and shook her head. "No. Why should he?"

Laurel shrugged. "He stopped by here and said a friend of his has some puppies to give away and he was wondering if you'd allow Becky to have one."

Julia's hazel eyes lit up. "That's a wonderful idea! How nice of Stephen to think of it! Since we always lived in apartments, she never had a chance to have a dog before. Tell him yes, will you?" she added as she happened to glance through a window to see a car pulling to the curb, the first of the arriving parents dropping off their children. "You'll have more time to call him this morning than I will," she finished before she went to open the door. "And be sure to tell him thank you for me."

An hour later, Laurel had picked up the telephone receiver and recradled it three times before she finally worked up the courage to dial Stephen's number. After last night, the last thing she wanted today was to have to talk to him. Darn him! Darn Julia, too! Both of them were using her as a go-between for their messages when there was no reason in the world why they couldn't communicate directly and a lot of reasons why she shouldn't be involved.

Finally she dialed the number, then crossed her fingers in a childish gesture of superstituous hope that he wouldn't answer. But the little magic action didn't work; perhaps it never did after one became an adult. Stephen's voice came strong and clear across the line.

"This is Laurel Patterson," she announced from a dry, scratchy throat.

Almost as though she could feel the vibrations emanating from him even across the miles, she knew he had grown stiff and cold after she had identified herself. "Yes?"

The stiff reserve in his voice was intimidating, and Laurel licked her lips before going on. "Julia asked me to call you. About the puppy. She thinks it would be wonderful for Becky to have a pet of her own, and she asked me to thank you for suggesting it."

"Certainly." He paused for a moment, as though thinking, then said, "I'll be free around four-thirty this afternoon. How about if I stop by then and pick Becky up to take her to choose which one she wants?"

"That'll be fine," Laurel said. "I'm sure she'll be thrilled."

"All right." Stephen's voice was brisk, as though he had already wasted too much time talking with her. "If there's nothing else, then?"

"No. Nothing," Laurel said in a rush. "Goodbye."

When she hung up the phone she went limp with reaction. Thank God, she told herself, that's over. Now she could get on with the business of the day and think no more about Stephen Tanner.

Around noon Laurel drove to the school to pick up her kindergarten charges. When she returned, Julia asked one of the assistants to see that they were occupied for a few minutes. "I need to speak to Laurel in the office for a moment," she told the woman, "but I'll be back shortly to help you get them all settled down for their naps."

After the two sisters entered the office and closed the door, Laurel looked at Julia curiously. "More trouble with Becky today?" she asked.

To her surprise, Julia's face turned a delicate shade of pink. "No," she answered, "but it does have to do with the school principal, Clark Baskin. He called while you were out."

Laurel frowned. "Has he decided against using us to care for his son, David, then?" Yesterday he had made definite arrangements with Julia at the school

conference to enroll the child at the center beginning
the following week.

"No," Julia said again. "It's nothing to do with
any of the children. He . . . he called and asked me
to go out to dinner tonight with him."

No wonder her face had gone so flushed. Julia had
been asked for a date, and she was embarrassed
about it. Laurel hid her smile of amusement over
Julia's self-consciousness. "Did you accept?"

Julia nodded. "Yes. Yes, I did."

Laurel was faintly surprised. Not once since her
separation and divorce from Bert had Julia gone out
with another man, though she had been asked a
number of times. Maybe she was finally emerging
from her shell.

"Good for you," she said firmly. "It's about time
you started going out."

"There's only one thing," Julia said. "Becky. Can
she stay the night with you, Laurel, so I can be free
to go? I can't leave her at home alone."

Laurel laughed. "Sure. No problem."

At four-thirty that afternoon, Becky waited excitedly in Laurel's office. Julia had told her about the
puppy as soon as she had arrived from school, and
now she was impatient for Stephen to come for her.

When he did, Annette Pharr was with him. She
preceded him into the office, and a cloud of heavy
perfume suddenly stifled the air in the small room.
She was dressed casually in slacks and a red silk
blouse, but everything about her was neat and well
groomed, understated elegance and sophistication.

She smiled and spoke civilly to Laurel. "I hope the
opening of your center has gone well."

Laurel forced her lips into an answering smile. But
she was thinking that it wasn't fair for Annette to
look so beautiful, so perfect, in the late afternoon,
while Laurel herself felt grubby and unkempt after a
long day at work. There was no way Stephen could
help but notice the difference in the two women's

appearance, and no way that Laurel could not lose heavily in the comparison.

She hoped she kept her frustration hidden as she gave a calm reply. "So far, we're doing fine, thank you." Now, for the first time, she dared to lift her gaze and meet Stephen's unfathomable eyes. She murmured politely, "Would either of you care for a cup of coffee?"

"No, thank you," Stephen answered. "We don't have the time. I promised my friend we'd be at his place before five, and I imagine Becky is eager to see the puppies. Aren't you?" He directed the last question to the child, who stood near the door.

"Yes," Becky responded, almost hopping on one foot. "I can't wait! What color are they, Stephen, and how old are they?"

Julia entered the room at that moment, spoke a few polite words to Annette, thanked Stephen for his kindness, and added, "Please bring Becky back here when you're done. She's going to spend the night with Laurel."

"I am?" Becky asked with faint curiosity. "Why?"

Julia shrugged casually. "I need to be out tonight, and Laurel said you could stay with her."

"Okay," Becky said indifferently. She tugged at Stephen's sleeve. "Can we go now?"

He smiled down at her and gave a playful tug to her long silky hair. "Yes, Miss Impatience," he told her. "We'll go now."

Laurel watched them leave with something akin to envy lodged in her throat. She wished Annette had not been there; she wished that she had been invited along on the jaunt instead. It was a silly thought—after Stephen's coldness last night there was no reason why she should wish to be with him, but she did. She felt left out, forlorn, and she was hurt that he had brought Annette here. He had done it deliberately just to show her how little she meant to him, she was positive.

She was exhausted when she finally climbed the

stairs to her apartment after the long day, but Laurel knew her fatigue was mental rather than physical. It came from the strain of having to see Stephen and the cold indifference with which he had looked at her.

Laurel went straight to the bathroom, where she ran a tub of steaming hot water, threw in some bath-oil beads, and began stripping off her clothes. Then she stepped into the water and slowly lay back until her entire body was covered except for her face.

Gradually she relaxed, and with a lessening of tension came clearer thoughts. There was no need for her to be so upset over Stephen and his opinion of her. She still wanted her independence from men, and that did include him, so she ought to be glad he had shown up today with Annette. It merely proved that though he was still seeing someone else himself, he hadn't wanted her, Laurel, to do the same. It was the age-old chauvinistic approach all over again— the man doing as he darn pleased, while the woman was supposed to sit home faithfully and wait for him while he went out and had *his* fun!

By the time Becky arrived with a wiggly bundle of sandy-brown fur in her arms, Laurel, dressed in her nightgown and robe, had their dinner of spaghetti and meat sauce almost ready and was tossing a salad.

"Come see," Becky shouted as soon as she opened the door. "Come see my puppy, Laurel."

Laurel rushed from the kitchen into the living room and quickly admired the tiny animal. The front door stood open, and she asked, "Stephen didn't come up with you?"

Becky shook her head. "No. He walked with me as far as the stairs, but when he saw the kitchen light he said he was sure you were home and that he had to go. I think he's going to drive Annette back to San Antonio tonight."

Laurel pursed her lips, closed the door, and then held out her hands for the puppy as she pushed all thoughts of Stephen from her mind. "He's a darling," she said as she cuddled the little ball of fur. "I brought up one of the large cardboard boxes I used for moving and put it in the bathroom, lined with an old towel. That can be his bed for the night."

"Stephen bought me a bag of puppy food," Becky said, pointing to it on the floor near the door, "and he said we should put an alarm clock in his bed tonight. The ticking makes them think it's their mother's heart beating, and then maybe he won't cry so much."

"Yes," Laurel said, handing the puppy back to Becky. "I've heard that before, and I think I have an old alarm clock. I'll go find it. Why don't you feed him and then wash up so we can eat?"

A half hour later the two of them sat down to eat while the puppy curled up beside his bowl of food and took a little nap. Only then did Becky think to ask, "Where did Mom have to go tonight?"

Julia had told Laurel to explain, since she could hardly have done it herself earlier with everyone around. Laurel sucked in a breath and said, "Your mother went out to dinner this evening with Mr. Baskin."

Becky's hazel eyes, so like her mother's, rounded, and she dropped her fork to her plate with a little clatter. "You mean she has a *date* with him? The *principal?*" Her voice was shrill with shock and disapproval.

Laurel nodded and calmly took a sip of her tea. "Sure. Why not?"

"Why not?" Becky exclaimed. "Because she's my mother! Because she should be with my daddy, not with some other man!" Her lower lip trembled, but her chin jutted out implacably.

Laurel reached across the table and covered Becky's hand in a comforting gesture. "I know none of it is easy on you, honey," she said gently. "But what you just said doesn't make sense, you know. She can't be with your daddy because he's married to somebody else now. Just because she's your mother is no reason she shouldn't have an occasional date with another man. Mothers need to have some sort of social life, the same as children do. You like to have friends. Remember how happy you were when Pat and Matt invited you over to their house? Well, it's exactly the same thing. Your mother needs friends, too."

"Not *men* friends!" Becky said obstinately.

"Yes," Laurel contradicted. "She does. Maybe you're still a bit too young to understand that, but it's true. And it was bound to happen sometime, Becky, so you're just going to have to learn how to accept it."

"No!" Becky shook her head, pushed back her chair, and stood up. "No, I won't accept it! I hate it! I hate Mom, and I hate Mr. Baskin!" Her eyes flashed dangerous sparks and her lips pressed into an uncompromising line.

Laurel stood up and went to her, gathering the child into her arms. "You really must stop saying you hate everything and everyone, sweetheart," she said softly. "Hate is a poison, and it poisons the one who does the hating. And you don't really mean it, anyway." She lifted Becky's chin so that she could smile at her and added, "Now, cheer up and be glad your mother is getting out and enjoying herself for a change."

Although Becky calmed down, she remained firmly opposed to the idea of her mother's going out with a man, any man. At last, helplessly, Laurel dropped the subject.

The puppy was the salvation of the remainder of an evening that had started so dismally. He distracted Becky from her dark thoughts to the point where she would actually laugh.

She named him Rascal, and both she and Laurel enjoyed watching him waddle across the floor. He was so pudgy that he could only stagger. He was friendly enough while they played with him, his little pink tongue often darting out to give an affectionate lick to his new mistress. But when it came his bedtime, matters changed.

Becky slept with Laurel that night instead of in the spare room. Laurel knew she was really upset about her mother, so she made no demur when the child asked to sleep with her. But though Becky drifted off almost at once, Laurel was kept awake for a long time by the puppy's unhappy yapping from the bathroom, by her sympathy for both Julia and Becky, and by her own uncomfortable thoughts about Stephen.

In the morning Laurel went downstairs while Becky finished her breakfast and stayed behind to feed Rascal and play with him until she had to leave for school. When she reached the foot of the stairs, Julia was just entering the front door.

"How did your evening go?" Laurel asked.

Julia gave her a glowing smile. "Wonderful. He asked me out again, too, so I guess he likes me."

Laurel laughed. "Of course he does. And you? How do you feel about him?"

"I really like Clark a lot," Julia admitted frankly. "We talked for hours. Honestly, Laurel, it's almost unreal how much we both like the same things." She glanced toward the stairs leading to the apartment and asked in an undertone, "How did Becky take the news?"

Laurel grimaced. "About as badly as possible," she said truthfully. She hated to wipe away that happy expression on her sister's face, but she would have to find out how things really stood sooner or later.

A moment later Becky tripped down the stairs, and Julia went to meet her, a hopeful smile on her lips as she asked, "Did you get your puppy? Will you take me up to see him?"

"He's in Laurel's bathroom if you want to see

him," Becky said defiantly. "I'm leaving for school now." She brushed past her mother and toward the main door.

"Becky!" Julia called sharply.

Becky half turned to glance back over her shoulder. "I don't want to talk to you, Mother," she snapped. "Just leave me alone, okay?" Then she rushed out of the house.

Julia turned a helpless gaze upon Laurel, but there was nothing Laurel could do except say, "She'll come around. She's just got to get used to the idea, that's all."

The doorbell rang, and the subject was necessarily shelved as their workday began.

At ten, while the others were serving the children their midmorning snack of cookies and juice, Laurel drove to the bank to make a deposit. It was a gorgeous sunny day in early March that felt almost like summer. Laurel felt the pull of the day and wished she could be outside enjoying the weather.

Her business at the bank did not take long, and just as she pushed through the heavy glass doors and started down the steps outside, Stephen was coming up them.

Both of them were taken by surprise, and for a moment they paused and merely gazed wordlessly at each other. Laurel had time to drink in the sight of him: his white western-cut shirt that made his hair appear Indian black; the blue denim jeans that hugged his lean, muscular legs; the way the sunlight played light and shadows across his angular face. She had time, too, to be glad that she was wearing a flattering yellow print dress that curved gently around her breasts and flared softly at her hips.

At last Stephen broke the spell that imprisoned them. Slowly he ascended the remaining steps between them until he stood at her side, and when he reached her a smile came to his lips.

"Good morning," he said as though he were really glad to see her.

"Good morning," she answered, unable to conceal a smile of her own that showed her gladness at meeting him.

"You look very lovely today," he said in a low voice. "Like a sunflower."

"Thank you." Laurel felt stupid because she couldn't think of anything bright and interesting to say. But at that moment she could only feel, not think. Her heart tripped unsteadily beneath the admiration of his gaze, and his nearness was doing insane things to her senses. This morning he smelled faintly of aftershave lotion, and the warmth, the vitality, of his presence seemed to be sapping her of her strength, rendering her weak-kneed and breathless.

"I've got to go inside for a minute," Stephen said after another lengthy silence during which their gazes locked and held, "but I won't be long. My car's parked at the end of the block. Would you wait for me there? I'd like to talk to you . . . in private."

Almost mesmerized, Laurel found herself nodding. "All right," she agreed in a slightly thickened voice.

Stephen's hand reached out and lightly touched her bare arm. "Good." He gave another smile, and its radiating heat robbed her of all rationality. "I'll join you shortly."

Once she was inside his car, Laurel's mind cleared and she asked herself what she was doing here. She should have said no and gone straight back to the center where she was needed. But even as the thought ran through her mind, she knew she would stay. Today there was that magnetic pull between them again that was stronger than her independent will.

When Stephen came, he didn't, as she had supposed, plan to speak to her there, parked along the busy business street. He started the car and set it in motion.

"Where are we going?" Laurel asked after a while, not really caring.

"Where we can talk without being interrupted," he replied.

"But my car . . ."

"We'll come back for it," he answered.

"I can't stay away too long," she told him. "About noon I have to pick up the kindergarteners at school."

"I'll have you back in plenty of time, I promise," Stephen said. He turned a corner, then threw her a smile.

Laurel returned it and leaned back against the seat, content for the moment and unwilling to spoil it by insisting that she needed to get back to the center.

Stephen drove to the river and parked not far from where Laurel had the day she had taken Becky there. He cut the motor, and for a long while there was only silence between them as they both gazed at the rushing cold river waters that sparkled and glinted beneath the brilliant sun. Live oaks and cypress trees lined the banks and dappled the river with strange shadowy patterns. From the opened car windows they could hear the cheerful chirps of sparrows and, from a distance, the call of a bob-white.

At last Stephen turned to her, giving her the powerful force of his undivided attention. Laurel's throat went dry with emotion at the tender expression in his eyes.

His hand went to her shoulder and brushed against it, and then his fingers entwined in her curly, thick hair. "I can't forget our night together," he said huskily. "And I still want you, Laurel. I believe I want you more than I've ever wanted any other woman in my life." There was a sound of surprise in his voice, but the smile on his lips was hesitant, almost uncertain, as though Stephen were unsure of her reaction and prepared for her rejection.

But Laurel was beyond playing coy games. Her

own hand went up to his against her shoulder and she covered it with her slender fingers. "I . . . I can't forget that night, either," she whispered shakily.

Stephen drew her to him then, gathering her close against the hard strength of his body as his arms slid around her back. When his head bent to hers, Laurel unresistingly gave him her lips.

His kiss was ruthless and demanding, almost smothering in its intensity as his lips forced hers to part. White-hot desire swept through Laurel as her own lips responded. Her hands moved up his shoulders, caressed his neck, and then raked through his hair as she clung to him. Stephen uttered a groan, and one of his hands came around to cup her breast.

"Damn it, I want you!" he muttered thickly. His fingers slid inside her dress to touch the soft, tender flesh of her breast. "I want you *now!*" But, as though to deny his words, he pushed himself away from her, and for a time the only sounds were their labored breathing as they both sought to gain control of their emotions and the tinkling cadence of the river as it rushed its way across the rockbed.

Laurel was suddenly uncertain whether he was angry with her or with himself. Tentatively she reached out a hand and rested it against his still heaving chest. "You're not . . . you're not upset with me, are you?" she asked anxiously.

Stephen gave a short laugh, grabbed her hand, and raised it to his lips. "Hell, yes," he stated, but he said it with a grin. "I'm very upset with you! Here it is in the middle of the morning and we're out in broad daylight where anybody might come by and see us, and I want to make love to you here and now!" He sucked in a deep breath, then went on more calmly. "But I won't. It's neither the time nor the place for it, much as I ache for you. I need to get back to the ranch and set out new salt blocks for the cattle and see if one of my men got our tractor repaired, and I know you have to get back to work, too. But, Laurel, will you let me see you tonight?

We can have dinner at my place like the last time, and I promise I won't give you any argument about going home later. Please come!" There was a husky urgency to his voice.

"Yes," she answered, knowing it was what she wanted more than anything else. "Yes, I'll come, Stephen."

He bent and gave her a quick chaste peck on her lips. "Thank God!" he exclaimed fervently. Then he laughed. "I'll take you back to town now before I forget my good intentions for the time being. If I'm lucky, I might actually manage to concentrate on my work today, knowing I'll be with you tonight."

"Me, too." Laurel smiled almost sadly, thinking of how much time she had wasted in fruitless day-dreaming these past few days.

There was a wicked gleam in Stephen's eyes. "Oho!" he said. "So what happened between us has been gnawing away at you, too! That's good! I hope you've spent as many sleepless hours as I have! You deserve every form of punishment there is for putting me through such torture!"

Laurel pulled his head down and boldly gave him an apologetic kiss. "I'm sorry," she said a moment later. "Does that make up for it a little?"

"Only a little." Stephen laughed. "You can finish your apology tonight. Right now I don't trust myself with you a moment longer than necessary. Come to think of it," he added with a teasing grin, "I don't trust you either."

It was only when she returned to the center that Laurel remembered Annette, and a shadow darkened the bright day. Stephen was playing an ugly game, and chills suddenly climbed her spine. What was she doing? she asked herself fiercely. If she allowed herself to become involved with a man who she knew already had another woman, she was simply asking to be hurt again!

Bitter gall rose in her throat as she parked the car in the drive and slowly walked toward the house. She had been allowing physical magnetism and raw emotions to dominate over logic.

No more, she ordered herself. From now on she would keep her feelings sternly under the tightest of control. Her salvation depended upon it! She would not, she decided, go to Stephen tonight, after all.

It was very easy to tell herself so. But, all the same, an ache of loss lodged in her throat and her eyes smarted with unshed tears as she entered the coolness of the house.

Chapter Seven

Since Stephen had said he would be by to pick her up early, around five-thirty, Laurel telephoned him at five to forestall him.

"I've changed my mind," she said in a slightly thickened voice. "I really don't think tonight is a very good idea, after all."

"Why not?" Stephen's voice was as hard as limestone.

"You know why." She lowered her voice. "We're simply becoming involved too fast, and I—" She never got to finish the sentence because Stephen hung up on her with a loud clang.

Tears smarted Laurel's eyes as she stared at the office wall. Well, what had she expected? she demanded of herself. That he would be delighted that once again she was backing out? What was wrong with her, anyway, she wondered dismally, turning hot, then cold, as she was doing? She was acting crazy, and Stephen could hardly be blamed for being furious with her. She was furious with herself. She didn't know her own mind anymore. She wanted him, yet she didn't and if her conflicting actions were confusing him, it was nothing compared to her own confusion and misery.

Abruptly, Laurel brushed the tears away, stood up, and went to join the others in the end-of-the-day routine. She hugged a tired and cranky two-year-old, reassured the first grader that the Tooth Fairy would surely visit him tonight even though he had misplaced the tooth he had lost at school today, and helped another child tie his shoelaces.

It was close to a quarter of six by the time everyone was gone and she could climb the stairs to her apartment. Even before she crossed the small upstairs hall, the scent of tobacco alerted her that someone was in the living room. Laurel stiffened with outrage that someone would dare to try to rob her, and she marched smartly into the room, too angry to even think of being afraid.

Stephen sat in an armchair, calmly smoking. A swirl of pale gray cigarette smoke wafted spirals before him. One black-trousered leg was casually crossed at a right angle over the other. He looked thoroughly comfortable, as though he had been there for some time.

"Make yourself at home, will you?" Laurel said in a deceptively sweet voice.

He inclined his head slightly. "I have, thank you."

"How did you get in here?" she demanded. She stood in front of him, hands on hips, and her eyes flashed with indignation.

"I'm the landlord, remember?" he answered indifferently. "I have a key of my own."

"Then maybe it's time I had a safety lock put on the door," she snapped. "I thought you were a burglar."

Unhurriedly Stephen rose to his feet. "In the time we've known each other you've thought me a number of things, all of them unflattering," he stated. "Now, what's all this nonsense about tonight? This morning you seemed eager enough to accept a date with me."

Laurel felt her face heat. "I told you . . . things are moving too fast, and I . . . ."

"You're afraid of it."

"Yes."

There was a short silence, and then Stephen said, "Go get changed into something a little dressier. And bring your coat."

"I won't go to your house," Laurel said doggedly, her gaze fixed at the open V of his shirt where she could glimpse his darkly bronzed neck. Somehow she lacked the courage to meet his eyes.

"We aren't going to my house," Stephen said. "But I promised you dinner, and we're going to have it . . . together. Now, get a move on. We've got a drive ahead of us." Laurel lifted her thick lashes and risked looking at his face, which was strangely unreadable. He didn't appear angry, but he didn't look as though he particularly liked her very much, either. More than anything he looked determined, and a second later he confirmed her suspicion by adding, "If you don't go change right now, I'll help you."

She could see that he meant it, that he was not going to allow her to back out of their date. Laurel wavered for an instant, then decided that if she was prudent, she had better do as he said. She gave a brief nod, then went toward her bedroom.

Thirty minutes later, wearing a dress of russet-red that blended with her hair and carrying her coat draped across her arm, Laurel accompanied Stephen to his car. When she slid onto the seat, she saw that his leather jacket was slung carelessly across the back.

To Laurel's surprise, Stephen drove though town and continued onward until they reached the highway. "Where are we going?" she asked, breaking the heavy silence that lay between them.

"We're going to San Antonio for dinner," he answered.

"Oh."

"Ever been to the *Paseo del Rio?*" he asked.

She shook her head. "No. On our way down to Mexico last summer Julia and I visited the Alamo and the HemisFair Plaza, but that's all."

"Then you missed the most scenic part of the city altogether, and it's very close to the Alamo. That's where we're going."

"Oh."

"Stop saying 'oh' every second, as though you're afraid I'm going to bite your head off if you say anything more," Stephen roared. Then he lowered his voice and added, "I think I understand, in part at least, your objections about us. Things *have* moved fast, so maybe it's time for us to slow down. So forget your fears. Tonight is strictly for fun, nothing more. Okay?"

Laurel was hesitant, but after a moment she nodded. "All right."

Stephen tossed her a quick smile that seemed to light up the dusky evening like a bright golden sun. Laurel lost her nervousness at being with him. Absurdly, all at once she was happy and carefree and she looked forward to the evening ahead.

"How does Becky like her puppy?" Stephen asked after a time.

Laurel laughed. "She adores him, and he adores her."

"A mutual admiration society, hmm?"

"Precisely. And she couldn't have gotten him at a better time. It helped her last night somewhat, anyway, to get her mind off her anger toward Julia."

"What's the matter there?" he asked, sounding genuinely interested and concerned.

"Julia had a date last night for the very first time since her divorce, and Becky just couldn't handle it."

Stephen frowned, pulled a cigarette from his pocket, and lit it. "Poor kid," he said. "I suppose it is hard for a youngster to get used to something like that."

"Yes." Laurel sighed. "Divorce can be so horrible, so cruel and hard on everybody concerned. I *never* want to go through what Julia has!"

"You want the till-death-do-us-part sort of marriage?"

"I'm not sure I even believe in it anymore," Laurel admitted. "I've seen a number of my friends end up in divorces, too. It's such a crazy world these days. There's no stability anymore, no loyalties, no guarantees for anybody. I'm not sure I care to ever get married. What if it ended in divorce and I had children like Becky? If it were only the couple involved, it wouldn't be quite so bad, but it's the innocent little children who get hurt the most."

"You've got something there," Stephen agreed. "But, on the other hand, if people never took chances on marriage, they would never find out if they could have been lucky in love and might have missed out on a lifetime of fulfillment and happiness."

They were entering the outer fringes of San Antonio then, and the conversation was dropped as Stephen concentrated on the heavy freeway traffic.

When they arrived at the *Paseo del Rio,* or River Walk, Laurel gasped with pleasure. It was a lush tropical paradise, and the walkways beside the river were bordered by shops, restaurants, and art galleries.

"Like it?" Stephen bent close to her ear to ask.

Laurel's eyes sparkled. "I love it!" She turned to him with a glowing smile. "Thank you for bringing me."

He gave her an answering smile. "My pleasure. Shall we walk for a bit first, or would you rather eat now?"

"Let's walk," she elected.

Casually Stephen took her hand in his, and they ambled slowly past boutique shops and restaurants. The river itself was alive with paddleboats and a large water taxi filled with evening sightseers. Though the night air was cool and bracing, it in no way infringed upon anyone's enjoyment. Laughter floated along the river's banks.

They passed spreading palm fronds and luxuriant shrubbery and mounted the steps to an arched footbridge spanning the river. Cottonwoods towered above them along both banks, and evening lights cast iridescent colors that shimmered on the river below. Laurel was enchanted with the loveliness of it all, and when she spotted tables and chairs in front of an outdoor restaurant, she exclaimed, "Oh, when the weather is warmer, I must bring Julia and Becky here to dine outdoors."

"It's a bit too chilly to enjoy a meal outside tonight, but already the days are warm enough that it would be pleasant," Stephen said.

At length they entered a restaurant and relaxed over the food and wine.

Stephen gave Laurel a teasing smile. "Glad I forced you to come?"

She laughed. "Yes. You're a terrible bully, but I am glad. Are you?"

His smile widened. "If I hadn't wanted to spend the evening with you, I wouldn't have bothered to practically kidnap you."

Laurel lowered her gaze to the snow-white tablecloth. "I guess you think I've been acting pretty ridiculous," she said softly.

"More like you aren't sure you know what you want. And I'd prefer it if you were sure, Laurel," Stephen said gently. "Because I'm very sure that I want you. But if you need time to sort out your feelings about me, I'm not going to rush you anymore." He smoothly changed the subject then, sparing her any embarrassment or uncertainty by asking, "Did you enjoy your trip to Mexico?"

"Yes. We went to Monterrey and had a wonderful time. It's very beautiful there."

He nodded. "I've been there a number of times. One of my mother's brothers still lives there."

"Really?" she asked, surprised. "Somehow I got the idea that you didn't have any relatives."

Stephen laughed, picked up his wine, and took a

sip of it. "Oh, I've got lots of cousins littering
Mexico and Texas, and even a few on my father's
side of the family somewhere in Pennsylvania,
though I don't know much about them. My mother's
family originally settled in Texas when her ancestors
were given a land grant by the Spanish government,
way back before this land *was* a state. My
great-great-grandfather on the Tanner side arrived
here as a very young man, bought some land, and
began ranching. Later, he fought in the Civil War.
Both sides of my family were among the earliest
settlers of the area."

"Do you enjoy ranching?" she asked curiously.

"It's my life," he answered simply. "I was born to
the land. It's where I belong, where I want my own
children to be born and raised someday."

"You were an only child?"

"Yes, though I can't say I was ever lonely. There
were always the ranch hands' children to play with,
besides a few local cousins. On the other hand, I
missed out on a really close relationship like you and
Julia seem to have."

Laurel smiled. "We are close, of course, but,
on the other hand, we don't have deep roots the
way you do here. The two of us were born and
raised in Boston, but my mother came from New
Hampshire and my dad was from Ohio. We have
no family in Boston, nothing to really keep us
there."

"Why did you come to Tierra Nueva of all
places?" he asked. "I've always been curious about
why you chose a small town instead of . . . say,
San Antonio."

Laurel laughed, told him the story of Julia's
antique search, then added, "We both felt we
needed a complete change in our lives . . . someplace different. When we saw Tierra Nueva, we fell
in love with its quaint, small-town atmosphere."

Stephen gazed at her intently. "I can understand
why Julia wanted to move after her divorce, but why

did you feel you needed such a drastic change as well?"

Laurel shrugged and toyed with a corner of her linen napkin, not answering.

"Was it a man?"

She nodded, avoiding his eyes. "Yes."

"Do you still love him?"

Her gaze flew to his face. "No!" she said quickly. "No, I don't."

A slow smile spread across Stephen's face. "Good," he said softly. His hand covered hers, warm and strong.

A quiver of longing shook Laurel. What was it about this man that had such a powerful sway over her emotions? she wondered. He had only to look at her in a certain manner with those liquid coffee-colored eyes, only to smile in that just off-centered way, only to touch her no matter how innocuously, for her to be reduced to a state where she no longer thought coherently.

After dinner they took a water-taxi ride on the river and then walked the few blocks to the car for the drive home. The parking lot was in semidarkness, and once they were inside the car, Stephen turned to her. All she could see was the deep shadow of his profile before she felt his hand on her arm as he drew her to him and softly kissed her.

The kiss bore no relation to the fierce hunger of the one they had shared that morning. Rather, this one was gently caring. When they drew apart, Laurel felt Stephen's smile through the darkness. "It wasn't such a bad evening, was it?" he whispered teasingly.

"It was a wonderful evening," she said, with a sigh of regret that it was almost over.

"Would it be asking too much of you," Stephen inquired, "or pushing things too fast if I asked you to sit here beside me on the way home instead of over there where I can hardly even see you? I want to feel your warmth next to me."

Obediently Laurel nestled her head against his shoulder. A lump in her throat prevented her from speaking, but there was really no need for words. Stephen brushed her forehead with a light kiss, then started the car.

They talked little on the drive back, but the silence between them was peaceful and contented. Laurel was enclosed in a wonderfully warm cocoon with Stephen's arm draped lightly around her. Occasionally his hand would stray to her arm and move up and down it in a sensual motion that sent tingles along her nerve ends.

When they reached Tierra Nueva and the car turned in the direction of her apartment, Laurel suddenly sat upright and protested boldly, "I don't want to go home yet."

Stephen's features were sharply etched, like a silhouette, as they drove past a streetlight, and the glance he threw her was penetrating. "What do you mean?" he asked bluntly.

"I mean . . ." She hesitated only a fraction of a moment, sucked in a deep breath, then went on in a rush. "I want to go home with you . . . for a while."

There was an odd little silence; then Stephen asked in a tight, strained voice, "Do you realize what you're saying?"

"Exactly."

"But this afternoon you . . ."

"Had changed my mind," she finished for him. "Now I'm changing it again . . . if you still want me."

"Want you?" Stephen's voice cracked over the words. "Are you sure this time, Laurel? You're not playing games?"

"I'm not playing games," she murmured softly. And she wasn't. This morning she had wanted to be with him more than anything; tonight she felt the same. Once again all doubts and uncertainties were swept away. Laurel was only aware of this man beside her and of their mutual attraction and desire for each other. Just now there seemed no justifiable reason to deny those feelings.

The ranch house was in darkness except for a dim light in the hall, but it was enough to illuminate their way upstairs. Stephen's arm was secure around Laurel's waist as they went, and the moment they entered the bedroom he drew her to him, lowered his head, and kissed her with all the longing he had displayed that morning.

His eyes blazed as he gave her a tender smile. "Still sure?" he asked huskily. "Because if you're not, you'd better leave right now. I want you very much, darling." His thumb was tracing the delicate outline of her face.

"I'm sure," Laurel whispered just before she was crushed against the strength and hardness of his chest.

Stephen picked her up and carried her to the bed, then lowered himself beside her. His fingers went to the buttons on her dress while his lips again sought the sweetness of hers.

The dress was tossed aside, and Stephen unhooked her bra while Laurel tugged his shirt loose from his waistband. Once her breasts were free of restraint, Stephen bent over her and cupped one in his hand as his lips covered its nipple. Delicious shivers of desire danced across her bared skin, and Laurel slid her hands under his shirt and up his back, pressing him closer to her. Stephen's own hands then went to her back and he half lifted her against him so that his lips could touch her throat. His kisses were flames that burned every place they rested upon her. Laurel, knowing she was totally consumed, could utter not a single protest. Her body had been rendered weak by the needs he aroused in it, and a moment later, when he drew away from her, she cried out in protest.

"I'm not going anywhere," he said hoarsely.

She opened her eyes and saw by the dim light that he was removing his clothes. Almost immediately he

was back. Until then she hadn't even realized she
still wore her panty hose and half slip. Stephen slid
them down over her hips and legs before at last
stretching out full length beside her.

His mouth sought and found hers once more as he
gathered her to him, pressing her soft breasts against
his lean, furry chest. His hands traveled from her
back down to her hips, drawing her yet closer to the
hardness of his body. An ache of warm need was like
a leaden weight in Laurel's lower limbs, and she
trembled both with a heightened awareness of his
nearness and with a torturous craving for him to end
her agony.

At last he pressed her back against the pillows and
came to her. Laurel arched toward him, her heart
thudding as a primitive passion swept them both into
its maelstrom current, tossing them where it would,
relentlessly claiming its victims with no regard to
whether they might drown or live. This moment
alone contained them, disassociated from past or
future.

A half hour later they lay close together, a sheet
covering their bodies. Laurel's index finger made
circles on Stephen's shoulder. All their pent-up
desires had been expended, and for the moment
there was nothing more either of them wanted
except the contentment of being together, their
warm bodies lightly touching.

Tonight had been more wonderful than the first
time, Laurel marveled to herself. Stephen's eyes
were closed, and so she gazed openly at him. Her
senses drank in the chiseled ruggedness of his
features, the stone-hardness of his sun-browned
shoulders and chest, and she was bemused by his
masculine, virile looks. Never before had any man
stirred her emotions as this man did, and she was uncertain what it all meant or where it would lead.

Stephen opened his eyes abruptly and caught her
gazing at him. His lips stretched into an easy smile.
"A penny for them," he said softly.

Laurel's face warmed and she shook her head. "Nothing," she said hurriedly. "I wasn't thinking about much of anything, really."

"That's too bad. I was hoping you were thinking how devastatingly attractive I am and how you can't bear to be away from me," he teased softly. Then his voice grew more serious. "That's how I feel, you know. You're the most beautiful creature I've ever known, and I adore you, Laurel. I don't want to be apart from you."

Laurel smiled uncertainly. "You're talking nonsense," she said lightly. Briskly she sat upright. "Right now I'd like a shower before you drive me home," she stated. As a sudden modesty and shyness assailed her, she grabbed the top sheet from the bed and wrapped it around her nude body.

Stephen reached to a nearby chair and, picking up his bathrobe, shoved his arms into it while Laurel gathered her clothes. "Maybe it would be a good idea if you brought a spare toothbrush and a few extra clothes to leave here," he said mildly. Then he lifted a quizzical eyebrow at her, awaiting her reaction. Laurel's face heated, but she said nothing. When she turned in the direction of his adjacent bathroom, he added, "You might prefer the one across the hall. I believe Annette left a shower cap and some bath-oil things the last time she was here."

Laurel went perfectly still, and slowly a tremendous rage spread through her. "You're actually suggesting I make use of things your other women have left here?" she asked with frigid incredulity.

She heard Stephen's quick indraw of breath. "I didn't mean it that way," he said calmly. "Annette won't—"

He got no further as Laurel turned on him like a wildcat and screamed, "The last thing I want to hear about is your girl friend! What sort of man are you, anyway?"

Black anger smoldered in Stephen's eyes and his face was dark, like a threatening storm. "I'm not the

sort of monster you think me, that's for damn sure!"
he seethed. "I'm not a kiss-and-tell sort! The women
who have shared my bed in the past are none of your
business, and if you believe I'm going to discuss
them with you, you're much mistaken!"

"Oh, I was mistaken, all right!" Laurel raged.
"Mistaken in coming here tonight. But that's a
mistake I have no intention of repeating! There's no
way I'm going to allow my life to be messed up by
becoming involved with a man who spreads himself
around!" Swiftly she turned toward his bathroom,
where she would dress. She would rather die before
using the other one . . . the one with Annette's
belongings in it!

But she was brought to a shocking halt as a hand
gripped her arm. "And would you," Stephen asked
just behind her, "become involved with me if you
knew *positively* that you were the only woman in my
life at the present?"

Though her back was turned to him and she
couldn't see his face, she could sense Stephen's
waiting stillness. Laurel wavered, but then her pride
came full force, protecting her. "No," she croaked
out. "I won't. I don't want to belong to any man, to
be owned or possessed or controlled. The . . . the
time would come when we would eventually part,
and I don't intend to be hurt that way. I want my
independence."

"In other words"—Stephen's voice dripped with
ice—"you'll sleep with me occasionally, but you
won't belong to me in any meaningful sense?" He
released her arm and added in a flat tone, "Go get
dressed and I'll drive you home."

Laurel's fingers trembled as she dressed. She was
wildly furious with Stephen for making her sound so
little, so cheap. And she wasn't like that! She wasn't!

But the next day his words returned to mock her.
Calmer now that she was away from his disturbing
presence, she wondered if she had meant what he
had said—that she would have an affair with a man,

him, yet not allow anything deeper to grow between them.

The trouble was, she thought despondently as she ignored the menu plans that were spread before her on the desk, that she already did feel something deeper for him. There was an undeniably magic spark between them physically, but what she felt for him was much more than just that. Stephen exuded vital masculine charm the way some people simply breathed, and she was sharply aware of his compelling, magnetic attraction. No one could be more conscious than she was of his overt sensuality or of the devastating impact of both his body and his personality. When he chose to, Stephen could be great fun and a marvelous companion. She already had proof of how kind and generous he could be, not only to her but to others, as well. Julia liked him, and Becky was crazy about him; and Laurel had even had the opportunity to notice how popular and respected he was in town by other people. He was the Rock of Gibraltar type, a man of decision, one who easily took command and responsibility upon his shoulders. He was a man who was sure of his own worth, yet at the same time he had a sense of humor. He was everything she had ever dreamed of in a man who would make an ideal husband.

Husband! The word jerked Laurel's head up, and she stared blankly out the window. Her eyes took in the loveliness of the spring day, the children playing on the climber and the tire swings and the assistant who was standing nearby watching them. But her mind never saw any of it at all. Why had she even thought of such a word in connection with Stephen? That was crazy, she told herself severely, crazy and completely out of line. First of all, she had no desire to marry any man, no matter how many good qualities he might possess. Secondly, she did not love him. And third, he had never, by a single word, given her an indication that such a step was in his thoughts, and she would do well to remember that.

Stephen liked her and enjoyed her company, and there was no doubt that she appealed to him physically. But that was all there was to it. If and when the time came for Stephen to marry, he would most likely choose someone like Annette Pharr who came from a background similar to his, one of wealth and position. In the meantime he would continue to enjoy himself with all the ladies, exactly as her ex-fiancé had done.

Except her, she reminded herself grimly. There would be no more incidents between them such as had happened last night. That was playing with fire, and Laurel knew it. So what if he had practically assured her that she was the only girl in his life at the moment? That proved nothing except that he wanted her now, for a time. But, for Laurel, that wasn't good enough.

Early Saturday morning Laurel drove to Julia's house and for the first time got to meet Clark Baskin. He was calmly sitting in the living room sipping a cup of coffee when Laurel arrived. As soon as he saw her, he stood up politely.

Laurel flashed him a quick smile. "You must be Clark," she stated.

He smiled and nodded. "You must be Laurel."

The two of them shook hands, and then Laurel motioned for him to sit down again as he said, "Julia's still dressing."

"Is Becky awake yet?" she asked.

"I don't believe so." He shook his head. "It's too bad we couldn't convince her to come with us today. I think she would enjoy Nuevo Laredo."

"Perhaps another time," Laurel said. She sat down in a chair across from him and studied him curiously. He was a pleasant-looking man with sandy hair and kind blue eyes. Otherwise, he was average in every way—average height, average appearance. Though he probably wore a business suit every day at school, today he was dressed in casual slacks and a short-sleeved tan shirt that was open at the neck. He

was utterly unlike her sister's former husband in
looks, and in personality as well, if his quiet-spoken,
serious manner was anything to go by. Laurel could
scarcely believe that Julia was actually attracted to
him. Somehow she had expected someone more like
Bert . . . a handsome, lighthearted extrovert.

Just then Julia entered the room, wearing a soft
pink sundress and a matching jacket. She looked
lovely this morning, and her eyes sparkled with
anticipation of a day's shopping and browsing at the
Mexican border.

"Hi, Laurel," she greeted. "I suppose you two
have introduced yourselves."

"We have," Laurel said.

Julia glanced toward Clark. "Well, I suppose I'm
ready to go if you are. Laurel, thanks for keeping
Becky."

Laurel laughed. "It's nothing. I had no other
plans, anyway." She turned to Clark and asked,
"What about your son? I never thought about
offering to take care of him earlier, but . . ."

Clark smiled. "Thanks for the offer, Laurel, but
David is staying the weekend with his grandmother
in Houston. My mother-in-law came for him yesterday."

Julia was checking her purse. "Becky's still asleep,
Laurel, so if you have things to do at home, you'll
have to wake her. Otherwise, there's coffee already
made in the kitchen and the morning paper's on the
table if you want to just relax here for a while. I
called Stephen last night to tell him Becky would be
at your place when he comes to get her. Both Clark
and I tried to talk her into coming to Mexico for the
day with us, but she's more interested in those
horses than a day of shopping and sightseeing."

"So Clark told me. Well, you two get going.
You've got a long drive ahead of you. Be careful,
and have fun."

When Stephen arrived three hours later at her
apartment to pick up Becky, Laurel was purposeful-

ly busy out of sight in the kitchen. Vigorously, as
though her life depended on it, she was polishing the
exterior of the refrigerator. She was certain that he
would not come inside to seek her out. Since the last
thing she wanted today was another confrontation
with him, she felt the safest thing was to make
herself scarce.

But, to her chagrin, Becky led him through the
living room and into the kitchen. "Here's Stephen,"
she announced brightly, completely oblivious to
what she had just done to her aunt's strained nerves.

Laurel's hand stopped its activity as she glanced
across the length of the small kitchen, and her heart
seemed to do a double flip when she saw him
standing there. He was wearing faded Levi's and a
multicolored print western shirt, and on his head
was his Stetson. His face was somber and unsmiling
as he gazed at her, and in that one split second
Laurel knew positively what she had been denying to
herself. She loved him. Wholeheartedly, without
reservations, she was deeply and forever in love. She
knew it. Her feeling for Stephen was so strong, so
intense, that it made the fond infatuation she had
felt for Ken almost laughable by comparison. Only,
just now, she saw nothing funny about the situation.
The realization was a shock, a dreadful blow, and for
the moment her head spun, as though she were
riding a merry-go-round.

"Good morning." Stephen's strong, matter-of-
fact voice brought her back to normal.

"Good morning." she answered in soft politeness.
"It looks like you two will have a lovely day for your
ride."

"Yes," Stephen agreed. "It does. And Julia and
Clark will have a lovely day for their trip to the
border." He happened to glance down at Becky and
noticed her drooping lower lip. "What's eating
you?" he demanded. "A minute ago you were all
sunshine and smiles."

Becky stared at the floor. "I just wish Mom hadn't gone with him, that's all."

"Clark? But why?"

"Because I don't like her going places with him."

Again Stephen asked, "Why?"

Becky jerked her head up and glared at him. "Just because, that's why!"

Laurel could see the unshed tears building up in Becky's eyes and she made a move to go to her, but Stephen forestalled her. He turned Becky toward him, one hand on her shoulder while the other lifted the child's chin until she was forced to look up at him.

"You're being a little brat, you know that?" he scolded. "You're going off for the day to have *your* fun, so why shouldn't your mother do the same? Surely you're not so mean and selfish that you would deny your own mother any pleasure?"

"I'm *not* mean and selfish," Becky stoutly defended herself. "It's just . . ."

"Just that you want to pick her friends," Stephen said, uncompromisingly harsh. "Does she pick all your friends for you, or does she allow you the freedom to do that yourself?"

Becky hung her head, shamefaced. "No. And I'm not a brat, either."

"Good! It's a sign you're growing up if you can understand your mother's needs for friendship and fun, too!" Again Stephen raised her face until their eyes met, only this time he was smiling. "That's my girl! I knew I couldn't be wrong about such a nice girl as you are!"

At last he won a smile from Becky, and then, while he patted her shoulder, he turned to Laurel and asked politely, "Would you care to come riding with us?"

"Oh, no, thank you," she said hastily. "I've got a lot of work here to do today."

"Come on, Laurel," Becky urged. "You just

heard Stephen say Mom needed to get out and have fun. Well, *you're* a grown-up, too, and you need to have some fun!"

Laurel carefully avoided Stephen's gaze, but when she tried to explain to Becky all the reasons why she shouldn't go, she failed. Becky became maddeningly obstinate and absolutely insisted that she join them.

At last Stephen intervened in a bored tone, as though he, too, were tired of Laurel's flimsy objections. "Becky wants you to come . . . and who knows . . ." he added tauntingly, "you really just *might* have fun."

But though she was at last persuaded, Laurel did not enjoy the ride, despite the beauty of the day. The grasses on the range land were lush, billowing like a brilliant green sea beneath the breeze. Here and there a pin oak or a cottonwood cast a cool shade. The horse she was riding, an Appaloosa named Indian, was spirited, yet controllable, and followed her bidding as she guided him from a trot to a canter. At another time and in other company, Laurel could have derived wholehearted pleasure in the swaying movement of the animal beneath her and the cool, gentle breeze on her face. Instead, she was tense and nervous and acutely conscious of the man who rode beside her, a man who was doing his best to ignore her as she did him, while at the same time both of them tried to hide their animosity from the child.

At length they approached the cabin where Stephen had found them one afternoon, but they did not pause today. Farther along there was a clearing where the winding river was visible, and, without speaking, they all headed toward it.

Near the fence Stephen suggested, "This seems a good place to stop for a while and allow the horses to rest. Becky, did you know that in the shallow part of the river just over there"—he pointed beyond a thicket of trees—"there is a dinosaur track?"

"Can I go look for it?" she asked eagerly.

Stephen nodded as he slid from his saddle, then lifted Becky from Daisy's back. "Sure. Just be careful and don't fall in, okay?"

Becky raced off, and Laurel was suddenly alone with Stephen, an intolerable circumstance. Awkwardly, stiff from the unaccustomed exercise, she attempted to get out of the saddle, intending to follow Becky.

Strong arms gripped her waist and she was pulled free of the saddle and stirrups and came in touch with a warm, rock-hard body.

She flinched and mumbled in embarrassed chagrin, "I could have done it myself without your help." Roughly she thrust his hands from her and backed away a step, needing a safe distance from him.

Stephen cursed beneath his breath. "Damn it, Laurel!" he said bitingly. "You have nothing to fear from me. I don't intend to try to make love to you every second we're alone together!"

"I never supposed you did!" she threw back.

"The hell you didn't!" he snapped. "I felt you trembling just then. You're terrified for me to so much as touch you because you know how fast that can ignite a fire between us. You don't trust me or yourself. But right now you're yearning for me to make love to you as much as I want to, even though you won't admit it."

"That's absurd!" Laurel answered vehemently.

"Is it?" Stephen came to her and cupped her face in both his work-roughened hands. Laurel's lips quivered as their gazes met and locked, their faces only an inch or so apart. A rippling shudder ran through the entire length of her body, and Stephen felt it. A grim smile parted his lips. "Is it?" he repeated. He shook his head and, dropping his hands, stepped back from her. "You're a liar, Laurel Patterson, and we both know it!"

Chapter Eight

Laurel dreaded the long, empty weekend ahead. Despite the hectic, busy week just past, her thoughts had often strayed to Stephen, but he neither telephoned nor came. Apparently he was through with her for good, and while she told herself it was for the best, it did not stop the dull ache in her heart.

Why, she asked herself a hundred times, had she been so stupid as to fall in love with a man who wasn't right for her, a man who had wanted to enjoy the pleasures of the present with her but nothing more? And now he didn't want anything to do with her at all. He had called her a liar last Saturday, and he had been right, of course. She *did* want him, but she couldn't have admitted it, knowing that she loved him but that his feeling for her did not flow so deep. A fierce pride had overtaken her and saved her from allowing him to see the truth.

When the telephone rang, she ran eagerly to answer it, suddenly as hopeful as she had been despondent only a moment earlier. But the caller was not Stephen. It was Dan Silsby.

"I thought if you weren't busy tonight we could take in a movie together," he suggested.

Laurel weighed her options. She had no interest in seeing Dan again. But, on the other hand, only a long, boring evening faced her at home alone. And

Stephen was not going to call . . . ever. His silence this past week told her that loud and clear. It would be senseless for her to cut herself off from any social life whatsoever just because she couldn't have the man she wanted.

"Sure, Dan," she replied. "That would be nice."

They spent a pleasant, if unexciting, few hours together. Over coffee in a small café after the movie, Dan invited her to a western dance coming up at the club. "It's still a couple of weeks away, but if you'd like to go, I'll make our reservations tomorrow."

Laurel couldn't remember the last time she had gone dancing. It had been with Ken, of course, but ages ago. The idea appealed to her. It sounded like fun, and it would be an evening out and away from her brooding thoughts and silent apartment. "I'd like that, Dan," she said. "But if it's western, what do I wear?"

He laughed. "No problem there. Just wear jeans, and get yourself a western-style shirt if you don't already own one. My dad's got a couple of hats we can borrow."

When he took her home a little later, Dan kissed her good night. Though she supposed it shouldn't have, it took Laurel by surprise, an unwelcome surprise. She stepped away from him quickly, and in the darkness she could just barely make out his face . . . and see his frown.

"What is it?" he asked quietly. "I thought you liked me, Laurel."

"I do," she assured him. "But I don't want . . . I don't want a romantic relationship, Dan. I'm sorry."

He smiled faintly. "You told me once before that you didn't want to get involved with anyone," he admitted, "but surely just a good-night kiss can't hurt anything."

"Of course not. It's just that I'd rather not, that's all. Look," she added swiftly, "perhaps you had better invite another girl to the dance. I like you a lot as a friend, Dan, but I'm definitely not interested in—"

"You're my date for the dance," he told her firmly. "And as for the rest, well, that's my problem, tough as you're making it for me. But maybe if I keep on seeing you, you'll change your mind."

"Please," Laurel urged, "don't count on that."

"Someone must have hurt you pretty badly. Are you still in love with him?"

She nodded. She knew Dan believed she was referring to a man back east, and she thought fleetingly of Ken. But the hurt she had felt over finding out his true character was nothing compared to what she was suffering now. Like a thief, one large Texan had come along and stolen her heart, and he didn't even realize it.

Dan squeezed her hand in sympathy, "I know the feeling," he said solemnly.

"Your ex-wife?"

He nodded. "I'm still crazy about her," he confided.

"Is there any chance of your getting back together?"

Dan shrugged. "I doubt it. She moved to Houston and I haven't seen her since the divorce."

"Maybe you should," Laurel suggested gently. "Maybe she's missing you as much as you miss her."

Dan laughed. "That's a thought! In the meantime, our date's still on for the dance, okay? Just as friends?"

Laurel smiled. "Its a deal," she told him.

The rest of the weekend was just as dull as Laurel had dreaded, and by Sunday night she was heartily sick of her own company and looking forward to Monday morning and the workweek ahead. Small children and office work had a way of commanding one's full attention and left little time for unhappy thoughts or self-pity.

But morning brought a bit more excitement than she had either anticipated or desired. At first, everything was smooth and routine. The children arrived and the day's schedule began. Laurel spent an hour in the office working on the payroll while Julia organized the three- and four-year-olds for a finger-painting session.

It was close to nine-thirty when the telephone rang. With her mind still on her task, Laurel answered it a bit absently, mechanically saying, "Good morning. Tiny Tots' Palace. May I help you?"

"Laurel?" a faintly familiar voice asked.

"Yes?"

"This is Clark Baskin."

"Oh, hello, Clark," she said. "I suppose you want to speak to Julia, but she's pretty busy right now. Could I have her call you back later?"

"Maybe you can tell me what I want to know," he said. "I'm calling in my capacity as principal. We call all the children's parents whenever they are absent to find out why. Is Becky sick today?"

Laurel stared blankly at the pen she held in her right hand. "Sick? Not that I know of. At least, Julia didn't mention it when she arrived this morning."

"You mean Becky isn't at the center with you?"

"No, she isn't. Hang on, Clark. Maybe I'd better go interrupt Julia, after all. Just a minute."

She went quickly, told Julia that Clark was on the phone, and then asked one of the other girls to watch the children as she followed her sister back to the office.

Julia picked up the phone with a smile, but an instant later it had vanished and she turned deathly pale. "Not there? Are you *sure?* But I dropped her off myself just before eight! Oh, my God, Clark, where can she be?"

Laurel closed the door for privacy and crossed the room, forcing Julia down into the desk chair because she was swaying as though she might faint.

Laurel took the receiver from Julia's nerveless fingers and spoke into it. "Clark, this is Laurel again. Will you please double-check with Becky's teacher, and maybe her classmates as well, and call me back if you learn anything? If you can't find her, maybe someone happened to see her leave. I'll wait until I hear from you before I call the sheriff's office."

"Certainly," Clark said. "I'll get back to you as soon as I can."

"Where can she be, Laurel?" Julia asked tearfully after she had hung up the telephone. "You don't suppose she was kidnapped?"

"Don't even think it!" Laurel ordered. "Besides, it's much more probable that she's playing hooky. Is she still having trouble at school?"

"I don't know," Julia said. "Her grades haven't been so bad lately, but otherwise I just don't know. She doesn't confide in me like she used to, and we had a big fight last night because I wouldn't allow her to stay up past her regular bedtime. Clark was there and we'd put David to sleep in my bedroom, but Becky was just being obstinate because she resents Clark, I suppose. Anyway, she claimed I was sending her to bed only because I wanted to get rid of her, but that wasn't true; it was the time I always send her to bed." She shuddered and sighed heavily. "We used to be so close, but it seems like all we ever do anymore is argue."

"Well, the first thing we've got to do now is to find her. Do you have any idea where she might have gone, Julia?"

"No. Laurel, maybe we ought to call the sheriff's office now instead of waiting for Clark to call back."

Laurel glanced at her watch. "Let's give him a few minutes," she suggested, struggling to remain calm for Julia's sake. "She *could* be at school, you know, and was just late for class or something and . . ."

The sound of the office door opening from behind her caused Laurel to break off the rest of the sentence and turn around. Then her mouth fell open in surprise at seeing the two people who were entering the room. One was a very tall, dark-haired man; the other was a pint-sized girl who wore a decided pout on her face.

"Becky!" Julia cried. She got to her feet, skirted the desk, and fairly flew across the room to kneel in front of the child and gather her into her arms. "Oh, Becky, where have you been?" she asked shakily. "I've been so scared, so worried about you!"

When Becky didn't reply, Stephen said, "I found her walking along a street near the highway, and I thought I'd better bring her here."

Julia got to her feet and gave him a grateful smile. "I can't thank you enough, Stephen. Clark only called a few minutes ago to tell me she wasn't in school." She glanced down at her daughter's sullen face and demanded, "Why weren't you in school? Where on earth were you going?"

Becky shrugged nonchalantly. "Nowhere in particular. I just didn't want to go to school today. I hate it, and I knew I'd get in trouble during English class because I didn't have my paragraphs written."

Julia was suddenly trembling with anger, and she seemed to lose all her professional training and poise at dealing with children. She gripped Becky's shoulders and shook her, her voice rising to a near-hysterical pitch as she exclaimed, "Do you have *any* idea what you've put me through, young lady? I was terrified that something dreadful had happened to you! You will definitely be punished for this little episode. Becky, *when* are you going to straighten out and start behaving yourself?"

Becky's shoulders squared with rebellion. "I want to go live with Daddy!" she cried hotly. "I don't want to live with you anymore!"

Her pronouncement startled all three of the adults. Stephen glanced questioningly at Laurel, and she gazed blankly back. Julia dropped her hands from Becky shoulders and stared at her small face in disbelief.

"You don't mean that!" she whispered.

"Yes!" Becky said defiantly. "I do. I want to go home and live with Daddy!"

Julia burst into sobs and covered her face with both hands. Laurel went to her and put her arms around her shoulders in a comforting gesture.

"Becky," she said quietly, "why don't you go upstairs to my apartment right now? I'll be up in a few minutes and—"

Stephen interrupted her. "I have a suggestion," he said calmly. "Since she's already missed part of the school day and she's obviously upset, how about letting Becky spend the rest of the day with me out at the ranch? I'll put her to work helping with a few chores and bring her home late this afternoon. It'll give everybody a chance to cool off a little."

Since Julia was still crying and seemed incapable of making a decision, Laurel nodded. "It sounds like a good idea," she said in a soft voice. "But are you sure you want her for the entire day?"

"Sure." Stephen glanced down at Becky. "If I let you come out to my place for the day, do you promise to do your homework tonight and go to school tomorrow?"

Sullenly Becky lowered her gaze to the floor. After a moment she nodded. "I promise," she said in a small voice.

"That's fine. Let's get moving," Stephen said. He started toward Julia to say goodbye and accidentally brushed against Laurel's arm. When it happened, he glanced at her face, and their eyes met. Laurel shivered to see the coldness in his gaze. She stepped back from him in consternation; there was an utter lack of feeling in the depths of his eyes, and she bit back a cry of dismay.

"I'll see Becky home around six, Julia." For her, there was a thawing in his eyes and voice. "Will that be all right with you?"

Julia nodded, struggling to contain her tears, and said in an unsteady voice, "Yes. Fine." She turned away abruptly, unable to look at her daughter.

Becky saw the movement, and an odd expression crossed her face. For a moment Laurel thought the child was about to go to her mother, to throw herself into her arms. But the moment passed, and Becky remained silent and still.

After they left, Laurel turned her full attention back to Julia, who was crying hard, as though her heart would break. A lump lodged in her throat, and once again she tried to comfort her sister.

"It'll be okay," she said gently, this time not even sure she believed what she was saying. "Everything will work out, Julia. You'll see."

Julia shook her head, not accepting this. "No, it's just getting worse."

The door opened and closed, and Laurel looked up to see Clark. His face was ashen. "She's not at the school, Laurel. We searched everywhere and—"

Laurel said quickly, "She's all right. Stephen Tanner found her, and we've let her go out to his ranch for the rest of the day."

He crossed the room to Julia's side. Laurel moved away, and Clark gathered Julia into his arms. "What is it?" he asked gravely. "Laurel says Becky is safe, so why are you crying?"

Julia wiped her tears away and then gripped his hand as though it were a lifeline. "It's just that everything is such a mess. I don't know what to do about her anymore. You saw the way she was last night, Clark. And today she left school because she didn't have a homework assignment done." She gave a shivering sigh. "I just don't understand her now. She was never this way before."

"I wish there were something I could do to help," Clark told her. "But Becky seems to resent me, no matter what I do or say to her."

"I know," Julia replied. "I suppose it's natural for her to resent you. She still loves and misses her father."

"Of course," Clark agreed. "But Julia," he added

urgently, "you can't allow Becky to stop you from living your own life."

"I know that," Julia said softly, "but, oh, Clark, she says she wants to go live with Bert, and I just can't bear it!"

The tears spilled again. This time, oblivious to Laurel, Clark gathered Julia close to him once more and began raining kisses on her face, murmuring softly.

Laurel tiptoed toward the door. She was no longer wanted or needed here. As she went out into the hall and pulled the door quietly closed behind her she couldn't quell a tiny surge of resentment. Here was her family having a crisis, and it was outsiders who were comforting and helping them instead of herself: Stephen for Becky, Clark for Julia. It was almost as though she had no important place in either of their lives anymore.

With a determined effort, she thrust the thought from her and walked briskly into the kitchen to see how lunch preparations were coming. The business of the day still had to go one, regardless of personal events.

"Was that Mr. Tanner I saw in the hall a while ago?" Carmen asked as she stirred some green beans she was preparing for lunch.

Laurel nodded. "Yes, it was."

"Do you know whether something's bothering him?" the cook went on. "My mama says he's been in a real bad mood around the house lately."

"No, I really couldn't say," Laurel answered. She had no desire to discuss or even think about Stephen anymore this morning, so she quickly changed the subject. "Do we have enough oranges for tomorrow's lunch, or do I have to order more?"

"There's plenty," Carmen replied, "but I'm running low on paper napkins and flour and a couple of other things. I started a list . . . it's over there on the counter."

Laurel picked up the list, about to take it to the

office, where she would add the items to her master grocery list. But then she remembered that Julia and Clark were there. Instead, she pocketed the paper. "I'll order the supplies this afternoon," she told Carmen. Then she went out to the sunroom to take over Julia's position and relieve the assistant who had been holding double duty the past hour.

A little while later, Julia emerged from the office. Though her eyes were swollen and red, she was smiling and appeared calm. "I'll take over now," she told Laurel. "It's almost time for you to go pick up the kinders."

Laurel studied her intently. "Are you okay?"

Julia nodded. "I'm fine."

"Is Clark gone?"

"Yes. He had to get back to the school." She sighed wearily. "He's really wonderful, Laurel. I don't know what I'd have done without him this morning."

That evening, Laurel stood before the refrigerator, trying to make up her mind between a quick and easy sandwich or going to the trouble of grilling a pork chop and tossing a salad for her dinner. A knock on the door interrupted her concentration.

She glanced down to see if her robe was belted well enough to conceal the nightgown beneath before going to the door and opening it.

Stephen's tall form loomed in front of her, and Laurel was so surprised at the unexpected sight of him that for a moment she couldn't speak. Her senses immediately came alive as she took in the somber angular face, the usual western shirt and jeans he wore. This time a leather vest hung loosely open across his shoulders and chest and he held his Stetson in his hands. But, most of all, her attention was drawn to his face, to the dark eyes that met hers, and to the sensuous lips that even now were beginning to curve into a smile.

"What's the matter?" he challenged at last. "Cat got your tongue tonight?"

"More likely it would be Vaquero," she retorted, coming out of her daze. She peered out into the soft darkness surrounding him. "Where is he, anyway?"

"I left him home tonight," Stephen answered. He paused, then asked, "May I come in?"

"Certainly." She backed away so that he could enter and then closed the door.

Stephen turned to glance down at her and smiled. "You look very fetching," he said, indicating her robe. "And very young without any makeup. Were you about to go to bed?"

Laurel ignored the dubious compliment and instead answered his question with a shake of her head. "No. I just got out of the bath and was about to fix something for supper." She hesitated only an instant, then asked, "Have you eaten yet? I have a couple of thick pork chops."

To her amazement, he accepted her invitation. "No, I haven't eaten. That sounds good. What can I do to help?"

Laurel moved ahead of him toward the kitchen and pointed to the cupboard above the refrigerator. "There's some liquor up there, if you'd like to mix us each a drink." Suddenly self-conscious as he continued to gaze at her, she added, "If you'll excuse me a minute, I'll go get dressed."

"Don't," Stephen said easily. "I prefer you in what you're wearing. Much more cozy. Or even," he added wickedly, "nothing at all."

"Now, Stephen," Laurel protested, hoping her cheeks didn't look as red as they felt, "I don't . . ."

He held up a hand to stop her flow of objections. "I remember," he said dryly. "You don't want me. Anyway, I didn't come here tonight to try to persuade you to change your mind." He turned from her, lifted an arm, and easily opened the cabinet door above the refrigerator, from which he extracted a bottle of vodka.

Laurel watched, thinking vaguely how she had to climb atop a chair to reach it. "Why did you come?"

She moved toward the refrigerator and pulled out the package of meat as soon as he was out of the way.

"To talk about Becky," Stephen replied, unerringly opening another cupboard that contained glasses. "But that can wait until after we've had our dinner."

For the next hour Laurel put everything out of her mind except the enjoyment of the moment. As he had demonstrated in the past, Stephen could be great fun as a companion. He grilled the chops while Laurel made the salad, and they kept up a running stream of conversation the whole time. With the spring weather so warm, they talked of outdoor sports, and when Stephen mentioned tennis Laurel confessed the game was her passion, but an unsatisfied one since she had come to Texas. "Julia hates sports of any kind, and I don't know anyone to play with here."

Stephen gave her an easy grin. "Well, now you know someone who likes to play. Me. We'll set up a date soon."

"I'd love it," she said with pleasure. "But I have to warn you, I've got a wicked backhand."

Stephen laughed. "I'll take my chances," he said bravely.

After they finished their meal, he helped her wash up. But when Laurel offered to make coffee, he declined.

"No, thanks. I must leave in a few minutes." They walked into the living room and sat down on the sofa. Stephen's face lost the lighthearted expression it had worn the past hour and his eyes darkened like a muddy pond. "Why," he asked straight out, "does Becky hate her mother?"

Laurel sucked in a deep breath. "Did she actually tell you that?"

He nodded.

Laurel laced her fingers together and gazed down at them. "*Hate* seems to be one of Becky's favorite words these days," she answered, "so I don't put a great deal of stock in it. But the fact remains that she *is* upset and unhappy." She sighed, and her anxious eyes met his. "Becky still resents the divorce, even though Bert's been remarried over a year now. But somehow she's gotten it into her head that Julia's the one who sent her father away, and he wouldn't have gone to another woman otherwise. It's crazy, of course." She gave a harsh laugh. "The truth is that Bert walked out on Julia, that he had been cheating on her. But how can Julia tell that to a ten-year-old? He sends small gifts to Becky from time to time and he telephones her, yet he's slow with his child-support checks, or else they don't come at all. Becky doesn't know that, of course. To her, Daddy's a hero, the handsome, generous, fun-loving person who has always loved and spoiled her. And Julia . . . well, despite all the problems, she refuses to tell Becky the truth or to tarnish her image of her father."

"Hmm," Stephen murmured thoughtfully. "Becky does have a confused picture, then. From what little she said to me today, I gathered she does blame her mother for everything that's wrong in her life."

Tears of frustration filled Laurel's eyes and glittered like dewdrops on her thick lashes. "It just isn't fair!" she exclaimed. "Julia's been hurt so much, first by Bert and now by Becky."

"Hey," Stephen said gently as he gathered her into his arms and pressed her head down to rest against his shoulder, "don't cry. Becky is a bright child, you know. She'll soon realize how much she loves and needs her mother, and she'll also adjust to the move here."

"Maybe," Laurel said unsteadily. "Or maybe it would be better for Julia to send her back to her father. Maybe if she lived with him and his new family for a few months she would be ready to come back to her mother. Last summer, when she spent a couple of weeks with them, she claimed she hated it there. So today, when she said she wanted to go back to him, I just couldn't believe it."

"I'm sure she doesn't really mean it," Stephen said. "She's just hurt and angry, and hitting out at her mother is a way of venting her feelings." He dropped a light kiss on her forehead. "Well, I guess I'd better be going," he added, withdrawing his arms from around her.

Laurel didn't want him to leave. They had spent a pleasant time together, and just now he had been sympathetic and supportive over the problem with Becky. She didn't want to be alone the rest of the evening, yet she knew that if she didn't broach the subject herself, Stephen would go. She had rejected him once too often, and unless she was bold enough to admit that she wanted him, he would walk out the door.

Her fingers clutched at the sleeves of his shirt, and she lifted her face so that she could look into his eyes. "Don't go," she whispered pleadingly. "I know I've said before that I didn't want you, but I *was* lying. I do, Stephen. Please stay."

Stephen gazed silently at her for an endless time before he lowered his face to hers and kissed her. His mouth on hers was warm and sensual, sending a shiver of happiness through her. But a moment later the happiness faded. Stephen drew back, gently putting her away from him before getting to his feet.

"I'm truly sorry, Laurel," he said in a genuinely sincere voice, "but I can't. I have a meeting to attend." He thrust back his sleeve and glanced at his watch. "If I don't leave right now, I'm going to be terribly late for it."

Laurel was horrified, and her face flamed with embarrassment and shame. She had actually been forward enough to ask him to stay with her, and he was refusing. Self-contempt raged through her at the thought that she had exposed her weakness to him—

had actually said that she *needed* him! She stiffened and, still seated on the sofa, she drew her shoulders back and her jaw went rigid as she looked up at him.

"Please forgive me," she choked out. "Of course you're busy. I shouldn't have presumed that . . ."

Stephen came to her and gripped her shoulders. "Laurel, I *really* do have a meeting," he said, "and I'm honestly sorry I can't stay. Perhaps I could come back later?"

Laurel shook her head. "No. No, don't do that. Actually, I'm quite tired and I think I'll go to bed early. Don't think another thing about it, Stephen," she added with stiff pride. "I understand perfectly. Good night."

Stephen hesitated, as though he were about to say more. In the end, he withdrew his hands from her shoulders. "Good night, Laurel," he said softly. "I'll call you tomorrow."

Laurel held herself in stern control, and only after he was gone did she go limp and allow a scalding tear to trickle down her face.

Chapter Nine

$\mathcal{L}$ aurel spent a routine, dull Saturday morning. First she cleaned the apartment; then she gathered up all her laundry and headed to the laundromat. After that, she stopped by the supermarket and picked up her weekly groceries.

When she returned home, she carried in the groceries first and put them away. Then she trekked downstairs again for her clean laundry.

She was cleaning the bedroom, when someone knocked on the front door. Laurel frowned, hoping it wasn't Julia or Becky. After last night she wasn't in the best of moods, and she didn't feel like putting on an act that everything was fine.

She didn't recognize the young man who stood at the door, however.

"Miss Patterson?" he asked politely.

Laurel nodded.

"This is for you," he told her, holding out a long white florist's box.

Laurel stared at it blankly. "For me?" she asked, with obvious doubt in her voice. "Are you sure?"

"If you're Laurel Patterson, I'm sure." The young man smiled.

"Well, thank you." Laurel accepted the box, and as the man ran lightly down the stairs she turned and went inside.

She sat down on the sofa and opened the box.

Nestled inside green tissue paper were a dozen long-stemmed red roses. Their delicate scent rose up to tantalize her senses.

For a long moment, bemused, Laurel simply gazed at the lovely blossoms, not attempting to remove them from the box. But then she began searching for a card. There *had* to be a card!

She found it tucked at the base of the box, enclosed in a tiny white envelope. Laurel's fingers trembled slightly with excitement and anticipation as she slid the card from the envelope.

"Roses for a rose," the card read. "Please forgive me for having to leave you last night. Have dinner with me tonight. I'll come for you at seven." The bold signature below the message said simply "Stephen."

Laurel laid aside the card and reached into the box. She lifted one of the roses to her face so that she could enjoy its heady fragrance and then brushed the soft velvet petals against her cheek. A smile flitted across her lips.

She honestly didn't know whether to be happy or annoyed. The roses were exquisite, of course, and the gesture of sending them was a wonderful and thoughtful thing to do. She couldn't help but be glad Stephen had done it. She would be less than a woman if she weren't. On the other hand, there was a certain arrogance to his message. He didn't ask her to have dinner with him; he *told* her. He didn't ask her to call and let him know whether she would or not; he simply informed her he would be there at seven.

Throughout the afternoon Laurel debated with herself whether or not she should go. She wanted to—there was no point in attempting to fool herself by denying it. But was it wise? She loved Stephen, and she had made an idiot of herself last night by showing him how much she wanted him to stay, and then she had had to suffer the agony of his rejection. True, he was doing his best to apologize for that rejection today. Perhaps he honestly *had* had a meeting. But none of that altered the fact that by seeing him again she was involving herself in a dangerous situation. The danger was to her emotions; she would get involved again so deeply that she would be hurt a second time. Somehow she instinctively knew that the pain of it, if it came, would be far worse than anything she had yet experienced. There was something about Stephen, her feelings for him, that touched a part of her that had, until now, been inviolable. Ken had never reached that very core of her being, and she was wary of that most vulnerable part of herself being exposed. She yearned to share it; and yet, if Stephen did not care about her to the same extent and saw her soul thus bared, she would be left empty and drained.

Precisely at seven, Stephen knocked on the door. Laurel was dressed and waiting for him. Her mental debate had ended late in the afternoon. She wanted to see him and he had asked her out. It was as simple as that. If she got hurt later, well, she would just have to contend with that when the time came.

Stephen was dressed in a dark suit, and the formality of his attire at once gave him an aura of mystery, of a stranger, someone she did not know at all. At the same time, a tingle ran along her spine. She thought she had never seen him look more wonderful. Her heart tattooed against her breast as he smiled at her and she smiled back.

"You look sensational," he said with a slight catch to his voice. He had entered the room, and for a moment they simply gazed at each other. Stephen's deep chocolate eyes were almost as black as the night as they took in her appearance.

"Thank you," she said unsteadily. She was unable to withdraw her gaze from his. It was as though some magic spell held her imprisoned. "You . . . you look very grand yourself," she added almost shyly.

Stephen came to her and gently cupped his hands around her face. Then he lowered his head until their lips met.

"If we didn't already have dinner reservations," he said huskily, "I'd suggest we just stay in all evening." His meaning was unmistakably clear.

With a nervous little laugh, Laurel stepped away. "You promised me dinner," she reminded him, "and I'm holding you to your promise."

"You're a cruel, hardhearted woman, you know that?" he told her, but there was a twinkle in his eyes as he said it.

Laurel picked up her purse from a lamp table, and as they went toward the door she said, "I want to thank you for the roses. They're beautiful."

"No more beautiful than the woman who received them," Stephen said in a low voice. "But I'm glad you like them."

They had dinner at the country club and afterward went to a party given by some friends of Stephen's. It was a party for a married couple's tenth anniversary, and at first Laurel was reluctant about going; after all, she didn't know the people and she hadn't been specifically invited. But Stephen brushed aside her objections. "You'll enjoy it," he promised, "and besides, you *are* invited. I was told to bring a date."

Laurel was surprised to discover that she did indeed enjoy the party. Even though Stephen did not remain at her side throughout the evening, the other guests were so friendly and kind that she soon relaxed and felt as much a part of the group as anyone else. A few of the people she had already met casually since she had been in Tierra Nueva, and a couple of the guests had children at the center. The anniversary couple, Nick and Jan Colts, were most cordial and Laurel liked them.

When Laurel and Stephen were about to leave, their hosts walked with them to the door.

"Perhaps the two of you can come to dinner some night soon," Jan suggested.

"That would be nice," Laurel replied. But she felt a bit shy and uncomfortable about the invitation and didn't dare lift her eyes to Stephen's face. Maybe he wouldn't want the two of them to be issued a joint invitation. What was happening was exactly what Laurel had feared. People were starting to pair them off as a couple without any real justification.

"We'd like that," Stephen said heartily, just as though he thought it was a wonderful idea. "Say, do you two have any plans for tomorrow afternoon?" he went on. "Laurel likes to play tennis. Maybe we could get together for doubles?"

Nick glanced at his wife. "What do you say, honey? Think we can beat them?"

Jan laughed and nodded. "We can give it a try, but I *am* out of practice. I haven't played in months!"

Stephen grinned at her and teased, "You're just the sort of opponents we want. Meet you at the club around two?"

"We'll be there," Nick said.

They said their good nights and walked toward the car. Stephen's arm was around Laurel's waist, just as though it belonged there.

On the short drive back to her apartment, they talked casually about the party they had just attended and the people who had been present.

"Well, did you enjoy yourself?" Stephen asked.

Laurel smiled at him through the darkness. "You know I did. It's been a lovely evening."

"You'll like Jan and Nick, I think, once you really get to know them."

"I like them already," Laurel stated. "But, Stephen . . . do they *really* have five children?" she asked in awe. "Jan hardly looks old enough to be married, much less the mother of five!"

Stephen laughed. "It's true, all right. You didn't see them tonight because they were all spending the night at their grandparents' house. But they have five little Colts, all under nine, and they keep Jan on the run all the time. Nick, by the way, is the one who gave Rascal to Becky." He chuckled. "He said five kids were okay because they're deductible on his income tax. But five puppies, too, was going a little too far!"

A few mintues later they had reached Laurel's apartment. As soon as they entered the living room and closed the door against the night, Stephen took her into his arms and kissed her. Fire raced through Laurel's body as it always did at his touch, causing her senses to reel so that she was only aware of the present and the wonderful feelings that consumed her.

Stephen buried his face against her throat, lightly dropping kisses there, and Laurel went limp in an agony of desire. Her arms circled him and her hands ran up and down his broad back. When his hand came to cup her breast gently, Laurel shuddered with emotion and pressed close to the long, hard frame of his body.

Tonight, when they entered her bedroom, there was no argument, no backing down as there had been once before. They were both smiling at each other in complete understanding, in mutual desire.

Their clothes were scattered on the floor, and when Laurel looked toward Stephen, her throat ached. His body was so wonderful, so perfect in every way. His legs were long, yet molded with powerful muscles; his back gleamed, golden and smooth, in the soft lamplight.

She went to him and rested her head against his warm back, and her lips moved slowly, sensually, over it, up to his shoulders. Stephen turned, gave a exultant laugh, and, scooping her from the floor, carried her to the bed.

"You're adorable," he murmured as he came down beside her and gathered her into his arms, crushing her soft breasts against the crisp dark mat on his chest. His eyes were tender and glowing. "You're very special to me, Laurel."

Their lovemaking was exciting and perfect. Laurel

responded to Stephen's every caress with delight and wonder at the tremulous sensations he gave her. She thrilled at the knowledge that the pleasure she gave him was equal to his own. Each anticipated the desires and needs of the other and gave freely. It was as though they were meant to be together down through the ages, had finally discovered each other and could only find fulfillment through one another. The completion of their individual selves seemed possible only by coming together in this intimate closeness.

Laurel sighed with contented happiness when they rested at last, with their arms still wrapped around each other.

"We're perfect together," Stephen said huskily as he planted loving kisses on her earlobe. "Why do we ever argue?"

Laurel shook her head and her hair brushed against his shoulder. "I don't know. Whenever we're together like this it . . ."

"Feels so right," he murmured. "You realize that something of major importance could be happening between us, don't you?"

He meant that they might be falling in love, of course. Laurel knew that, for her, it had already happened. But she merely answered, "Yes. Yes, I do." She wasn't ready, quite yet, to commit herself with words. Too, despite their closeness tonight, she wasn't sure that Stephen actually felt the same.

He nibbled at her earlobe, then propped himself up on an elbow so that he could gaze down at her. A smile softened his lips as he tucked a strand of her hair behind her ear with his free hand. "Let's not spoil anything by fighting it, Laurel," he said urgently in a low voice. "Let's allow this feeling time to grow and develop. Whatever this is between us it's delicate and fragile. Let's not do anything to destroy it until we're really sure where we're headed. I'd hate for either of us to make a mistake that we might regret for the rest of our lives."

"All right," she whispered hoarsely. "All right, Stephen. We'll give it a chance," she agreed.

His smile broadened. "That's my girl." He lowered his face to hers and kissed her longingly. Then he said, "I suppose you're about to tell me now that I must go?"

Laurel toyed with the idea of taking a chance that no one would know, that no one would find out that Stephen had stayed the night. But again she wasn't quite ready for that sort of open declaration about their relationship. It wasn't that she didn't want him to stay, because she did. With an exquisite pain she ached to have him stay, to be allowed the privilege of sleeping in his arms, to wake up in the morning to find him there beside her, warm and sleepy-eyed. But, as Stephen himself had just pointed out, this thing between them was still very delicate and fragile, like the roses he had sent to her today. Neither of them knew what the future held, and if it became common knowledge that they did have a serious interest in each other, it could cause them both pain, and awkward embarrassment later on if they stopped seeing each other. This feeling they shared was still too new, their commitment too untried, to put it to the test of public scrutiny just yet.

With regret, she nodded. "Yes. I want you to stay," she told him earnestly, "but for both our sakes, I think you should go."

Stephen heaved a loud sigh. "I was afraid that's what you would say." His lips lightly brushed hers again, and then he smiled. "But I understand your reluctance and I don't want to do anything that might hurt you or embarrass you, so I'll go."

Laurel slept late on Sunday and was only awakened by the ringing of the telephone.

"Good morning, Glory." Stephen's voice was warm and vibrant.

"Good morning." Laurel smiled into the telephone. "What do you think I am?" she asked. "A flower garden?"

"What do you mean?" A hint of amusement thickened his voice.

"Well, you've called me a rose and a sunflower and now a morning glory."

"Ummm," he murmured sensuously. "You can be my flower garden anytime you want. Tell me, did you dream of me last night?"

"Actually," Laurel said dryly, "I dreamed about this devil with horns, and he had a huge dog who looked exactly like Vaq . . ."

Stephen's thunderous laughter drowned out her voice. "I can see a man gets nowhere with you by fishing for compliments! I've a good mind not to take you out to lunch after all!"

"Oh? Were you planning to do that?"

"I was . . . but if you're reluctant to share a meal with the devil . . ."

Laurel laughed. "I'll even cook for him if he likes." Her stomach grumbled as if on cue. "Come to think of it, I'm starved."

"I'll take a rain check on the home-cooked meal," Stephen said. "Be ready in half an hour and we'll eat at the club. Don't forget to bring your tennis gear."

"I'll be ready."

They spent a wonderful afternoon together. It was a gloriously beautiful day, with a high, wide cloudless sky, and the earth below seemed to be gilded from the sun's rays.

The tennis game with Jan and Nick was fun, and afterward they all sat around a patio table outside the club with cool drinks and lighthearted conversation. Laurel enjoyed herself thoroughly. By the end of the afternoon she felt she had made a new friend of Jan, despite the differences in their personal lives.

When they arrived back at the stately old Victorian house, they found Julia's Volks parked in the drive. As they walked around the side of the house they saw her coming down the stairs that led to Laurel's apartment.

Julia's eyes widened in surprise when she saw Laurel and Stephen together, but she didn't say anything about it. "There you are," she called out with a smile. "I was just about to leave."

"Hi," Laurel greeted. "What's up?"

Julia shrugged. "Nothing much. Becky's at her friend Pat's house for the afternoon and I was at loose ends, so I just thought I'd drop by for a while." She glanced at the tennis rackets they both carried and asked Stephen, "Have a good game?"

Stephen nodded. "Your sister is fantastic on the courts."

"I know." Julia grimaced. "Me, I never could hit the ball."

Stephen turned to Laurel. "Well, I'll leave you two alone so you can visit. I'll call?"

Laurel nodded. "Yes, that'll be fine. 'Bye."

She knew that questioning was unavoidable, and as soon as they were upstairs and had entered the cool dimness of the living room, Julia demanded, "What's going on here? I didn't know you were seeing Stephen."

Laurel laughed and shrugged her shoulders as she dropped her racket to the sofa. "Just goes to show you don't know everything, right, big sis?"

Julia grinned reminiscently. "How many times did you say that when we were kids?" That question was rhetorical, but the next one wasn't. "Is it serious?"

"I'm not sure," Laurel sighed. Then, in a rush, she said, "Julia, I'm really drawn to Stephen, and he seems to be drawn toward me, too. He . . . he even admitted last night that something important may be happening between us. But I . . . ." With a nervous gesture, she brushed a strand of hair back from her face. "I'm scared."

"Scared you'll end up being hurt again?" Julia asked shrewdly.

Laurel nodded. "What I feel for Stephen is different from what I felt for Ken. More intense, somehow." She gave a shallow laugh, then added, "It scares the daylights out of me."

"But if he cares for you, too—" Julia started.

"That's just it," Laurel interrupted. "I know he does . . . but as much as I do? How do I know he won't turn out to be another Ken? How do you measure somebody else's feelings?"

Julia shook her head. "You're asking the wrong person," she replied. "I thought all those years I knew Bert's feelings, but it seems I didn't." She shrugged. "Love is a gamble, Laurel. I don't know what else to tell you. But that doesn't mean we can shut ourselves away from it. We all need it in our lives, or else we're incomplete." She grimaced, then said in a different tone of voice, "Speaking of Bert, I've got a problem. Can we talk?"

"Sure. What is it?" Laurel sat down at one end of the sofa and brushed her hair away from her face. She yearned for a bath and shampoo after the strenuous tennis game, but she tried to hide her desires as she sat back to listen.

Julia perched on the arm of an overstuffed chair. "There won't be a child-support check from him again this month. I called today, and he said he still hasn't found work and that they're feeling the pinch, too." She sighed. "I'm really in a bind, and since neither of us is drawing a salary yet, I hate to ask. But, Laurel, could you lend me some money? I promise to pay you back just as soon as I can."

"Of course," Laurel answered quickly. But mentally she was going over her bank account. It was reasonably healthy at the moment, and since the center was at least paying its own expenses, she had expected, so long as she was careful, to have enough to last until there were enough profits to provide them both with salaries. But if she lent Julia money, it was going to make a serious dent, and she wasn't sure just how long it might be before she, too, was in financial difficulties. But, all the same, she had no choice. They were sisters, and she knew that if the situation were reversed, Julia would do her best to help her out.

"Thanks," Julia said with obvious relief as Laurel found her checkbook. "I don't know what I'd do without you."

Stephen didn't call during the following day, and with each passing hour Laurel's spirits sank a little further. He had told her he expected to be back in town by midday and promised to call when he arrived. But the telephone in the office remained cruelly silent. Throughout the afternoon Laurel kept her ears alert for its ring above the shrill voices of the children as she led them in a singing session. Somehow she managed to smile as she automatically did the hand motions and funny noises that went along with the various songs. But when the period came to an end she could scarcely remember what they had just sung.

At the end of the day, Julia invited her to supper. "David will ride home with me," she said. "Clark's going to meet us there for supper. I bought a large ham, and there'll be plenty if you want to join us."

"Thanks, but I'm pretty tired," Laurel refused. "I think I'll just take it easy around the apartment tonight."

Julia eyed her with knowing curiosity and asked, "You won't be seeing Stephen?"

Laurel shook her head. "He hasn't called."

Julia patted her arm. "Maybe he will later."

Laurel hoped so, but she was afraid to count on it in case he didn't. He had said he would call early today and he hadn't done it. She didn't know whether it meant he hadn't made it back home today, after all, or whether he had changed his mind about her. And if he had . . . Quickly she dismissed the dreadful thought.

When she got upstairs there was a heavenly scent of broiling steaks. There was only one person besides herself with a key to the apartment, and Laurel's pulse quickened along with her footsteps that carried her through the living room and into the kitchen.

Like the time before when she had found him lounging in the living room, Stephen sat at the kitchen table, a cigarette in his hand and a mixed drink before him on the table. He didn't see her immediately because he was leaning forward, his elbows on his knees, deep in thought. Laurel's heart twisted with love as she gazed at him.

Stephen looked up, suddenly aware of her presence. When he saw her standing there, he dropped his cigarette into the ashtray and came to her, with a teasing smile on his lips. "Hello, Marigold. Did you think you had another burglar?" he asked.

Laurel shook her head and laughed. "Not this time. I've never heard of a burglar who breaks in, brings along his own food, and stays to cook it! It smells delicious!"

"I hope you're not angry because I illegally entered your apartment again."

She shook her head a second time. "I'm just happy you're here," she said honestly. "When you didn't call like you said, I thought . . ." The words choked in her throat.

Stephen's hands went to her arms and traveled slowly to her shoulders before he bent and gave her a long kiss.

"You thought I'd just decided not to call again? That a mere twenty-four hours apart was enough to make me forget you?"

"I . . . don't really know what I thought," she murmured.

He smiled, and the warmth in his eyes melted away all her uncertainties. "I just got back later than I'd thought, that's all. I got home a couple of hours ago, showered and shaved, and decided instead of calling I'd just surprise you with a cooked meal instead."

"I'm glad you did," she said contentedly. "It's a lovely surprise."

"Did you miss me?" Stephen's eyes became serious and intent.

Laurel nodded without prevarication. "Yes. I did."

He laughed softly. "That makes two of us. I even got a speeding ticket on the way back, I was in such a hurry."

"You didn't!"

"I did," he insisted, "and it's entirely your fault. As a matter of fact, I think *you* should pay the fine!"

Laurel stuck out her tongue at him, and then they both laughed. She went into the bathroom to freshen up and change into a comfortable pair of slacks and a knit top while Stephen mixed her a drink. A little later the dinner was ready, and they ate leisurely as they talked about his trip.

It was just after they had finished washing the dishes that the trouble started. Stephen mentioned the upcoming western dance at the club and invited Laurel to go with him. When a stricken look crossed her face, he went very still and asked in a low, controlled voice, "What's wrong?"

Laurel went cold, then hot, and she felt near tears as she explained. "Oh, Stephen, I'm *so* sorry! I forgot all about it until you mentioned it just now. But . . . I promised I'd go to that dance with Dan."

Like a black tornado dipping toward the earth, Stephen's face abruptly lost its relaxed pleasantness and turned stormy. His eyes flashed with threatening danger. "You're going with Silsby?" he asked incredulously. "But I thought we had this understanding between us . . . just you and me now!"

"We do," she agreed swiftly. "But I accepted this date before we decided that."

"Then break it," he ordered curtly.

"I can't," Laurel answered miserably. "It's this weekend . . . only a few days away. I can't do that to him, Stephen. It wouldn't be right."

His jaw was rigid; every inch of his face was stiff and unyielding, as though carved into rock. "It's not right for you to go with him," he said icily. "Not if you care about me."

"I do care!" Laurel cried. "But we made this date weeks ago, Stephen! I can't just break it at the last minute! Please understand, I . . ."

"I understand perfectly," he said in the coldest, most remote tone of voice she had ever heard. "I falsely believed there was something really important developing between us, Laurel, but I was obviously mistaken. If you really cared deeply for me, you wouldn't think twice about breaking a date with some other man. You told me once you didn't want to get involved with a man who spread himself around. Well, that goes double for me. I want a woman who's my own, unquestionably. Apparently you're not that woman." He snatched his jacket from the back of the sofa where it had been draped, strode toward the door, paused as though he had just remembered something, and dug into his jacket pocket. From it he pulled a small white box and carelessly tossed it in Laurel's direction. "By the way," he added in an iron-hard voice, "this is for you. Keep it as a little memento of other days."

Chapter Ten

The next few days limped by with agonizing slowness for Laurel. The continued silence from Stephen seemed to shriek like the blustery spring winds. Each morning Laurel woke up with the hope that today would be the day he would call or come by, and each night she went to bed more despondent than she had been the one before because he did not.

A dozen times or more she had opened the small velvet green jeweler's box and gazed at the gift he had bought for her, the one he had tossed at her so carelessly. On a dainty golden chain hung the most beautiful pendant she had ever seen. It was a flower, each petal fashioned from an exquisitely shaped diamond, the leaves and the stem glittering emeralds. It was a beautiful symbol of his pet nicknames for her, of course—Rose, Sunflower, Morning Glory, Marigold. Her throat tightened as she thought of what care he had taken when he chose it. Surely, if ever anything could indicate a man's love for a woman, the necklace did it. Yet now she could not bring herself to even try it on, much less wear it, because of this new and most serious estrangement between them.

She told herself that perhaps this time she should go to him, apologize, and beg him to understand her feelings, but, in the end, she lacked the courage.

Stephen *didn't* understand. If he had, he would have said so. He still believed she was in the wrong to insist upon keeping her date with Dan, even though she had tried to explain that the date had been set before she and Stephen had grown so close.

It was utterly hopeless, she told herself on Thursday evening as she drove to Julia's, where she was expected for dinner. Stephen couldn't understand her principles against deliberately hurting someone else because he didn't want to understand. She was positive that if he thought about it calmly, he would see, would know, that she didn't want to go with Dan but only felt that she must. If Stephen had even tried to be reasonable about it, she would have promised him that there would be no future dates with any man except himself.

When she arrived at Julia's house and got out of the car, she thrust her unhappy thoughts about Stephen to the back of her mind. Before she reached the door, she carefully arranged a pleasant smile on her face. It had been a desperate struggle the past few days, pretending that she was happy so that Julia could not guess the truth.

She opened the door and walked inside without ceremony. A delicious scent of Julia's marvelous meat loaf enticed her toward the kitchen.

"Set five plates around the table, Becky," she heard Julia say just before she walked into the room.

"Five?" asked Becky.

"Yes. Clark and David are coming, too."

"Rats!" Becky muttered.

"Is that what you say about me, too?" Laurel kidded as she made her presence known.

Becky just grimaced without replying, and over her head Laurel saw Julia give a helpless shrug.

Pretending that they did not notice Becky's sour mood, Julia and Laurel talked casually while they finished preparing the meal. Julia whipped cream topping for the strawberry shortcake they would have for dessert while Laurel mashed the potatoes for her.

Ten minutes later, Clark and David arrived, and they all went into the living room to greet them. Clark carried a large, flat brown paper bag under his arm. When he saw Becky emerge from the kitchen, he went to her and held the thin package toward her.

"I brought you a little something, Becky," he said with a smile. "A couple of record albums." When she didn't take the package from him, the smile wavered, but, with determination, he went on in a cheerful voice. "I remember you saying the other day that you were saving up for these, so I thought I'd just give you a head start and let you keep the money for something else you want." He pulled the two albums from the bag and showed them to her.

"How nice of you to think of it!" Julia exclaimed in an equally determined cheerful voice. "Isn't Clark thoughtful, Becky?" When Becky didn't answer but instead stared stubbornly at her feet, Julia's tone changed and she said softly, but with steel firmness, "Where are your manners? You must thank him, Becky."

"No, I won't!" Becky said rebelliously. "I don't want his dumb old record albums!"

"Becky!" Now Julia's voice, tinged with horrified embarrassment, was sharp. "You will apologize this instant for your rudeness, or else there won't be any dinner for you."

"I don't care!" Becky cried. "I'm not hungry, anyway!"

Julia's face was splotched with angry red and she was trembling with emotion. She sucked in a deep breath and said in a controlled tone, "All right, then. You may go to your room and stay there the remainder of the evening. And since you've been so rude to Clark about the wonderful gift he brought, you're not to play your stereo for the next week."

Becky's chin quivered. She lifted her face and

glared with tear-glazed eyes at her mother. Then, whirling, she dashed toward the hall door as a ragged sob tore through her throat.

"I wish you hadn't done that," Clark said. He was clearly unhappy. "Punishing her will only make her resent me even more."

"Maybe so," Julia conceded, "but I'm not going to let her continue to get away with being rude to you, Clark. Enough is enough."

"I'll go have a talk with her," Laurel offered.

Julia shrugged. "Suit yourself, but you're wasting your time. If I were you, I'd just leave her alone and let her sulk all by herself all night."

But Laurel knew she had to try. She went softly toward Becky's room. She couldn't help but reflect how wonderfully Julia dealt with the children at the day-care center, how patient and good she was with them, how talented she was at coaxing a little one out of a bad humor. But, with all her training and experience, these days she seemed to be totally inadequate at dealing with her own child.

She might as well have saved herself the effort of talking with Becky, she told herself a half hour later. Usually more open with her, this time Becky refused to talk to Laurel. She was sprawled across the bed, her face buried in her pillow, and the entire bed trembled with her sobbing. In the end, Laurel gave up any attempt at reasoning with her and merely sat on the edge of the bed, patting Becky's back in an effort to comfort her. At last, exhausted form her turbulent storm, the child fell asleep. Laurel brushed the golden hair away from her tearstained face and bent to kiss her cheek before tiptoeing softly to the door, turning off the light, and leaving the room.

The remainder of the evening was less than a huge success because of the earlier scene, although they all tried to behave normally, more for little David's sake than anything else.

"I want to play with Becky," he said a number of times, though they tried to explain to him that Becky didn't feel well and had gone to bed.

Laurel was glad when the evening came to an end. At last she climbed the stairs to her apartment, feeling unbelievably tired. She was tired of her own problems, tired of Julia and Becky's problems, tired even of the daily problems of running the center. She was just plain tired, and she spent a moment or two indulging herself with the fleeting idea of taking a vacation. But since that was out of the question, she soon put it from her mind.

The night of the dance arrived, and as Laurel dressed in the green-and-white-checkered western-style shirt she had bought with its pearl fasteners and a pair of fashionably faded Levi's, she felt she had never been less enthusiastic about a date in her life. Stephen's anger and his silence ruined the event for her, and Laurel wished she could just crawl into her bed and hide away from the world.

But by the time Dan arrived she had a welcoming smile for him, and she even made a little joke about the hat he handed her to wear. Laurel had refused to break this date despite Stephen's objections because she didn't want to hurt Dan's feelings. She was determined to get through the evening without his ever knowing how much she actually dreaded it.

When they reached the club, there was already quite a crowd assembled. Some of the men were a little more formally dressed in western-cut suits and long, thin black ribbons at their necks in place of ties, and a few women wore satin pants and shirts, trimmed in fringe; but most were dressed as she and Dan were, in simple shirts and jeans.

An acquaintance of Dan's accosted them almost as soon as they were in the door. Since the discussion was about some real-estate deal and seemed likely to continue for some time, Laurel politely excused herself and went to the ladies' room so that she could comb her hair.

Seated on one of the pink-cushioned chairs before the vanity was Jan Colts. She was applying a fresh coat of vivid red lipstick to her mouth. When their gazes met in the wall mirror above the vanity, Jan gave a little wave with her free hand. Then she turned and smiled up at Laurel.

"Well, hi," she greeted with pleasure. "I've been intending to call you all week, but somehow I just never found the time." She gave an exaggerated sigh. "With five kids, I have a lot of good intentions that never get carried out. How long have you and Stephen been here? I didn't see you earlier."

Laurel dropped into the chair beside her and, opening her handbag fumbled around inside it, searching for her comb. With her gaze still averted from Jan's, she murmured in embarrassment, "I . . . I'm not here tonight with Stephen."

"Oh."

Laurel chewed nervously at her lower lip before finally looking at the other woman again. "I came with Dan Silsby."

"I see." There was a small pause; then Jan said in a rush, "I'm sorry for my assumption, Laurel. But after seeing you together before, I just naturally thought . . . and besides," she added, mixing one sentence with another, "Nick happened to run into Stephen downtown today and he mentioned that he was coming."

That bit of news caused Laurel's heart to hammer. She found her comb and began assiduously rearranging the mass of copper curls that protruded from beneath her borrowed western hat. She ran her tongue over her dry lips and swallowed hard. "Is he?" she said as casually as she could manage.

"Um-hmm," Jan murmured as she took a tissue and lightly blotted her lips. "I suppose, since he's not with you tonight, that he'll probably bring

Annette. If her father's well enough to leave, that is."

A vise squeezed Laurel's heart and she felt as though she were suffocating. "Have . . ." Her voice quavered ever so slightly, and she only prayed Jan didn't notice. "Have they gone together for a long time?"

Jan protruded her bright red lower lip in an attitude of thoughtfulness and then shook her dark head. "I'm not sure how to answer that," she said. "If you mean have they known each other long, yes. They've known each other just about all their lives, I guess, and they're certainly very close friends. But I would be very surprised if they ever got married, if that's what you're asking."

Laurel was aching to ask for more details and learn exactly why Jan sounded so positive, but she didn't have the opportunity. The door opened and two other women walked in, obviously acquaintances or friends of Jan's, because they all greeted one another with smiles and laughter. Laurel was introduced to them by Jan, but shortly after acknowledging the introductions, she left the room. She had no desire to remain and listen to talk that held no interest for her.

Only one thing interested her just then . . . that Stephen would be here tonight. She wasn't sure whether she was glad about it or dreaded it, but she couldn't help but be immeasurably cheered by Jan's revelation that Stephen and Annette were merely good friends.

At first Laurel enjoyed the dance. Mrs. Ramirez from the center was staying with Becky and David for the evening, and Clark and Julia had come, also. They joined Dan and Laurel at their table, and the four of them laughed and joked with good-natured ease. In between dances a number of people stopped by the table to greet them, mostly friends of Dan's or Clark's, but sometimes people whom Julia and Laurel had already met as well.

Although she laughed and smiled along with the others, Laurel's senses were keenly attuned to the rest of the huge room as her eyes searched constantly for Stephen.

And then, finally, she saw him as he arrived through the main entrance. How could she help it when he was so tall, so outstanding above the crowd, and was dressed in black from head to toe? Ridiculously, her heart lifted when she saw that he was alone. Through partly lowered lashes she observed him as he stood casually surveying the dimly lit room before someone among a group at a nearby table hailed him. With a slightly crooked smile, he went to join them.

Laurel lost sight of him then, for others blocked her view and, anyway, Dan was speaking to her. Reluctantly she turned her attention back to the party at her own table.

It was a half hour later, while Dan and Laurel were dancing, that Stephen saw her. He was on the dance floor himself with an attractive blond partner. As they glided past, Laurel happened to glance up and felt a tremor of shock to discover his brooding eyes upon her.

For a long moment they stared at each other across the shoulders of their dance partners, and there was a grim, forbidding set to Stephen's lips. Laurel felt hypnotized, powerless to look away, as her own eyes beseeched him to forgive her, to understand the principles behind her insistence upon keeping her date with Dan tonight. But suddenly, with ruthless deliberation, Stephen swung his partner around so that now his back was to Laurel, effectively cutting off their gaze. Laurel winced, for the action seemed just as cruel as if he had slapped her face.

That was only the beginning of her misery that evening. Several times more Laurel saw him dancing with other women, and each time it was like a knife blade plunged into her heart. Later, when he came toward their table, straight and tall, a small flicker of hope flared in her.

"Good evening, ladies," Stephen said urbanely, with a cordial smile on his lips. "Clark . . . Dan." He inclined his head politely toward the two men. "Are you all enjoying the dance?"

"We're having a great time," Clark responded. "Pull up a chair and join us."

"Thanks," Stephen answered, "but I'm at a table across the room with some other friends tonight. I just wondered if you'd be kind enough to allow me a dance with Julia?"

Clark turned to Julia with a questioning look. She smiled and nodded before she stood up. "I'd love it," she said and went to join him.

Laurel's heart plunged, though it wasn't yet at rock bottom as she supposed. That came later in the evening as it slowly dawned upon her that Stephen was not going to ask her to dance with him, not even once. He continued to dance with others, and twice more he danced with her sister. Each time he approached their table, Laurel tensed in an agony of suspense and hope and then was forced to swallow her disappointment and pain and smile in a casually friendly way, just as though it didn't matter.

By the time the dance ended and Dan drove her home, Laurel had a pounding headache, both from the smoke-filled room and from her turbulent emotions.

"You're very quiet," Dan observed as he pulled the car into the driveway.

"I suppose I'm just tired," she replied.

When they got out of the car, Dan moved close to her with an obvious intent to kiss her good night, but Laurel effectively avoided it by stepping to the side. "I'm sorry, Dan," she said in a low voice. "I truly had a wonderful time with you tonight, but I'd rather you didn't kiss me . . . or try to see me again. It would just be a waste of time for both of us."

"You're sure about that?" he asked. "You know

we enjoy each other's company and that we're both lonely. What can it hurt?"

"Us," she said bluntly. "There's just no sense in either of us attempting to make something out of nothing. The last time we were together you said you still love your ex-wife. Go see her, Dan. What have you got to lose except a little pride?"

Dan's lips stretched into a tiny smile. "Maybe you're right," he said softly. "Maybe I'll do just that. But what about you? You'll still be lonely yourself, won't you?"

"Maybe so," she acknowledged. Laurel averted her eyes from his and stared down at the purse in her hands. "But it's better than compounding the hurt we both have suffered already."

Dan touched her arm in a comforting gesture of sympathy. "Maybe you ought to take a little of your own advice, Laurel," he said gently.

Her eyelashes swept upward and she glanced at him with surprise. "What do you mean?"

The little smile on his face broadened. "You just told me that all I had to lose by contacting Marcy is a little pride. That's all you've got to lose, too, by reaching out to the man you love." Quickly, before she could even react, Dan bent toward her and brushed a light kiss against her soft lips. Then he straightened, stepped away from her, and said, "Good night, Laurel."

Laurel watched him drive away before she slowly mounted the stairs to her apartment. Once she was inside, she locked the door and went into her bedroom, where she undressed and slipped into a nightgown.

Although the hour was very late and she felt drained and exhausted, Laurel did not fall asleep for a long time. Her mind continued to conjure up torturing pictures of Stephen as he had been tonight, smiling and laughing and dancing with others while he very carefully ignored her.

She tossed and turned fretfully throughout the

night. Her dreams were filled with the same man who possessed too many of her waking thoughts. He was dressed all in black, and the cruel smile on his lips was cold and mocking. Beside him stood Vaquero, baring his teeth and growling at her. "I love you," she was saying, but Stephen only laughed at her and answered, "I don't understand." And then Annette was there, dressed in a beautiful gown that seemed to float about her. Stephen put his arm around her waist before they both walked away, ignoring her tearful pleas.

"You must understand," she moaned. "I love you." The words woke her and her eyes fluttered open. There was a heavy sadness in her chest, and she marveled at discovering that her face was wet with tears. She flipped over in the bed, turned on the lamp, and then lay down again, waiting for the effects of the nightmare to drain away, just as she had done when she had been a little girl.

You must understand. I love you. The words she had been mumbling swirled over and over in her head. All at once it struck her that Stephen couldn't understand that she loved him because she had never dared to say the words to him! He only understood that they had a mutual agreement that they cared about each other. In his opinion, she had broken that agreement by keeping a previous date with Dan. Naturally, he had been angry and upset with her. But what if she went to him and told him how she really felt . . . that she was in love with him? Would that change things, for better or for worse?

Worse? she asked herself. What could be worse than the hell she had already endured this past week, being completely alienated from him? Just as she had told Dan last night and he had tossed back at her, she had nothing more to lose than pride by going to Stephen and making a clean breast of things.

Laurel glanced at the bedside clock. Five a.m. Far

too early to drive out to the ranch. Stephen would still be asleep and would little welcome being awakened at this hour, no matter what she had to say to him.

Laurel chewed thoughtfully on her lower lip as she thought very hard about what she would say when the time came. First she would tell him again that Dan did not matter to her and that she would not see him again. Then would come the hard part. She would need to utilize all the courage she possessed and as much as she could pretend to have to tell him what was in her heart.

Laurel shuddered, and uncertainty and doubt began their inevitable course. Perhaps she shouldn't go, shouldn't be so honest, after all. She didn't believe she could bear it if Stephen laughed at her, if he rejected her love. On the other hand, she would never know unless she tried, and one thing was for certain: Stephen was *not* going to be the one to break the impasse and come to her.

So . . . she was just going to have to take her chances. She could either remain here alone, a frightened, timid mouse, or be as bold as a lioness and state her feelings. At this point, all that was really important was that Stephen know the truth. The rest would be up to him. She would point out clearly that she wasn't asking for any guarantees for the future, nor was she asking for him to lie and say he loved her, too, if he didn't. She didn't want that from him. She only wanted to be with him once again, if he would allow it, and she would take only what he was willing to give, just so long as things weren't at a total end between them.

Laurel laughed raggedly as she thought about her fine talk of independence only months ago. Well, so much for lofty words, she told herself. It only went to show how wide a gap there was between ideals and primitive emotions. She would be careful in the future about making such rash declarations.

Strangely enough, after she had definitely made

her decision about a course of action, Laurel relaxed, and her heavy eyelids fluttered down until her thick lashes fanned their golden tips outward and she fell into a peaceful sleep.

The lamp was still burning and sunlight flooded the room when she next awoke. Laurel glanced toward the clock and was appalled to see that it was past ten. Almost immediately she remembered her resolution, and in a leaping bound she threw back the covers and got out of bed. As late as it was, it would be past eleven before she had showered and dressed and eaten a little breakfast. She only hoped that Stephen would be home when she got there. Since it was Sunday, there was a likelihood that he was, but she also had to face the prospect that he might have gone off somewhere for the day.

When she did leave at last, wearing a cream-colored lightweight cotton dress, she walked toward the car with a certain amount of self-confidence. She knew she looked her best today in the well-cut dress that gently skimmed over her breasts and hips, and her russet hair tumbled in a flattering mass against her shoulders. She hoped that Stephen would notice how good she looked and be disposed to hear her out. Beyond that . . . well, beyond her own little rehearsed speech she dared not think.

Though the sun shone brightly, banks of clouds were building up in the sky, a warning that it might rain later. Laurel was unconcerned about it; she was far too tense over the scene ahead of her to be worried about the weather. Despite her nervous tension, she couldn't help but appreciate the day. The sunshine was warm on her skin, and once she reached the highway, there was a sprinkling of dazzling bluebonnets, the state flower, interspersed with a few early primroses and buttercups along the roadside.

When she reached the ranch house, an unfamiliar car was parked in the drive. Obviously, Stephen had company. A lump clogged Laurel's throat as she slowed to a stop. She shouldn't have come without calling first, she chastised herself bitterly. Sure, she had wanted to surprise Stephen, to catch him off guard and thus disarm him. But it was she who was surprised now . . . and utterly dismayed.

Her knuckles went white as her hands tightened around the steering wheel. Her mind grappled frantically with the problem of what to do. It wasn't enough that she realized she shouldn't have come unexpectedly; what should she do now . . . put the car in reverse and race away, or put on a brave face and approach the door? If anyone was in one of the front rooms and saw her scurry away, it would excite comment she didn't want. But if she knocked on the door knowing Stephen wasn't alone, what on earth could she possibly say when he answered it? Carrying out her original purpose was naturally out of the question.

Her mental debate was ended a moment later when the massive front door swung open and two people emerged from the house.

Both of them paused briefly on the steps when they saw her car. With a sigh, knowing she had to muddle her way through this thing now, she opened the door and stepped out.

"Well, hello, Laurel." Annette Pharr smiled pleasantly. "How nice to see you again."

Laurel forced a smile to her lips, and it seemed like the most difficult thing she had ever done. "It's nice to see you again, too," she lied politely. She eyed the other woman's pale green silk dress and her stunning golden hair beneath the sunlight, and suddenly she felt dowdy and unkempt by comparison. She wished fervently that she were anywhere but here.

"You wanted to see me?" For the first time Stephen spoke to her, and for the first time Laurel dared to meet his gaze.

Today, instead of his usual western-style clothes, he wore a pair of dark blue trousers and a sky-blue

sports shirt. Without his Stetson he appeared faintly
unfamiliar, and a light breeze ruffled his midnight-
black hair, draping a curly strand across his forehead. He was sinfully good-looking today, Laurel
thought resentfully as she forced herself to maintain
a casual air.

"Well, yes and no." Her laugh was a little nervous
and unsteady, and she prayed he didn't notice even
while her mind, with amazing rapidity, improvised.
"I'm rather at loose ends today, and I wondered if
perhaps Becky was out here this morning horseback
riding. I . . . um, I thought that if she was, you
might lend me a horse so that I could join her."

An evil, amused smile tugged at Stephen's lips.
His sharp, dark eyes traveled with maddening slowness up and down her body, lingering insolently at
strategic points on the journey. Laurel felt her skin
growing hot, and she knew it had nothing to do with
the heat of the blazing sun.

"You wanted to go horseback riding . . . dressed
like *that?*" Stephen drawled with open skepticism.

Damn! Laurel's teeth caught her lower lip in
vexation. Why hadn't she thought of how she was
dressed before she came up with such an idiotic lie?
Now she had to think up another. "Oh, I have some
jeans in the car," she added in a rush.

"I see." Clearly, he didn't believe a word she was
saying, and Laurel silently prayed that he wouldn't
ask her to produce the extra clothes. "I'm sorry," he
added, "but Becky isn't here today. She came out
yesterday morning. I'm about to leave to spend the
day with Annette in San Antonio, but you're quite
welcome to stay and ride by yourself, if you like."

"Oh, no . . . no, thank you," Laurel replied. "I
don't really care to go alone." She took a backwards
step, glued a smile to her face, and said, "I won't
keep you. I hope you have a nice day." Quickly she
turned and made her way back to the car.

By the time she was almost back into town,
Laurel's heart was still racing and every muscle in

her body was stiff, contracted and pinched from
sheer nerves. What a disaster, she thought, and what
an idiot she had been to go!

Jan had been wrong, she reflected, so very wrong,
when she said Stephen and Annette were only
friends, and Laurel had been wrong to allow herself
to believe it. They had looked so happy together just
now when they came out of the house, and Stephen's
arm had been around her waist in a casual, familiar
manner. Of course they meant more to each other
than mere friends.

Laurel shuddered and went limp as she realized
just how close she had come to making a complete
fool of herself! What if Stephen *had* been alone and
she had told him how she felt about him? It would
have been agonizingly embarrassing for the both of
them, and she could only thank God that at least she
had been spared that humiliation.

Chapter Eleven

"There aren't any swings left," a little girl named Kathy cried as she ran to meet Laurel, who had just come outside to the playground to assist Julia.

"That's okay, honey," Laurel soothed as she gently brushed the tears away from the child's face. "Someone will soon find something else to do, and then you can have your turn. Right now why don't you join Corey in the sandbox? Look what fun he's having!" She took the girl's hand and led her toward the sandbox, where she was soon happily settled.

Laurel watched for a moment and then went to join Julia on a bench beside the fence where they could easily keep an eye on all the children.

"I had a wonderful time at the dance Saturday night," Julia said. "Didn't you?"

"Yes," Laurel said untruthfully, hoping a bolt of lightning didn't suddenly strike her from the cloudless, gentle blue sky. "It was a lot of fun."

Julia smiled. "I think I'm falling love, Laurel," she confided. "Clark is so marvelous, and we get along so well together. I've never known such a gentle and kind man as he is."

"He does seem nice," Laurel agreed, "but still, you'd better be careful, sis. You don't want to make a second mistake and be hurt again."

"That's true," Julia agreed seriously. "But I don't

think I'm making a mistake this time. After all, I am older and wiser the second time around. At least," she amended, "I *hope* I'm wiser. Anyway, I'm not like you, wanting to be independent and completely self-sufficient. I need a man in my life. I always have and I always will. I'm not saying Clark is necessarily the right one, but someday there will be one, even if it isn't him." She paused, then asked, "What happened with you and Stephen? I thought something was developing between you, but you went to the dance with Dan, and Stephen didn't seem to mind when he stopped by our table."

Laurel knotted her fists in her lap and gazed toward the playing children. She gave a negligent shrug of her delicate shoulders. "We had a big argument because I already had the date with Dan and I wouldn't break it," she admitted. "So I guess it's over between us."

"That's exactly what I mean about my not being like you!" Julia exclaimed. "I just can't even visualize myself dating several men at the same time. One at a time is all I can handle . . . or want!"

Same here, Laurel thought, but she didn't have a chance to voice her feelings. One of their young charges came to show them a caterpillar he had just found, and the two sisters paused to admire it. A glance at her watch showed Laurel it was time for them to usher the children inside to wash up for lunch.

Late that afternoon, when the center closed for the day, Julia was swift to collect her purse and head toward the door. "Don't forget dinner tonight around seven," she called to Laurel, who was clearing the desk in the office.

"I'll be there," Laurel called back. "I bought a bottle of rosé to bring along."

"Great," Julia answered. "See you later, then."

Laurel locked up and went upstairs to her apartment and a few minutes later sank into a hot bath. As usual, whenever she had a moment to herself,

her thoughts strayed to Stephen. Yet no good could
come of it. She was only making herself unhappy.
She wished she could have had time to discuss the
situation thoroughly with Julia. There would be no
private moment to do so tonight because Clark
would also be at her sister's house for dinner, and
she would have liked to have had Julia's opinion.
Maybe, she thought, she *had* been wrong in insisting
upon keeping her prior date with Dan. She wasn't
sure about anything anymore. But Julia, given all
the facts, could be counted upon to tell her the truth
about the right or wrong of it, whether it was
palatable to hear or not.

Sighing and realizing she hadn't done a very good
job at keeping Stephen off her mind, Laurel got out
of the water and dried herself. Then she went into
the bedroom and slipped into a simple cream-
colored dress.

She was brushing her hair when a knock sounded
on the door. Wild, illogical hope soared in her heart
that it might be Stephen, and her feet almost seemed
to have wings as she flew from the bedroom and
toward the door.

When she opened it, shock assaulted her with the
heavy blow of a hammer. Laurel's eyes widened;
then she pressed them closed, positive that she must
be hallucinating. But when she opened them again,
the tall, blond-headed man still stood there, smiling
at her.

"Ken!" she gasped.

"Hello, love," Ken Waters said easily. "I came a
long way to see you. Don't you think the least you
could do is to invite me in?"

Numbly she stood back and allowed him to enter.
But when she closed the door and he reached for
her, obviously intending to pull her into his arms,
Laurel backed away.

"*Why* are you here?" she demanded sharply as
her equilibrium returned.

Ken frowned, and it marred his smooth, handsome face. "That's not very difficult to figure out, is it?" he countered. "I'm here because I love you and I want you back, Laurel."

"Then you wasted a trip," she said flatly, though her voice was not unkind. "It's been over between us for a long, long time, Ken."

He took a step toward her and again tried to touch her, but swiftly Laurel moved to the side. "You've allowed your resentment to drag on far too long," he told her. "Laurel, be reasonable. I've apologized to you every way I know how for what happened. I swear, if you'll only come back to me, I'll never look at another woman for the rest of my life. I want *you*, and I know now what a fool I was to hurt you the way I did."

Laurel sank weakly to the sofa and shook her head as her eyes sought his. "Ken," she began, carefully searching for the right words, "I'm truly flattered that you came all this way to see me, and I do accept your apology."

"Then . . ." Ken's voice took on a hopeful note, and a light flashed in his eyes until Laurel shook her head.

"What you're asking isn't possible any longer," she told him. "You see, I'm . . . I'm engaged."

"Engaged!" Ken's voice went hoarse. "When? Who?"

"Just this past weekend, as a matter of fact," Laurel improvised hastily.

"And who is this man?" Ken demanded.

"His name is Stephen Tanner. He's a local rancher." The instant she said it, Laurel was appalled at herself. Had she taken leave of her senses? she wondered wildly. She groaned inwardly, and the only comfort she could derive was from the knowledge that Ken would never meet Stephen and therefore no real damage had been done. Still, it was outrageous that she had ever dragged Stephen's name into this at all!

Defeat whitened Ken's face. With burning eyes,

he stared at her for a long time, and then, seeming to believe what she had told him, he said in a dull voice, "I . . . see. I came too late, didn't I? I hope you'll be very happy, Laurel. You deserve the best."

"Thank you," she answered huskily.

"I suppose I'd better be going," Ken said.

Laurel got to her feet. "You don't need to rush off, Ken. As you said, you came a long way to see me. I was just about to go to Julia's for dinner. Why don't you come with me? I'm sure she'll be happy to see you again."

Ken hesitated. "Are you sure I won't be intruding?" he asked wistfully.

"Positive. Let me just get my purse and the bottle of wine I'm taking, and we'll be on our way."

When they got downstairs, Ken said, "I've got a rental car here. I'll follow you to Julia's, and that way I can go straight back to the motel from there. I'll probably want to make an early night of it so I can get to San Antonio in the morning and catch an early flight home."

When they arrived at Julia's, Laurel received her second shock of the evening. Parked at the curb behind Clark's car was a familiar Buick. Stephen was here! Panic seized her, and it took all the willpower Laurel possessed to get out of her car and walk with Ken toward the door. Her heart pounded with sickening thuds and she had only a sense of impending doom as they entered the house.

Stephen was alone in the living room, sitting in a comfortable chair and flipping through a magazine, but he stood up politely when Laurel and Ken entered. His dark gaze was inscrutable, and Laurel's throat felt parched and dry as she performed the necessary introductions.

Naturally Ken picked up on Stephen's name immediately, and, with a bitter smile twisting his mouth, he extended his hand toward him. "Laurel told me the two of you just became engaged. I suppose I must offer my congratulations, though, to tell you the truth, I wish I were wearing your shoes instead. You're a very lucky man, you know."

Laurel held her breath without even realizing it, but Stephen never even batted an eyelash. He accepted Ken's handshake and said in the most cordial of voices, "Yes, I know I am. Thank you." He smiled, then moved to Laurel's side, put his arm around her waist, and drew her close before kissing her soundly on the lips. "Hello, darling," he said. "You didn't tell me you were expecting an out-of-town visitor."

"Be-because I didn't know myself," Laurel dazedly heard herself replying. Just then she caught sight of Julia at the kitchen door, and by the look on her face Laurel could tell that she had overheard everything. Laurel gave a slight, imperceptible shake of her head, and, to her relief, Julia apparently read her silent message correctly. When she came forward to greet Ken, she didn't say a word about the surprising news of the "engagement."

After Julia spoke to Ken and assured him he was welcome, Laurel asked, "Where is Clark? I saw his car outside."

"He's in the kitchen carving the roast for me. Stephen, would you be a jewel and fix Ken a drink? Clark will be in to join you in just a minute." As Stephen moved over to the table with the decanters Julia turned to Laurel and added, "Would you give me a hand and toss the salad?"

Laurel was delighted to have an excuse to escape from the two men in the living room, but as soon as they reached the kitchen, Julia turned on her. *"What is going on?"*

"Complete disaster, can't you tell?" Laurel said bitterly. "Ken showed up without warning, and when he wanted us to get back together I told him I was engaged to Stephen."

"What on earth made you do such a lunatic thing?" Julia demanded.

"Because I'm a lunatic, of course," Laurel

snapped. "What made *you* invite Stephen to dinner? Everything would have been fine if he hadn't been here!"

Julia grinned with wicked glee. "But now your lie has caught up with you! That's just what you deserve! As to why Stephen is here, I was merely trying to play Cupid, since the two of you are obviously as obstinate as mules." She chuckled, then turned to Clark, who was slicing meat and placing it on a platter. "We'd better warn you, Clark. For tonight, while Laurel's ex-fiancé is here from Boston, she's engaged to Stephen."

Clark lifted his eyebrows. "Does Stephen know?"

Julia giggled. "He knows . . . and, to give him credit, he played his impromptu part like an old pro. If he ever gives up ranching, he can always find work in Hollywood!"

"This *isn't* funny!" Laurel seethed, but her sister seemed to find the situation hilarious. In disgust, Laurel went to the counter and began tossing the salad with a vengeance.

At the table, Laurel was seated next to Stephen, while Ken and Becky sat opposite them. At the ends were Julia and Clark. David, Clark had said, was home with a baby-sitter for the evening.

Laurel was so tense and uncomfortable she could scarcely eat a bite of the meal Julia had cooked, and it didn't help that Stephen was solicitous in his attention to her. "Are you feeling all right, sweetheart?" he said once. A little later, it was, "These peas are delicious, darling. Would you like more?"

Laurel set her teeth and gave him the most natural smile she could muster while she coped admirably with the urge to kill him. He was enjoying this farce as much as Julia and Clark, and she ached to wipe that smile off his face and the devilish twinkle from his eyes. But of course she was helpless to do anything except endure it all. Ken, across the table, often glanced curiously toward them, and she didn't dare allow him to see what torture she was suffering.

Becky had been warned privately in her bedroom about the fake engagement, and she was game enough not to give her aunt away, either. But, unlike her elders, she didn't take any undue interest in the situation. She merely accepted it unquestioningly, more interested in her food and the table conversation than in Laurel's illogical pretense.

Except for Laurel's own acute discomfort, the dinner progressed well. Julia's meal was delicious, and she and Clark smoothly kept the conversation going. For once, Becky was on her best behavior and was acting like the sweet, sunny-natured girl she used to be. She even laughed with Clark over an amusing incident that had occurred at school that day.

"Mrs. Tribble slid on a wet floor in the hallway and fell." She giggled. "Mr. Baskin went to help her up, only he couldn't do it by himself because she's so huge!" She laughed again. "You should have seen Mr. Baskin's face! It was all red from trying to help her up, only he couldn't, until finally the janitor came along and they both did it!"

Clark laughed, too. "On top of that, I strained my back from trying to pull her up. But, Becky, if you repeat what I just said at school tomorrow, I swear I'll haul you into the office and give you a good spanking!"

Instead of growing angry over the threat of corporal punishment, Becky giggled again. "You *did* look funny! Like an ant trying to lift an elephant!"

"You shouldn't speak of Mrs. Tribble in such terms," Clark said repressively, but the grin on his face gave him away.

Laurel herself did not enjoy a moment of the evening. She was too sharply aware of both Ken and Stephen. While the men spoke politely to each other, she sensed the reserve and even antagonism between them. The situation in which she found herself made her so tense and nervous that she could do little to ease the situation. Whenever Ken engaged her in conversation, Stephen seemed not to like it and would then either put his arm around her or call her by some endearing term as a brand of his "possession" of her. Whenever he did that, Ken frowned and looked angry. All of it left Laurel confused and exhausted. Finally, as soon as they had finished drinking coffee in the living room, she had had all she could take and decided to make her escape.

She stood up, smiled pleasantly at Ken, and said, "It was nice to see you again, and I hope you have a safe trip home." She turned quickly to Julia, adding, "I need to get home early tonight and work on the payroll."

It was a blatant lie, since Julia had seen her doing the payroll that afternoon, but her sister graciously accepted the excuse. But, to Laurel's dismay, when she moved toward the door Stephen unwound his long limbs from the chair he was sitting in and said, "I'll walk with you to your car, darling. I need to be getting home myself."

In front of the others, especially with Ken's gaze upon her, Laurel could not object. She stood in impotent anger while Stephen thanked Julia for the dinner and said his goodbyes.

"Did you enjoy yourself the other evening at the dance, my love?" Stephen asked conversationally when they reached her Chevy.

Laurel's spine stiffened beneath his intense gaze, and she paused, her hand on the door handle, before turning to look at him. Idly, as though he intended to make himself comfortable for a nice, long chat, Stephen leaned against the car, propping one hand against the hood.

"It was fine," Laurel replied shortly. She opened the door. "Now, if you'll excuse me, I'd like to get home."

"Did Dan also enjoy himself?" Stephen asked, just as though she hadn't spoken.

"If you really want to know, why don't you ask him?" she answered with exasperation.

"And how about tonight?" Stephen taunted. "Did you enjoy it, too? It was really a nice gesture," he added musingly, "for your old beau to come all the way from Massachusetts to congratulate us on our engagement."

"Drop dead!" Laurel hissed. She pulled the car door open wider and moved to get inside.

Instantly Stephen left his position against the hood and came around the opened door. His strong fingers clasped her upper arm, imprisoning her. "Not so fast," he said sternly. "As my fiancée, I figure the least you owe me is a good-night kiss before you go."

"Since I'm *not* your fiancée, I owe you nothing."

"Yes," Stephen ground out, suddenly angry himself, "but you can make use of me for your own purpose, can't you? What was the point of it, anyway? Just to make your friend in there"—he jutted a thumb over his shoulder—"jealous? To bring him up to the wire so he'll declare *his* intentions?"

With swift fury Laurel's hand flew out and made a sickening thud against Stephen's face. The instant she did it, she was appalled at herself and tears gathered in her eyes and choked her throat. "I'm sorry," she whispered hoarsely. "My God, Stephen, I'm really sorry."

Stephen's dark eyes narrowed. Gingerly he rubbed his cheek. "Who are you angry with?" he asked shrewdly. "Yourself . . . or me?"

"Both. You for what you said . . . myself for making up such a lie." Laurel lowered her head, shamefaced, so that she could avoid his penetrating gaze. "I'm sorry I involved you," she added softly. "It . . . it was very good of you to play along, and I shouldn't have slapped you. I . . . I'll be going now." Once again she turned toward the car.

Stephen's hand, more gently this time, touched her arm, halting her flight once more. When she half turned back toward him, she saw his eyes glittering beneath the slender thread of moonlight. He was so close she could feel his soft breath on her face. For an endless time they gazed at each other wordlessly, and Laurel's heart began to beat a quick tattoo against her breast. Then, slowly, Stephen's arms went around her and he pulled her to him until their bodies melded, making a single dark silhouette against the dark night sky.

Stephen's lips came to hers, warm and firm, and Laurel's own parted in a response she could neither conceal nor deny. Primitive passion spread through her veins like a potent drug as Stephen's hand traveled up to her throat and then buried itself in her hair at the nape of her neck. The pressure of his mouth on hers grew to almost violent intensity as it explored and devoured hers with masterful possession.

"You've gotten under my skin, Sweet Pea," he muttered in a sensuous, vibrant tone. "More than anything, right now I'd like to be making love to you." One of his hands slid upward from her waist to cover her breast, and then, unsatisfied with the cloth that separated them, he began to fumble with the buttons on her dress.

Laurel went limp with surrender. Her own hands were caressing his shoulders as she abandoned herself completely to the fierce, hungry desires that caused her entire body to tremble. Bemused, she was lost in the wonderland of ecstasy that his touch always evoked within her. At last Stephen lifted his head and she murmured, "Oh, Stephen, I . . ." She opened her eyes and immediately forgot whatever she had been about to say as she realized with horror that they were standing beside her car in Julia's front yard. The only thing that shielded them from possible view of the house was the thick dark night and the opened car door. Abruptly she thrust his hand away and began rebuttoning her dress. "We can't . . . here . . ." she stammered. "We might be seen."

A sardonic smile flitted across Stephen's lips, cruel and harsh. "Yes, and that would be dreadful, wouldn't it?" he chided. "If Ken saw us he might be utterly convinced of the truth of our engagement, after all, wouldn't he? And that would never do! Then you'd have a hard time explaining me away if you suddenly decided you wanted to pick up where you left off with him. Please forgive me!" he added sarcastically. "For a minute there I got carried away and forgot two vitally important things."

"What . . . things?" she asked in a cracked voice.

"Number one, that you don't want a relationship with me; and number two, that I don't want a woman who isn't mine alone. You've got too many men on your string to suit me." He raised his right hand to his forehead and gave a mock salute. "See you around sometime, my sweet prickly pear blossom."

Taking long strides, he walked briskly toward the curb and his own car.

During the following week Laurel stayed as busy as possible in order to keep her mind off Stephen. Neither the center nor her own apartment had ever shone quite so brightly as they did now, because she worked early and late at scrubbing both in between her normal duties. As far as the center was concerned, the hard work paid off. One morning the state health inspector arrived without warning, and the spotless yet cheery-looking center passed his scrutiny with flying colors.

The morning after the health inspector's visit, Julia interrupted Laurel during storytime and said somberly, "I've got a personal errand to run. I may be gone for a good while. Will you hold the fort down?"

"Certainly," Laurel answered quickly. "But is there anything I can do to help?"

Julia shook her head. "No." Now she seemed eager to get away. "I'd better run. See you later."

She was gone for two hours. When she returned she looked depressed, yet so forbidding that somehow Laurel lacked the courage to ask her what was wrong. But there was definitely something the matter. Though Julia resumed her duties with the children, her natural sparkle and easy smile were missing, and that left Laurel feeling uneasy.

That evening, shortly after six, when all the children and staff were gone for the day, Julia approached Laurel. "Can I talk to you?"

"I wish you would," Laurel said emphatically. "I've been worried about you all day. What's wrong?"

Julia grimaced and sank into a chair on the opposite side of the desk where Laurel had been working. "I just don't know what to do," she sighed.

"Is it Becky again?"

"No." Julia shook her head. "At least, not directly. Last night I called Bert, and while he told me that he does have a job and is working again, he said he couldn't send me any child-support money for a while because one of his wife's children has a large orthodontist bill he must pay. Can you believe that?" she demanded. "He's more concerned with supporting some other man's children than his own!"

Laurel shook her head. "No, I can't believe it! Bert sure has changed since I knew him."

"Hasn't he ever?" Julia's tone was bitter. "I'm at my wit's end, Laurel. I can try to take him to court, of course, and sue him for the child support he owes me. But you know how it is . . . that could take months, if ever, before I recovered all the money he owes me! And right now I'm flat broke. Besides my regular bills, I need some carburetor work done on the car, my refrigerator is going on the blink, and

Becky is outgrowing clothes like a wild weed in summertime! I went to the bank this morning to ask for a personal loan, but since they lent us all that money to get the center going, they refused." She sighed again. "I can't blame them, really. Like the man said, until we're making enough to earn salaries ourselves, I don't really have a way of paying them back. Laurel . . . *what am I going to do?*"

"I don't know," Laurel answered. "But we'll think of something."

"What?" There was an edge of panic in Julia's voice. "I know you can't afford to lend me any more, not after you've already done it once."

Laurel nodded unhappily. "To tell the truth, I'm skating on rather thin ice myself. I was going over the books today, and the way we're growing here, I really think if we can hold out a couple of more months we'll both be able to start drawing small salaries for ourselves. But there *has* to be something we can do in the meantime."

Julia got wearily to her feet. "Well, it's not going to be solved tonight, and I've got to get home and cook supper. Since it's Friday, I promised Becky she could have a school friend spend the night with her, and I'm sure they're both starving."

During the weekend, Laurel mulled over the problem, went over the office ledgers again with a fine-tooth comb, and still came up with no answer. By Sunday afternoon she had come to the conclusion that she, too, would have to approach the bank for a loan, but she had little hope that she would have any more success than Julia had.

She was right. On Monday morning when she talked to the loan officer at the bank, though he was polite and seemed genuinely regretful, her request was denied. As she left the building her heart was heavy. There was only one thing left for her to do, and it was a vastly distasteful one, but she had no choice.

Laurel returned to the center and resumed her

morning duties. In the early afternoon, while the children were napping and she had some free time, she picked up the telephone receiver and dialed.

Ana Marie answered, and from a dry, scratchy throat Laurel asked to speak to Stephen.

"I'm sorry," the housekeeper said. "He's with the vet. One of the cows is having a difficult labor and they're trying to save her. But I'll take a message if you like."

"Yes, please. Would you tell him that Laurel Patterson called and that I need to talk to him? It's important."

"*Sí*," the woman replied. "I'll tell him."

For the rest of the afternoon Laurel worked mechanically while she waited with dread for Stephen's call. But he didn't get around to making it until almost seven that evening.

His voice was curt as he announced, "This is Tanner. You called?"

"Yes." Laurel hated the unsteady huskiness in her voice. "I need to see you, to talk to you."

"About us?"

"N-no. It . . . it's business."

There was a long pause while the line seemed to be dead. Then, in an icy voice, he said, "I see. Well, I'm busy tonight. If it's really important, I can see you tomorrow evening. Be here at eight."

"Yes." Laurel's heart thudded, and she was glad she was speaking to him over the phone so that he couldn't hear its pounding. "Yes. Tomorrow at eight is fine. Thank you."

She was in agony throughout the following day, and by seven-thirty, when she drove toward the ranch, she felt she was in danger of becoming a basket case. She couldn't get out of her mind the harsh coldness that had been in his voice, and she wondered miserably whether she wasn't going on a fool's errand. Given the state of affairs as they now stood, she must be insane to believe that Stephen would be in any disposition to do her a favor. Still, he was the only hope she . . . or Julia . . . had.

When she parked in the drive and got out of the car, Vaquero came racing around the house, barking wildly at this intrusion on his domain. But as soon as he recognized Laurel, the barks changed to short yaps of welcome.

"Down, boy," she ordered the exuberant animal. "I love you, but I don't want your paw prints all over my dress." With one hand she held his head still so that he couldn't jump up, while with the other she scratched behind his ear. As he tried to lick her hand she smiled faintly. "I wish I could dare to expect as warm a welcome from your master," she told him.

Vaquero wagged his tail, as though to say he hoped so, too. Then, as she straightened her shoulders and walked toward the house, he accompanied her.

Stephen answered the door, and for a tense moment they merely gazed somberly at each other. Laurel's breath caught in her throat from nervousness over her purpose in coming and from the reaction she always had at seeing him. Tonight, framed in the hall light, he was dressed in casual slacks and a white knit shirt. His inky black hair glistened beneath the light and his dark eyes were as unfathomable as Texas crude oil.

At last he invited, "Come in. No, not you, Vaquero," he added as the dog moved forward.

Vaquero's ears and tail drooped with disappointment, and if she hadn't been so tense, Laurel could have laughed.

Stephen ushered her into the living room and waved a hand toward the sofa, indicating that she should sit down. When she did, he asked civilly, "Would you care for a drink?"

She shook her head and moistened her lips. "No, thank you."

He inclined his head slightly. "As you wish."

Instead of sitting down himself, Stephen walked over to the fireplace and leaned an elbow against the mantel as he turned to look at her. "All right, you said you needed to see me about business. Let's get on with it."

His eyes, his voice, his entire demeanor, were so cold and off-putting that inwardly Laurel cringed. She wished that he would at least sit down. That way he wouldn't appear quite so intimidating. But obviously he had no such intention and was still waiting for her to speak.

She looked down at her clasped hands in her lap so that she could avoid his unyielding gaze. "I . . . I need a loan . . . a long-term personal loan," she explained, "of several thousand dollars. I . . ." Now she braced herself to look up at him as she stated her case. "I will repay you on a monthly basis, and I would like to do it over a two-year period."

There was a long silence while Stephen merely looked at her as though he could perhaps read her mind if he stared hard enough. On edge, tense, and expectant, Laurel endured it, not daring to look away from him this time.

"Why do you need so much money?" he asked at last.

"It . . . it's for personal reasons," she answered in a low voice. She hated to have to admit why she really needed it unless it was absolutely necessary. She didn't want to betray Julia's trust, since Julia didn't have any idea that Laurel had decided to approach Stephen.

"I see," he said, though clearly he did not. "And why haven't you approached the bank?"

This time she did lower her gaze. She was unable to bear the penetrating intensity of his any longer. "I did . . . but they turned me down."

"So I'm the last resort, am I?" His voice was hard and inflexible. "And supposing I make you this loan? What exactly can you put up for collateral?"

"My car," she answered promptly.

Stephen's harsh laugh drew her eyes to his face again, and there was a sneer on his lips. "That old rattletrap of yours?" he asked with scorn. "It's already practically worthless. No, Laurel, you'll need to do better than that."

She chewed anxiously on her lower lip. "Well," she said hopefully, "I could put up my half-interest in the center."

Her heart plunged as he shook his head. "Sorry, but I don't have the least desire to become a part owner of a nursery school."

Utterly defeated and fighting back the hot tears that scalded her eyes, Laurel rose to her feet. "I have nothing else to offer," she said in a low voice. "I . . . I thank you for taking the time to see me," she added politely. "Good night."

She had just taken her first step toward the door when his voice halted her and made her turn to look at him once more.

"There is a way," he said.

"What?" Her fingers were tightly clasped around her purse as she waited.

"I'll lend you the money," he said slowly, "if you'll put yourself up as collateral. For the next two years you'll have to be my woman, to move in here with me and allow everyone to openly see that you belong to me . . . and to me alone!"

Laurel felt lightheaded with shock and disbelief at the cruelty in Stephen's face, in his words. But his hard eyes were implacable, reflecting his steely resolve. There was no doubt about it . . . he meant what he was saying.

There had been a time when she had wanted this man any way she could have him, under any conditions, Laurel reflected, but this wasn't one of them. The man she had thought she loved apparently didn't even exist; this man standing before her was a stranger, a terrible stranger.

And yet she still needed the money. If she didn't get it, she had no idea what would become of Julia and Becky.

"Well?"

Knowing she had no choice, Laurel nodded. Tears glittered in her eyes, and angrily she brushed them away. "All right, Stephen," she said in a hard voice that matched the roughness of his. "If those are your terms, then that's the way it will be. But if you force this on me, I'll hate you. I will hate you until my dying day!"

"What does that matter to me?" he asked in a frigid, unfeeling tone. "I'll still be getting what I want." He paused, then smiled in a cruel, taunting way as he arrogantly ordered, "Come here to me now and we'll seal the bargain."

Chapter Twelve

This couldn't be happening, Laurel thought frantically. Surely it was just some horrible nightmare from which she would soon awake. She squeezed her eyes shut in an effort to block out the ugly situation, and as she did new tears spilled from her eyes and trickled down her face. But this time she wasn't even aware of them. She was chilled and trembling from head to toe, and her mind was swirling from the impact of Stephen's hateful words and her own weak acceptance of his deal. How cheap, how low, it all made her feel.

"I'm waiting, Laurel," Stephen said in a granite voice from across the room. "I told you," he reminded in a measured tone, "to come here to me. Now."

She opened her eyes, and through her tears his face wavered before her. The face was still cruel and menacing, the dark eyes narrowed and inscrutable, the mouth twisted into a hateful, mocking sneer.

"Please," she pleaded, and her voice quivered. "Please, Stephen, don't do this to me . . . or to yourself."

The smile on his lips stretched until his mouth was a taut, straight line. "Take it or leave it," he said carelessly. "It's entirely up to you."

Laurel hesitated for another full minute, praying desperately that he would come to his senses, that he would feel a spark of ordinary human compassion, that he would release her from such a shameful bargain. But at last she realized that he was not going to relent, that he was unswerving in his indomitable will, and that he was still waiting for her to come to him.

She sucked in a sharp, painful breath. Then, rigid and wooden, she slowly crossed the room. When she stopped directly in front of him, she knew that he expected her to offer him her lips in order to seal their bargain. A bargain with Satan, she thought almost hysterically. Then, with deliberation, she tilted her head back slightly, closed her eyes, and waited for the kiss that would be the signature of her imprisonment, her loss of freedom and independence and, worst of all, her self-respect.

The kiss came, ruthless and utterly contemptuous. Gone, as though she had only dreamed them, were the kisses of the past . . . those tender expressions of caring, of deep passion. Here instead was an assault upon her vulnerable lips and upon her deepest convictions. Stephen's mouth plundered hers as a thief might a jewelry chest, violently taking what he wanted with no regard for his right to possession, with no consideration of the right or wrong of it, without the slightest concern for her own bruised emotions. His hands intimately explored her body, traveling over her soft breasts and along the contours of her hips. But this time the touch did not arouse and inflame her senses as it had always done before. This time her shame was too overwhelming, her emotions too battered, until, finally numb, Laurel merely went limp, feeling nothing.

When he lifted his head at long last, Laurel expected the next and final step . . . the journey upstairs to his bedroom. Dully, almost dispassionately, she wondered if she had the strength to go through with it, not only for this one night but for the next two years. Sightlessly, she gazed at the pocket on his shirt so that she would not have to look at his cruel face.

But then he shocked her even more by shoving her from him so that she stumbled backward. Her eyes widened and her gaze flew to his face. The dark expression it wore frightened her even more than the one that had been there before.

"Did you *really* think I'd want a woman I must buy?" he asked bitterly. "Any woman I must buy?" He shook his head and his eyes glinted with black fury as his voice was laced with derision and ridicule. "Frankly, I'm not so sure the pleasures of your charms are worth that much money! And, to tell the truth, I really believed you would call my bluff and refuse. I never thought you'd actually be willing to sell yourself for any amount of money. You must," he added contemptuously, "need that money pretty badly."

Laurel was devastated, and her face drained of all color as he lashed out at her with his scorn. She should have known, she thought vaguely, that Stephen wouldn't have wanted her like that. In his raging anger, he had set her up for humiliation. Well, he had succeeded marvelously and had dealt her a blow from which she would never recover.

"I'm sorry," she said in deep mortification. She lifted a shaking hand to smooth her mussed hair. "I'll . . . I'll leave now."

"Surely you're not going to leave without what you came for, are you?"

"What . . . what do you mean?" Her gaze flickered nervously to his darkly flushed face, then back to the floor again.

"The money you asked for. Let's go into the study and I'll write your check now." Without waiting to see whether she followed, he strode quickly from the room.

Reluctantly Laurel followed. When she reached the study and saw him bent over the desk, scribbling into a checkbook, she forced herself to ask, "But . . . what about collateral?"

Stephen ripped the check from the book and held it out toward her. Once again his lips curled into that horrid, disdainful sneer. "Forget the collateral," he said harshly. "You have absolutely nothing that I want. *Nothing* at all. I'll just take a gamble on the chance that you'll repay me."

Laurel hesitated about taking the check until Stephen snapped impatiently, "Well, go on . . . take it. It's what you wanted, remember?"

She accepted it and tucked it into her purse without bothering to look at it. Her eyes were locked with his, and something odd seemed to flicker in the depths of those dark eyes, she thought in faint surprise. It was almost as though Stephen were as hurt over this ugly episode as she was, but that just didn't make any sense.

"Thank you," she murmured huskily. "I swear I'll repay every penny . . . with interest."

"As you wish." There was a suddenly bored tone to Stephen's voice. He broke the spell of their mesmerized gazes by glancing pointedly at his watch. "Now, if you'll excuse me," he said coldly, "I have another engagement tonight."

Laurel almost stumbled in her haste to get out of the house and away from Stephen. When she drove through the gates and out onto the highway at last, her eyesight was blinded by the tears she finally allowed to flow freely. Her entire chest ached with more, as yet unshed tears, and she wondered dimly whether the hurt would ever go away. Unquestionably, Stephen hated her. But why? Why? What, after all, had she ever done that was so dreadful?

She spent a sleepless night, and by morning her eyes were gritty and she ached from fatigue. The memory of the previous evening returned, torturous in its brilliant clarity. Stephen had hurt her with cruel deliberation, proving once and for all how he truly felt about her. Renewed pain ballooned in her chest until she felt as though she were going to suffocate with it.

It was an effort to get moving this morning. All Laurel really wanted to do was stay in bed and pretend the rest of the world had vanished. But that was impossible. She still had work to do and people who depended on her.

Unable to face breakfast, she dressed listlessly and went downstairs early to unlock the door for the stream of parents and children who would be arriving within the next half hour. Then she went into Carmen's kitchen domain and brewed enough coffee for the entire staff.

She was just sipping her first cup when Julia arrived. "You look as though a steamroller just drove over you," she observed unflatteringly.

"Thanks for the bouquet," Laurel replied dryly. "Remind me to toss you one sometime."

Julia's eyes narrowed as she studied Laurel. "Are you sick?"

Laurel shook her head and with a weary gesture lifted a hand and brushed her hair away from her face. "No. I just didn't sleep well, that's all."

Fortunately, one of the parents arrived then with a two-year-old and a three-month-old baby. Laurel took charge of the baby while Julia invited the older child to help her choose songs for the group to sing later in the day.

By midmorning everything was running according to a smooth routine, and Laurel took time out to go to the bank. She had never felt more reluctance to do something in her life than she did to endorse and deposit the check Stephen had made out to her. For a long time she simply stared at it with revulsion. If she *had* asked for the money simply for herself, no matter how urgently she might have needed it, she knew that after the scene between them last night she would tear the check up and starve before using it. But it wasn't for herself . . . it was for Julia; and no matter how much she hated the idea, she was going to have to deposit it in her account.

After lunch, while the children were napping and the staff was enjoying a much-deserved break chatting on the sun porch, Laurel called Julia into the office. When, wordlessly, Laurel handed a check to her, Julia stared at it in blank amazement for a long time before her searching gaze went to Laurel's face.

"Where did you get this much money?" she gasped. "Or have you completely wiped out your own savings?"

"No, it isn't my money," Laurel replied truthfully. "I got a loan."

"The bank lent it to you?"

Laurel shook her head. "No. They turned me down, too. It . . . it's from Stephen."

"Stephen!" Julia exclaimed. "It never occurred to me to go to him!" Impulsively she hugged Laurel and laughed happily. "You're a lifesaver, Laurel! And Stephen, too, of course!" She glanced down at the paper in her hand. "I can't thank you enough, and I promise I'll repay it on time every month." She paused, then looked up once more, and there was a curious expression in her hazel eyes. "It must have been a bit embarrassing for you, going to him and asking for a loan."

You don't know the half of it, Laurel thought almost hysterically. But that part of the matter was best left unmentioned, and so she shrugged her shoulders indifferently and said as lightly as she could manage, "It was, somewhat. But what's important is that you now have the money you need."

The next morning Becky's teacher called Julia and asked to have another conference with her. Julia sighed heavily after she hung up the phone. "More trouble, apparently—and I thought she was doing better at school." She got to her feet. "I said I'd be there in half an hour, so I guess I'd better get ready."

"Maybe she wants to tell you how Becky's grades have improved," Laurel said with a tiny smile of encouragement.

"Oh, sure." Julia's smile was wan. "And I'm about to inherit a million dollars from some long-lost relative, too."

Laurel grinned. "If you do, half of it's mine. Remember, it would be *my* relative, too."

Laurel was in the kitchen putting food on trays for Carmen to serve the children when Julia returned from her conference an hour and a half later. As soon as she walked into the room, Laurel could tell by her expression that she had been given more unpleasant news, and her own heart sank.

"What is it this time?" she asked anxiously.

Julia grimaced and leaned against the counter. "Same old thing. Becky's grades were up for a while, but they've fallen off badly again. She's not even bothering to try at all. She doesn't do her assignments, and she's constantly clowning around and distracting the other students from their work. According to her teacher," she added irritably, "I don't need to worry about her lack of friends any longer. She says Becky is the most popular child in the class, always pulling stunts or making funny, outrageous comments."

"Well, at least that part sounds like the old Becky we used to know," Laurel pointed out.

"Maybe so, but the old Becky pulled her cut-up capers outside the classroom, not by disrupting class routine."

"I suppose you're right," Laurel conceded. She put a small carton of milk on one of the plastic trays, then reached for another, continuing to work swiftly while she talked. "So . . . what now?"

Julia shook her head. "I only wish I knew. My lectures don't seem to help, and neither do restrictions. Nothing I seem to do or say gets through to her anymore. I'm beginning to wonder if maybe I should send her back to live with Bert, after all. It's what she says she wants."

"It might be what she *thinks* she wants, but I don't believe she really does, Julia. She would be utterly miserable in his house, having to share him with another woman and her children. Besides, Bert probably wouldn't want to have her."

Julia stiffened with indignation. "No 'probably' to it," she said with heat. "I *know* he wouldn't want to be bothered raising her, much less having to put up with her moods, not when he doesn't even support her like he should! Bert just simply doesn't care about her anymore, and that's the truth, Laurel! Not as any *real* father should, anyway! He'd probably have a fit if I sent Becky to him!"

Laurel didn't have a chance to see Becky that afternoon or the day after, because the girl didn't always come by the center after school these days; she had gotten into the habit of sometimes walking home with a friend, or having a friend go home with her. Because they were extremely busy with the children at the center, Laurel didn't have an opportunity to learn from Julia about the results of her latest confrontation with her daughter. But when she stopped by Julia's house on Saturday morning before going about her usual chores, she immediately discovered a measure of cool distance between mother and daughter. They were barely speaking to each other, and when they did, it was with the formal politeness of either total strangers or angry intimates.

"What's going on here?" she asked Julia as she helped herself to a cup of coffee while Becky went outside to feed Rascal his morning meal.

"It's the cold war, can't you tell?" Julia said in a discouraged voice. "I'm furious with her because she refused to promise to behave or try to better her grades at school. She's furious with me because I won't promise to stop seeing Clark. Impasse." Her shoulders slumped as her hands circled the coffee mug on her kitchen table.

Becky came back inside the house just then, so the discussion was hastily dropped. Laurel eyed her thoughtfully as the child took out a box of cereal, reached into the refrigerator for milk, and poured both into a bowl for her own breakfast.

"Have you got any big plans for today, Becky?" she asked.

Becky pulled out a chair at the table, sat down, and shrugged indifferently. "Nothing special. Why?"

"How about spending the day with me? I've got to do my laundry and shop for groceries this morning, but this afternoon we could go to a movie, or maybe have a picnic down by the river. It's a beautiful day."

Becky paused with a spoon halfway between bowl and her mouth. "If we have a picnic, can I bring Rascal?"

"Sure, only he can't go shopping with us. We'll come back for him later, if you want."

Becky nodded. "Can I choose to buy what we're going to eat?"

Laurel grinned. "It's a deal."

By noon they had accomplished all the necessary chores, and they set out for lunch. It was a day in late April with summerlike temperatures, and they both wore jeans, short-sleeved shirts, and sneakers. Becky had opted to buy a box of fried chicken for their meal. It rested on the front seat of Laurel's car between them while Rascal alternately bounced from the back seat to the floor and jumped back onto the seat, only to repeat the entire process again.

They parked on a level stretch of ground a few yards away from the riverbank. Since they were both hungry, they decided to eat their meal at once. There was a shady oak tree nearby, and they spread out their tablecloth beneath it while Rascal scampered around, darting here and there, pausing to sniff at a fallen twig or a growing weed. The spot was very peaceful. The gurgling water of the river was only steps away, and along its opposite bank were feathery green cypresses, their leaves swaying in the breeze.

"I like it out here," Becky said as she chose a chicken thigh from the box, leaned back against the tree trunk, and began to munch.

"So do I," Laurel agreed. "Everyone needs to get away from their everyday routine at times and go someplace like this where they can just relax." Today, she needed it very much, she thought silently as she took a sip of Coke. She needed the quiet peace of nature to flow through her and work its magical healing on her bruised spirit.

For a while they were both silent as they ate, but then they laughed when they saw Rascal come face to face with a large frog. Rascal backed away a pace, obviously uncertain. Then he crouched and barked excitedly. The frog calmly eyed him, seeming to hypnotize him, before it suddenly took a flying leap toward the water. Rascal was startled, and he came racing back to Becky's protective arms, whimpering with fear.

"It's okay, boy." Becky laughed as she cuddled him to her. "It was only a frog and it won't hurt you. Besides, you're bigger than he is."

"I don't think he believes you," Laurel chuckled. "Look how he's trembling!"

"He'll soon learn not to be afraid," Becky said, "and then he'll be a good, brave watchdog. Won't you, Rascal?"

Rascal shuddered and buried his nose in the crook of his mistress's arm.

Laurel began stuffing all the litter from their meal into a large paper bag. "I hear through the grapevine," she said casually, "that you've made a lot of friends at school. Do you like it here in Tierra Nueva now?"

"It's okay," Becky said without looking up. She stroked Rascal's silky back lovingly. "At least it's better than it used to be." Suddenly she giggled. "Yesterday, this girl in my class, Susie, dared me to swipe all the teacher's chalkboard erasers. So I did and hid them in one of the bookcases. Boy, was she mad! She made the whole class do conduct, and nobody squealed on me, either!"

"Do you think that was very nice?" Laurel asked without smiling.

Becky shrugged. "It wasn't so bad, and when the class ended I pretended to find them, so she got 'em back. It wasn't stealing or anything," she said defensively.

"No, it wasn't stealing, but it was an inconvenience to your teacher, besides making her angry. On top of that, the whole class was punished, even if they were loyal enough not to tell on you. But would you like to be punished for what someone else did?"

"I wouldn't care."

"Yes, you would."

Becky looked up at her. "Maybe so, but I wouldn't tell on them, either. Gosh, Laurel, you're making such a big deal about it. It was just a joke."

"I understand that," Laurel told her. She sprawled out full length on the ground. "But it wasn't a very kind joke for anyone involved. You can still be popular and have fun without making anyone angry or being a troublemaker, you know. And what I can't understand is why you're doing it. You used to be an excellent student, and now you don't try at all. Do you really believe you're hurting your teacher or your mother or even Mr. Baskin by refusing to do your work?"

"I don't care if I am or not," Becky answered defiantly. "None of them cares about me!"

Laurel sat upright and dangled her arms across her propped knees. "Not care?" she demanded. "How can you say that? Mr. Baskin cares, or he wouldn't keep trying to make friends with you, despite the way you act toward him. Your teacher cares very much, or she wouldn't bother calling your mother in for conferences about you. And your mother cares the very most, or she wouldn't bother trying to talk some sense into your head. But you resent that. That's the reason for the deep freeze at your house this morning, isn't it? Because your mother lectured you about behaving yourself at school and doing your homework. I care, too, Becky, or I wouldn't be discussing it with you right now. We all care about you, and it really wouldn't hurt a bit if you cared back a little sometimes! It's no fun when all the caring is one-sided."

Becky stared at the ground and looked as though she were fighting back tears. "I do care," she mumbled so low that Laurel almost failed to catch it. "I care about you . . . and Mom . . . and Stephen. Even my teacher's not so bad. But I *hate* Mr. Baskin."

Laurel sighed and cupped Becky's chin in her hand so that she could lift her face and look into her eyes. "There you go again with that awful word, honey. As far as I can see, Mr. Baskin is just as nice to you as Stephen is, or at least he would be if you'd allow him. Tell me the honest truth, what's so terrible about him except for the fact that he likes your mother?"

Becky refused to answer, and a moment later a tear fell from her face onto Rascal's back. When that happened, she wiped her face with an angry motion of the back of her hand and said, "Let's go for a walk."

Laurel stashed their picnic remains inside the car and made sure it was locked, and then they started off along the river's edge, with Rascal at Becky's heels. It was a pleasant walk, and since Becky soon regained her good spirits, they enjoyed their customary rapport.

"Pat says sometimes in the summer her dad brings a bunch of kids down here to swim and have a wiener roast. He even hangs a rope on a tree so they can swing out over the water."

"Sounds like a lot of fun," Laurel answered.

"Yeah. Pat says next time they do it, she'll invite me. I wonder if the water's warm enough for swimming now?" To satisfy her curiosity, she went to the water's edge, dabbed her fingers in it, and exclaimed, "Brr! Not yet!"

They walked a good distance along the meandering river and found evidence at several points that people had once built campsites. Laurel could imagine that in summer the now deserted river would be clogged with splashing, happy children.

At last they began to retrace their steps back toward the car, though they both did so with reluctance. Becky was loaded down with souvenirs: a small, interestingly shaped rock, a wild flower, a few acorns, and a strangely crooked twig. But when they reached the point where she had once crossed the river onto Stephen's property, she suddenly pushed her treasures into Laurel's hands and darted toward the large stones in the water.

"I'm going to see the witch's house again," she called over her shoulder as, hair flapping away from her neck, she hopped from one stone to another.

"Come back this instant, Becky!" Laurel said sternly. "You know it's only a hunting cabin."

"I'll be back in a minute," Becky shouted before she crawled beneath the barbed-wire fence and vanished.

Laurel frowned, then sat down on the ground to wait. This time she had no intention of going onto Stephen's land herself. Besides, it wasn't as though Becky didn't know her way back. Rascal came to her and licked her hand, and she cuddled him into her arms.

But when about ten or fifteen minutes had elapsed and Becky had not returned, Laurel got to her feet, with Rascal still in her arms. She, too, jumped across the stepping-stones in the swirling water. Darn

Becky anyway, she thought irritably. She shouldn't have gone across in the first place, and what was she doing now that she hadn't returned already? Laurel answered her own question. She was collecting more souvenirs, no doubt.

While she scrambled up the other bank, eased herself and Rascal between the dangerous points of the barbed-wire fence, and fought her way through the dense thickets beyond, Laurel's annoyance grew. She practiced a blistering speech to deliver to her niece the instant she clapped eyes on her.

Once she had gained freedom from the bushes, Laurel glanced around, but she didn't see Becky anywhere. With a sigh of frustration she walked slowly toward the cabin. And then she saw a small form in a crumpled heap on the ground just in front of the cabin steps.

She broke into a run and a minute later had eliminated the distance between them. Laurel knelt down beside the child and asked hoarsely, "What's wrong?"

Becky grimaced with pain and pointed to her right foot. She had removed the shoe, and Laurel could see that the foot was badly swollen and already had a slight bluish tint. "I tripped and fell," she explained. "I can't walk on it, Laurel. I tried three times, but it hurts too much."

"Oh, great!" Laurel despaired. "And here we are, a long way from the car!"

"I didn't mean to do it!" Becky said, with a quiver in her voice. "I know you're mad at me, Laurel, but, honestly, I didn't mean to cause trouble."

"I know you didn't, honey," Laurel said in a calmer voice. "But, all the same, it wouldn't have happened if you had only minded me. I told you not to come over here."

"I know." Becky appeared close to tears. "I'm really sorry."

Rascal snuggled up beside her, as though to comfort her. Laurel stood up. "I'll look inside the cabin and see if I can find some sort of towel or cloth I can wet in the river and then wrap around your foot. We need to get that swelling down."

Inside the cabin, Laurel only barely noticed a double bed in one corner, bunk beds in another, and, across the room near the fireplace, a table and chairs, a work counter, and a wood stove. She searched in the drawers beneath the counter, found a kitchen towel, and went back outside.

"I'll only be a minute down at the river," she said. "Now, don't you dare try to—" Laurel broke off, and they both looked in the direction from which they heard the beat of horses' hooves. As though it were a bad dream being replayed, Laurel saw Stephen riding into view just as had happened another time. Only today he wasn't alone. A second rider came around some bushes, and Laurel recognized Annette Pharr.

Stephen looked in their direction at once and cantered toward them. Then he slid from the saddle with a lithe grace and strode forward. "What's going on here?"

"I sprained my foot," Becky answered.

"What were you doing here in the first place?" Stephen's voice was uncompromisingly stern.

"I . . . I just wanted to see the cabin again," Becky explained in a subdued voice. "Only I fell when I came out, and then Laurel came to find me."

Stephen knelt down to examine Becky's foot. "I don't want you to ever come out here again without someone with you. What if Laurel hadn't known where you were?" Gently he ran his fingers over her foot and ankle; then he looked up at Laurel. "I don't think anything is broken, but we'd better get her to the house and put an ice pack on it."

By then Annette had joined them, though she was still mounted on her horse. She smiled pleasantly at Laurel and asked Stephen, who was getting to his feet, "What happened?"

"Becky fell and sprained her foot. We'll have to

put her up in front of you for the ride back, Annette. Your mare can't take as much weight as my horse, so Laurel will have to ride with me."

"Oh, no," Laurel said swiftly. "I can walk. My car is parked a good way down on the other side of the river. I'll go back for it and then meet you at the house."

"You'll come with us now," Stephen said in an arrogant, grim voice. "What if you should have an accident yourself on the walk back? There would be no one to help you. I'll drive you back for your car later." Without bothering to wait for any further discussion of the matter, he gathered Becky into his arms and lifted her to sit in front of Annette. Then he turned back to Laurel and swept a hand toward his black stallion, indicating that she should mount.

Laurel was mortified as Stephen helped her up with his hands on her waist. Her face flushed with embarrassment and self-consciousness as he swung into the saddle behind her and his arms went around her to take the reins into his hands. Their bodies were pressed tightly together, her back against his broad chest, thigh to thigh, and his face so close to hers she could feel his breath upon her cheek.

The ride seemed interminable to Laurel, and it was filled with bittersweet emotions for her. This tantalizing closeness to Stephen was playing havoc with her senses. Her blood was racing white-hot, and her skin tingled from his touch. She ached to cover his browned hands before her with her own; she yearned to turn her head ever so slightly until her lips met his. But of course she didn't dare. There were Becky and Annette beside them; but even had they been alone, she couldn't have done it, because Stephen's body was rigid, his face colorless and without emotion. If he was suffering from the turbulent emotions that raged through her, it didn't show, and Laurel had a desperate struggle to appear unaffected as well.

Once they reached the house, Stephen carried

Becky to a chair on the patio and soon had an ice pack on her foot and a cold soft drink in her hand.

"I'm sorry we've been so much trouble to you and spoiled your ride this way," Laurel told Annette while Stephen tended to Becky's foot.

Annette smiled and shook her head. "Don't worry about it," she said. "I've got to be leaving in a few minutes, anyway. You didn't spoil a thing." She went to Becky and asked sympathetically, "How's the foot now? Are you still in a lot of pain?"

"It doesn't hurt so much now," Becky answered.

Laurel realized suddenly that if it weren't for her relationship with Stephen, she might have really liked Annette. She seemed to be a very kindhearted person as well as beautiful. But the fleeting thought vanished a moment later.

"I'd better be going now," Annette told Stephen. "As it is, it'll be dark by the time I get home and Dad will worry about me. Is our date still on for next Friday night?"

"You'd better believe it," Stephen said in a hearty tone. "I wish you wouldn't rush off like this, but I realize you need to get home." He placed both hands on her shoulders, then bent and gently kissed her cheek.

Laurel cringed and looked away. She had no business being here, she thought in an agony of embarrassment. She had no right to be witnessing this tender scene, and she wished desperately that the ground would open up and swallow her.

Chapter Thirteen

April relented and gave in to May, and some of the roses were already blooming beneath a benevolent sun. Because the weather was so fine, the children had extended play periods out of doors, their young bodies thriving in the fresh air and the warmth of the sunshine on their skin. Laurel wished their gaiety and happiness were contagious, but though she often smiled at their lively antics, her heart felt heavy and dark, like a leaden weight.

It had been two weeks since she had last seen Stephen, that day Becky had sprained her ankle. Although she had not seen nor heard from him, she knew Julia had. Her sister had mentioned that Stephen had stopped by the house a couple of evenings to visit briefly with Becky.

On the following Tuesday afternoon, just at closing time, when most of the children had already gone home with their parents and Laurel was holding a fretful one-year-old on her lap and trying to soothe him, she suddenly felt some strong reason to look up. Her heart stopped. Stephen stood in the doorway, gazing intently at her, and there was a tiny smile on his face.

"Good afternoon." He came toward her at once.

Laurel felt flustered and uncomfortable. Her hair was in disorder and her clothes were wrinkled from a day of holding children like the one who was still in her lap, with one little fist tightly clenched around a wad of fabric just above her breast.

"Good afternoon," she answered at last.

"You look very much the madonna just now," Stephen observed in a soft voice. "Did anyone ever tell you that you ought to be a mother yourself?"

"Not that I can remember," she replied crisply. "What can I do for you?" she went on. "I'm sure you didn't come here to talk to me of motherhood."

Just at that moment, Julia entered the room. "Laurel, do you know where the . . . oh, hello, Stephen. I didn't know you were here."

"Hello, Julia." Stephen nodded pleasantly. "I just arrived."

"What a nice surprise. Would you like a cup of coffee? I believe there's still some in the—"

"No, thanks," Stephen said, cutting her off. "I can only stay a minute. I just came to invite you both to a dinner party at my house on Saturday night. And naturally," he added with a twinkle in his eyes as he looked at Julia, "I expect you to bring Clark, as well."

Julia beamed at him. "That sounds lovely. Doesn't it, Laurel?" Without giving her sister a chance to respond, she added, "We accept. Thank you. What time should we be there?"

"Around seven-thirty." Now he turned to Laurel again. "I'll come by for you at seven." Then, before either of the two women could say another word, he strode quickly out of the room.

"Well, that ought to be fun," Julia said, still smiling. "I certainly enjoyed myself the last time he invited us."

"I'm not going," Laurel stated flatly. The child in her arms squirmed restlessly, and she set him down on a rug and gave him a yellow rubber lamb. He babbled happily as he clasped it, and Laurel stood up, smoothing her wrinkled skirt.

"Not going?" Julia's voice was sharp. "But why? I

thought you and Stephen were really hitting it off there for a while."

"For a while, yes," Laurel acknowledged. "A very brief while."

"What happened? Did you quarrel over the date you had with Dan?" Julia asked shrewdly.

"You might say that." Laurel began stacking chairs atop the tables. "But I really don't want to talk about it, Julia."

"That's fine," Julia said quickly. "But about the dinner party . . . Laurel, Stephen's *expecting* you to be his date for the evening. That was as plain as anything, since he said he'd come by for you. He must still feel—"

"He doesn't feel anything for me," Laurel snapped irritably. "He probably only offered because he's sorry for me and thought I'd need an escort."

"Sorry . . . for you?" Julia sounded amazed. Then, surprisingly, she laughed. "Stephen surely doesn't think that! Why, everyone in town knows that Laurel Patterson is independent and doesn't need men in her life. Who could possibly feel sorry for you when you're so strong and decisive?"

Somehow Julia's description sounded horribly unflattering, and Laurel's eyes darkened with anxiety. "Is my attitude *that* unbecoming?" she asked. "That apparent to everyone?"

The little boy tossed the lamb at Julia's feet. She stooped to pick it up and toss it back. Then she smiled at Laurel and answered, "Well, maybe I was a bit hard on you just then," she admitted. "Probably your attitude is known to only a few—to me, especially. But, honestly, Laurel, you *could* be just a bit more gracious to people who want to do nice things for you . . . such as accepting Stephen's invitation to his party. He wouldn't have invited you if he didn't really want you to come, so why resent it and turn him down? Are you afraid of Stephen, or of letting go and enjoying yourself . . . or both?"

Put like that, Laurel sounded like a coward. Which, of course, she was. She was terrified at the idea of having to spend an entire evening as Stephen's date. He had been so horrid to her the night she had gone to him for a loan, and she winced at the thought of a repeat performance. Yet, if she didn't go, she would be silently telling him, as well as Julia, that she was afraid of him, not physically, but of his ability to hurt her already bruised heart.

"I'll go," she said with reluctance.

"Great!" Julia nodded in satisfaction. "Wear that black cocktail dress you bought last summer. You're a knockout in that!"

The little boy's mother came rushing in then, full of apologies for being late and gushing distractedly about a boss and last-minute letters, a burning roast and guests arriving. She swooped up her child and dashed toward the door.

Laurel laughed. "There went a whirlwind."

Julia smiled with sympathy. "I know exactly how she feels. I've been there too many times myself." She sighed. "It's not always easy being a working mother, even if you have a husband around to help out."

"I know it isn't," Laurel said. "By the way, is Becky doing any better at school since your teacher conference?"

"A lot better," Julia replied with relief. "Better at home, too." She smiled and added, "On Sunday Clark and I are taking David, Becky, and one of her girl friends from school to San Marcos for the day to see the aquatic show. Becky is so pleased about it that she's completely forgotten to sulk and act resentful around Clark these past few days."

Laurel forced herself to give an answering smile and to act pleased for them, but after a moment she turned and busied herself storing away a few toy dishes in the learning center. She swallowed over a lump in her throat. Apparently Julia was so involved in her romance with Clark that she must have forgotten that Sunday was Laurel's birthday. Since they had always had special little celebrations for each other's birthdays, Laurel had just naturally assumed that Julia would plan a little something for her this year, too.

On Saturday, Laurel was on edge all day about the coming evening and she couldn't seem to do anything right. By mistake one of her best blouses, which she had always hand-washed, got mixed up with the rest of the laundry she took to the laundromat and came out looking raveled and old. Her shopping at the supermarket was slapdash, and when she got home she realized she hadn't bought half the things she needed. And when she cleaned out the refrigerator, she dropped and broke a bowl of stew all over her freshly mopped floor.

At six, she indulged herself in a bath scented with her favorite perfume, but though she tried to relax and let the steaming water soothe away her tension, the effort failed. She was a solid mass of nerves. She was sharply conscious of the passing minutes and of the fact that in less than one short hour Stephen would be here. Why, she wondered frantically, had she allowed Julia to talk her into going?

When the knock came on the door at seven, Laurel was just fastening her earrings. She threw one scrutinizing glance at herself in the bedroom mirror. The black cocktail dress, sleeveless and with a teasing, but not too low, V neckline, molded itself around her breasts, narrowed at the waist, and swirled softly around her legs. The severe color made her skin seem more golden than normal, and her hair, piled atop her head, looked like burnished copper with a hint of fiery red. Her makeup concealed the recent freckles that had cropped up across her nose from her hours in the sun. Around her throat was the necklace Stephen had given to her . . . or, rather, thrown at her one day. She had

not worn it before and she felt that she was very
daring to wear it tonight, but just once, at least, she
wanted to wear it. Her only fear was how he would
react when he saw it.

Laurel gave herself a grim smile and decided she
looked the best she could. With an erratically pounding heart, she left the room and went to answer the
door.

Stephen looked absurdly wonderful, she thought,
in his dark suit and wine-red tie. His hair was smooth
and rich, shimmering blue-black in the light that
spilled from the room. But it was his eyes, his face,
that drew her gaze, for there would be her clue to his
mood.

With something of a jolt, she found a soft warmth
in his eyes and a gentle smile lurking on his lips.
"Good evening," he said at last, after they had
gazed wordlessly at each other for some time.

"Good evening."

The smile, slightly crooked, widened. "Aren't you
going to invite me in?"

"Of course." Feeling flustered, Laurel moved
away so that he could enter.

The door clicked quietly behind him and Stephen
said, "You look incredibly lovely tonight."

Did she imagine it, Laurel wondered, or had there
been a faint catch to his voice? "Thank you," she
murmured. She started to move away. "I'll just get
my purse."

"Wait a moment," Stephen said. "I have something for you." He held out a square white box with
a cellophane top.

Laurel looked down at it in surprise. Inside was a
delicate, violet-colored orchid. "It's beautiful," she
said slowly. "But I never expected a corsage."

"Shall I pin it on you?"

"Please." She was glad when he took the box from
her so that she could hide her unsteady hands behind
her. But a moment later she realized that was a

mistake. When Stephen pinned the corsage just above her left breast, her skin tingled at his electric touch, and she sucked in her breath, trying to remain still, praying he wouldn't notice how his nearness affected her.

But once the corsage was pinned, Stephen did not immediately step away. His hand went to the necklace and he smiled deep into her eyes. "I'm glad you're wearing it," he said softly.

Laurel could not have replied if her life had depended on it. She was mesmerized by his tantalizing closeness, by the scent of his aftershave cologne, by the warmth of his fingers against her throat. A paralyzing weakness came over her, and she wanted nothing so much as for Stephen to take her into his arms and kiss her, to end the cold restraint that stretched between them like an icy ocean.

But he did not. An instant later he stepped away and said in a perfectly controlled, normal voice, "If you're ready, we'd better go. Since I am the host tonight, it won't look well if I'm away too long."

Laurel crushed down her disappointment, picked up her purse, and preceded him out the door. The drive to the ranch was accomplished with little conversation; when they did speak, it was only about mundane things like the good weather they had been having. Laurel was uptight, certain that the evening was going to be long and extremely difficult. The only good thing about it was that there would be others present, so at least she would not have to spend the entire time trying to think of things to say to this man beside her.

When they reached the house the drive was already lined with cars. "It would seem that all your guests are very prompt," she said in surprise. "What must they be thinking of you that you weren't here to greet them?" Her green eyes widened as she looked at him apologetically. "You shouldn't have bothered coming for me."

Stephen gave her an easy smile. "Don't worry. I had one of my friends come early so that she could greet them for me." He parked in front of the garage.

Annette? Laurel wondered when Stephen went around the car to open her door. But that didn't make sense. Why would he ask her to play hostess while he went to escort another woman to his dinner party? But then Stephen had her door opened and there was no time to speculate about it anymore.

They entered the house, and Stephen, with his hand lightly at her waist, guided her into the living room. The moment they entered, there were shouts of "Surprise!" and "Happy birthday, Laurel!"

Laurel stood as though rooted to the spot while the other guests converged upon them with greetings. Julia and Clark were among them, and Julia laughed at the baffled expression on Laurel's face.

"You didn't really believe I'd forgotten your birthday, did you?" she asked.

Laurel nodded. "Yes. Yes, I did. What . . . how . . . ?" Now she looked up at Stephen in her confusion. "How did you know?"

He laughed. "Becky happened to mention it a week or so ago. Julia and I got our heads together, and here you are!"

"It . . . it's a lovely thing to do," Laurel said in a quivering voice. She felt close to tears. "I never had a surprise party before!"

Stephen's eyes were tender, his smile one of amused gentleness. "I'm glad you like it," he said. "Now, would you care for a glass of punch or a mixed drink? I have to warn you: the punch is spiked. I'm not sure just what all Jan and Julia put into it this afternoon, but they sure were doing a lot of giggling and laughing at the time!"

Laurel grinned. "I'll take a chance on it."

Throughout the entire evening Laurel floated on a cloud of happiness. There was a buffet dinner with a dazzling array of luscious dishes, gifts to open, and, later, dancing on the patio in the silky warmth of the evening. Stephen had hired a mariachi band to play, and the musicians added a touch of romantic elegance with their silver-and-black-studded costumes and their soft, crooning voices.

Although he fulfilled his role of host with thoughtful consideration for the comfort of all his guests, Stephen was rarely gone from Laurel's side for more than a few brief moments at a time. At dinner, he was there, helping her fill her plate; when she opened her gifts, it was Stephen who handed them to her, one by one; and later, when the band began playing, he was the first to dance with her.

Politeness demanded that they both dance some of the time with others, but when Laurel returned to him after one dance, he whispered, "I'd rather be selfish and keep you all to myself tonight." She smiled at him in a way that let him know she felt the same, but then she was whisked away by another man.

After a particularly fast tune that she danced with Nick Colts, Laurel felt a need for a breather. She slipped into the house unnoticed and went to the kitchen to thank Ana Marie and Carmen for the wonderful food they had served.

"We enjoyed doing it," Carmen said as she towel-dried a large bowl. "Mama especially likes to cook for parties."

Laurel smiled at the older woman. "Stephen told me you baked the lovely birthday cake. You're a very talented lady, Ana Marie. I've never seen a cake before that looked like a basket of flowers! I hated to cut into it, it was so beautiful. You should open up your own bakery!"

"Hush!" a voice grumbled from behind her. "If she listens to your advice, I'll lose the best housekeeper and cook in all of Texas and Mexico combined!"

Laurel turned to find Stephen just behind her,

smiling good-naturedly at them all. Her heart leaped at the sight of him.

"You talk foolishness, the both of you," Ana Marie declared, but her face was wreathed in a smile that told them she was pleased by their compliments. "Now, go on . . . get yourselves back to the party."

Stephen's arm slid possessively around Laurel's waist, drawing her close to his side. "Come dance with me?" he asked.

With radiant happiness shining in her eyes, Laurel nodded, and they returned to the patio, where the mariachi band was playing a slow, romantic tune. Laurel drifted into Stephen's arms just as though she had always belonged there, just as though she always would.

"Did I thank you for the beautiful leather handbag you gave me?" Laurel asked as they swayed in unison to the music.

"Uh-hmm," he murmured close to her ear. "I've got another gift for you, too, but it's private. I'll give it to you later, when we're alone."

For a while they danced in silence, cheek to cheek, and the warmth of his body close to hers flooded Laurel with contentment. She closed her eyes and savored the moment.

"Why didn't you tell me that loan was not for yourself but for Julia?" Stephen asked.

Laurel's eyes flew open and she drew back from him so that she could see his face. "How did you find out?"

"Julia told me herself when she thanked me for it. Why couldn't you have just been honest with me?"

"If you recall, you weren't in the mood to give a sympathetic ear to anything I had to say. Besides"— she shrugged lightly—"I didn't want to be talking about Julia's problems."

Stephen drew her close again, and his voice was husky and deep. "I'm sorry about that night, Laurel. I behaved abominably toward you."

"Yes," she said unsteadily. "You did. But . . ."

She gave him a tremulous smile. "I accept your apology."

It was after one before the last of the guests left. The band had packed away their instruments and gone, and Carmen and Ana Marie had also left.

As soon as they were alone, Stephen returned to Laurel, who stood near the fireplace, feeling pleasantly tired but not really sleepy.

For a moment Stephen merely gazed at her with that odd little quizzical lift to one eyebrow and a hint of a smile lurking on his lips. Then he gathered her into his arms, and willingly Laurel offered him her lips.

"Will you stay the night with me?" he asked in a vibrant voice. "Just this once? The center is closed tomorrow and Julia and Becky will be away for the day, so no one has to know. I want to make love to you, and I want you with me in the morning when I wake up."

In her present bemused state, Laurel could deny him nothing. He wanted her, and she wanted him; and, just then, there *was* no tomorrow. There was only now . . . and her love for Stephen. She nodded slowly.

Laurel went upstairs alone while Stephen locked the house for the night. In his bedroom she went to the dresser and unpinned the orchid he had given her earlier in the evening. It had worn well and still looked lovely and fresh. She placed it on the dresser, and then she happened to catch a glimpse of herself in the mirror above it and saw that her eyes were darkened with passion, that her lips were soft and vulnerable. Her yearning for Stephen was almost frightening. She wanted him to hold her in his arms, to kiss her, to make love to her.

When he came, she was attempting to unzip the back of her dress, but he took over the job and did it for her. As the dress slid from her shoulders and down to the floor he bent his head and kissed the back of her neck, darting little shivers through her veins.

Without haste he undressed her, pausing often to kiss her. Laurel trembled with throbbing desire as his lips burned her skin from her throat down to her tender breasts. Her nipples tautened beneath his exploring tongue and her heart raced as her entire body became tinglingly alive at his touch. She tugged at his tie and unbuttoned his shirt so that her hands could revel in the sensuous enjoyment of his warm chest.

Stephen cupped her face with both his hands and his lips claimed hers in a long kiss that sent electrical charges through her as her own lips parted in response. Then his hands moved slowly down, to caress her breasts, then on to her hips. Laurel's hand was pressed against his bare chest, and she could even detect the beating of his heart beneath her fingers.

Stephen uttered a strange sound, like an agonizing moan, and then he pressed her backward onto the bed. Quickly he finished undressing and came down beside her. The upper half of his body crushed against her breasts as his arms slid around her and once again his mouth devoured her soft, kiss-swollen lips. It was as though this overwhelming passion that swept through them both seemed likely to drown them, yet they were helpless to escape.

"Oh, God, how I've missed you," he whispered hoarsely as he planted tiny kisses on her eyelids, her cheeks, her earlobes. He paused for a moment to gaze down at her, and his eyes were smoky-black with unbridled ardor.

"I've missed you, too," she whispered back. Her own lips sought a trail along the jugular vein of his neck. His lips possessed hers once more, with that same urgent, almost ruthless hunger as before, while his hands stroked her breasts and then gradually roamed down her silky body to her hips.

Laurel's fingernails raked his broad back, returning to cling to his shoulders. She whispered in frantic desperation, unable to bear the teasing and the longing a second more, "Please . . . please!"

Her body arched toward him and he joined her. Exquisite sensations enveloped Laurel, and she was submerged in a pleasure so marvelous that she was almost in awe of it.

When finally they had reached the heights together, Stephen buried his face between her breasts. "This was the most wonderful time yet," he said hoarsely.

"I know." Laurel lovingly threaded her fingers through his thick hair. Total peace and contentment overtook her, for now the desperate need that had gnawed at her senses had been satisfied.

"Know what else?" Stephen said after a minute as he lifted his head and smiled. A laughing gleam lit his eyes. "I'm suddenly starving. What about you?"

She laughed. "Come to think of it, so am I."

"Let's go raid the refrigerator. Ana Marie's bound to have had a lot of leftovers from the party."

Laurel brushed her hair back from her damp face. "I think I want a shower first."

"Excellent idea." Stephen grinned. "I'll be your back scrubber."

They showered together, splashing water into each other's faces and laughing a great deal. By the time they had finished with their antics, they really were ravenous. Stephen put on the bottoms of a pair of pajamas; Laurel put on the top and covered that with his robe. It was huge and dragged on the floor, but it only served to make them laugh again.

Downstairs, they made sandwiches of ham and cheese, and finally, near three in the morning, they climbed the stairs again.

"Happy birthday," Stephen whispered once they were snuggled close together in bed. His arm was across her middle, and her head was tucked between his shoulder and neck.

"Thank you," Laurel said drowsily. Her eyelids fluttered down. "It's the best birthday I ever had."

She was vaguely aware of Stephen kissing her forehead, drawing the blanket up beneath her chin, and then she sank into a deep, restful sleep.

Chapter Fourteen

*L*aurel awoke abruptly, instinctively aware that she was not in her own bed and that she was not alone even before she opened her eyes. When she did, her gaze first saw the ceiling before she cut her eyes sharply toward the space beside her.

Stephen was there, lying on his side, frankly studying her. An animated spark lit his eyes, like sunlight dancing through rustling leaves on a tree, and his lips parted into a warm smile. "Good morning," he said softly. "Did you sleep well?"

"Ummm. Like a log." Laurel yawned and stretched lazily, imitating a cat. "And you?"

Stephen's mouth stretched into a teasing grin. "Best night's sleep I've had in years. What do you say to getting married?"

Laurel's throat suddenly constricted. "Wh-what did you say?"

"You heard me." Stephen laughed and gently brushed her tousled hair away from her forehead with his index finger.

"You . . . you're joking, of course," she said after a minute.

He shook his head.

"But . . . why?"

Stephen shrugged one bare tanned shoulder and entwined one of her locks around his finger. "Why not?" he countered lightly. "You're very beautiful and intelligent, you're good with children, and I even happen to know you can cook. We're very attracted to each other, and I want you here with me, in my bed, every morning when I wake up. Anything wrong with that?"

Swift delight flooded through Laurel's being the way sunlight now beamed through the bedroom window. She was just about to give a joyous yes in response when she suddenly realized there had been one glaring omission in his reasons. Stephen had not said he loved her.

"Well?" he asked quizzically. "Did Vaquero get your tongue again?"

A lump clogged Laurel's throat, so that she was, for the moment, unable to speak. But she was spared having to make an immediate answer, because just then the telephone rang.

Stephen swore, then muttered, "I'd better get it, I suppose. No one would be calling this early in the morning without good reason." He flipped over in bed and stretched out a long arm toward the phone on the bedside table. While he answered it Laurel slipped from the bed, grabbed up his robe, and covered herself with it as she went to stand at the window, gazing out at the brand-new day.

What should she do? she wondered frantically. Here was the one man she would always love, body and soul, asking her to marry him. Should she just ignore the fact that he had not mentioned love and hope her own was enough to carry their marriage? After all, what Stephen said about their attraction to each other was true. Physically, they were highly attuned and thrillingly compatible. But marriage was more than just a physical relationship between a man and a woman, no matter how satisfying it might be. Marriage meant children and responsibilities, good and bad times, problems to be solved. Could a marriage without deep, abiding love on both sides ever survive the rigors of living together through the years?

The question made Laurel's head ache. She only knew that, for her, marriage meant forever. It was not something to be entered into lightly. Even when both partners started out in love, sometimes it wasn't enough—witness what had happened to Julia. Yet without that vital ingredient, surely a marriage could have no prayer of passing the test of time.

Yet . . . she loved him so much. Without Stephen in her life, she *had* no life! It was as simple as that. For her, he was what made the sun rise in the morning and the stars shine at night. Without him she would have no firm purpose, no direction for her future. What was it Julia had once said? Something about how love was a gamble, but one couldn't shut oneself away from it, that everyone needed it. She *did* need it. That was the problem! She *needed* Stephen's love, and though he offered marriage, he had not offered his heart.

She became aware that, across the room, Stephen was still speaking into the telephone. "Sure, Annette. Sure, baby. Now, try not to worry about a thing. I'll be there. Yes. I'll see you later. 'Bye."

Laurel froze. Annette again! How easily she had been forgotten! Always Annette. Annette *baby!* Annette, whom for some unfathomable reason Stephen did not plan to marry, yet who was still very much an important factor in his life! What a fool she was to even have considered for a moment Stephen's proposal! Clearly he had no intention of placing Annette out of his life just because he wanted Laurel in it!

She did not hear Stephen cross the carpeted floor, and she jumped when he touched her arm.

"Now, where were we?" he said in a throaty voice. "I believe I was in the middle of a marriage proposal."

"And the answer is no!" Laurel said in a rush.

"Why?" Stephen's voice was suddenly harsh. "If you're going to turn me down, the least you can do is give me a good explanation."

Laurel averted her eyes and stared out the window where the sun was burning away an early-morning mist that hung over the land. She took a long, shuddering breath and said, "Marriages don't last these days. Men aren't faithful to one woman forever, and I don't want to face that probability someday. When Julia and Bert were first married, you never saw two people more crazy about each other. And look how that ended. When I was engaged to Ken, he couldn't even bring himself to be faithful to me until the wedding! He tried to convince me that it didn't mean anything, that he only cared about me. But it *did* matter!"

With an effort, Laurel made herself half turn so that she was facing him, and she met his gaze unflinchingly. "I just heard you talking to Annette, Stephen. You're going to see her later today, aren't you? You see, you're just the same as the others." Her laugh was brittle. "Lucky for me she called, or else I might have made the mistake of accepting your proposal."

A hostile coldness hardened Stephen's eyes, and it froze the blood in Laurel's veins. "You're a fool." His voice was scathing. His hard gaze raked her face in merciless contempt. "I can easily explain my relationship with Annette, but in the face of your blatant suspicions and distrust, I see no reason to bother. You're tarring me with the wrong brush, my dear, and I refuse to accept any part of the blame for what other men may have done. Not all men cheat on their fiancées, or wives. My own father was faithful to my mother until the day she died. But then, she was woman enough to hold his interest through the years. He used to tell me that she was the most fascinating woman he had ever known. Perhaps it's your own ability to hold a man that you doubt?"

"That's a filthy thing to say!" Laurel gasped at his deliberate cruelty.

A sardonic smile flitted across his lips. "It's no worse than your condemnation of me based on what your philandering fiancé did!" He glared at her with distaste. "I obviously mistook you for a generous, warmhearted woman, but you're not. You're very cold-blooded about personal relationships, aren't you? You want everything spelled out in black and white, a written guarantee that you'll have a lifetime of sunshine without any clouds. But there *are* no such guarantees about life! I feel sorry for you, Laurel. It's a sad, pitiful individual who can never take a chance on getting close to another, who doesn't dare trust anyone. People need people. A man and a woman were created to give each other comfort and help and trust and the greatest fulfillment two human beings can give. But you're incapable of giving so much to another because you can't even accept it for yourself."

The tears burning in her eyes had begun to spill, unheeded, down Laurel's face during his speech. Now, in a choking voice, she cried, "That isn't true! I'm not like that!"

"Aren't you?" Stephen's voice was grim and forbidding. "I think you are. I guess I should thank you for turning me down before I could make a terrible mistake." He shrugged, as though dismissing all that had gone before. "Anyway, the subject is closed. You've refused, and my offer is withdrawn. Frankly, I don't want to marry you any longer. Now, if you'll get dressed, I'll take you home." He turned, stalked to his closet, from which he pulled some clothes, and left the room.

Laurel never knew quite how she got through the next half hour. Somehow she managed to gather up her clothes and put them on. When she went downstairs, Stephen was dressed and waiting for her. Without a word, he ushered her outside to the car. The back seat had already been loaded with her birthday gifts from the night before, and Laurel suddenly remembered that he had told her then that he had another gift he would give to her in private. Had his proposal been that gift? she wondered fleetingly as she got into the car.

Not that it mattered. Nothing mattered anymore except for this dreadful ache in her chest that seemed to be suffocating her. Stephen sent the car down the drive with tires squealing and dust flying, as though he could hardly wait to see the last of her. Laurel sat stiff and silent beside him.

When they reached the apartment, Stephen's face was rigid while he carried her gifts upstairs. In the living room he dropped them onto the sofa, went straight for the door, then paused to glance back at her over his shoulder. With an edge of finality to his voice, he said, "Have a nice life."

On Monday, Laurel was downstairs early. She had already worked out menus for the next two weeks, had written her grocery order form, and was doing the payroll that wouldn't be needed until Friday, and all before seven A.M. At four she had given up all pretense at sleeping, dressed, and come down to the office. It was better to work and get something accomplished than to fight her torturous thoughts in the darkness of her bedroom.

Julia arrived around seven-thirty and breezed into the office humming a tune. "Morning," she said with a glowing smile. "Isn't it a gorgeous day?"

"I wouldn't know," Laurel said dourly. "I haven't been outside."

Julia was oblivious to Laurel's mood. She did a little dance in the center of the room, then leaned across the desk and challenged, "Guess what? I'll give you a hint. It's something wonderful."

"You found that rich relative with the million dollars," Laurel said without interest. She bowed her head over the check she had been writing.

"Better than that," Julia exclaimed. "Much better! Laurel, last night Clark proposed to me, and I accepted!"

At last she had her sister's full attention. Laurel dropped the pen with a clatter and jerked her head up, her green eyes wide. "Run that by me again!"

Julia giggled and perched on the edge of the desk. "You heard right. We had the most wonderful day yesterday in San Marcos. The weather was great, the kids were great, and everybody enjoyed it. And then last night, after we got back home, Clark asked me to marry him! Isn't it thrilling? I'm so happy, Laurel!"

Laurel rose from her chair, went around the desk, and hugged her sister. "I'm delighted for you both," she said, mustering up a smile. "I hope you'll have a wonderful life together."

"Thanks," Julia said tremulously. "There's only one problem, though," she added, turning to gaze out the window.

"Becky?" Laurel asked shrewdly.

Julia nodded, then turned back to look at her somberly. "I haven't told her yet, and, frankly, I'm dreading it. Yesterday she had a good time on our outing and she seemed to like Clark more than she ever had before, but"—she shook her head—"how she'll take this is anybody's guess."

"When are you going to tell her?"

Julia sighed. "Tonight. I asked Clark not to come tonight so that I can spend the evening alone with her."

"That's probably a good idea," Laurel said. Then she smiled encouragingly. "Let's be optimistic, Julia. Maybe by now Becky is used to the idea of Clark being around enough to be able to accept him as your husband. You said she seemed to like him better yesterday, and you know she adores David. It'll work out. You'll see!"

"I hope you're right," Julia said.

Three parents arrived simultaneously with their children just then, and a moment later Mrs. Ramirez came. Their busy day had begun and there was no more time for private discussion.

But a few minutes later, when Clark arrived bringing David, both sisters did take a moment out to speak to him. Laurel offered him her congratulations and gave him a peck on his cheek, and then she led David away so that the couple could have a minute alone together.

Laurel was sincerely happy for her sister, but after what had happened between herself and Stephen, it was hard to work up any real enthusiasm about anything. She felt dead inside, listless, and uninterested in what was going on around her. Today it was harder to smile at the children and listen to their prattle with any degree of honest attention.

By the end of the day, Laurel had a pounding headache, a combined result of not enough sleep, too many cups of coffee, and inner tension. Whenever she thought of Stephen, her entire body ached with the pain of loss.

Once she was upstairs in her apartment, she completely forgot about Julia and her affairs as thoughts about Stephen intruded with no distractions. She could picture him here in her apartment, cooking steaks; she could remember the romantic evening they had spent on the Paseo del Rio. But most of all her tortured mind conjured up the wonderful thrill of being in his arms, of his masterful lovemaking.

And she had thrown it all away. He had asked her to marry him, and she had refused. Was she being a fool, after all? Or had she indeed made the right decision?

Her mind was in too much of a turmoil for her to know. After making a sandwich, for which she had no appetite, and taking a bath, Laurel crawled wearily into bed, hoping that oblivion would overtake her and end the throbbing pain in her head.

Exhaustion had taken its toll, and she slept deeply. The alarm clock's buzzing did not even awaken her the next morning, but the insistent jangling of the telephone finally did.

She fumbled with the receiver before finally raising it to her ear. "Hello," she muttered sleepily.

"Laurel, it's me, Julia!" Her voice was shrill, unlike her usually well-modulated tones. .

Laurel raised herself up on one elbow, her eyes wide open now. "Yes, Julia. What is it?"

"It's Becky!" Julia cried. "She's gone!"

"Gone? What do you mean, gone? Gone where?"

"I don't know!" Julia's voice broke over a sob. "Last night I told her about Clark and me, and she was violently against it. She must have run away in the middle of the night! When I went into wake her for school this morning, she was gone! What am I going to do? If anything's happened to that child, I'll never forgive myself!"

"The first thing," Laurel ordered sternly, "is to calm down. You sound practically hysterical, and that won't solve anything. Now, have you called anyone else?"

"No."

"Call Clark," Laurel said decisively. "I'm sure he'll help you call her friends' houses. She might have gone to one of them. I'll call the sheriff."

"All right," Julia said in a slightly calmer voice. "And, Laurel, would you call Stephen? Becky likes him, and she might have decided to go to his place."

Reluctance spread through Laurel at the idea of contacting Stephen. But of course Julia had no idea of what had happened between them, and this certainly was no time to explain. "Yes," she answered tensely, "I'll call him."

Because she dreaded it, she decided to telephone Stephen first. Better to get it out of the way so that there was no time to dwell on it. Besides, it was possible that Becky had gone to him, though Laurel seriously doubted it. The last time she had run away from school, he had found her and returned her to her mother immediately, so it wasn't likely that she would willingly have gone to him.

Stephen answered the phone on the first ring. Laurel sucked in a deep breath and plunged in with her reason for calling before he could have time to hang up on her if he had a mind to do so. She explained the situation quickly and succinctly.

His voice was sharp and to the point when she had finished. "I haven't seen her, though I'll take a look out at the stables. She might be hiding there. Have you called the sheriff yet?"

"I was just about to," she replied.

"I'll do it for you," Stephen said briskly. "Can you tell me why she ran away this time?"

"Last night Julia told her that she and Clark are going to marry."

Laurel was afraid the news might precipitate fresh anger on his part about his own recent proposal of marriage. But, to her relief, he made no comment beyond "I see. Well, I'll call the sheriff and then go out to take a look. Keep in touch if you hear any news."

"Yes. Yes, I will." They rang off, and Laurel hurried to dress. In a short time it would be business as usual at the center, and somehow she would just have to manage to cope with the job at hand despite her anxiety.

She had just barely reached the foot of the stairs when the front doorbell rang. Laurel frowned, then quickly went to open it, though it was still too early for either children or the staff to be arriving.

Clark stood there with David, and his face was grim and pale. "Is it okay if I leave David here with you now?" he asked. "I'm going over to be with Julia."

"Of course," Laurel said instantly. "Come in, David."

David scooted past her, but Clark made no move to leave. "You know Julia just broke off with me," he said dully.

Laurel stared at him. "Broke your engagement?"

He nodded. "Not that I can blame her, I suppose. If Becky resents me this badly, I guess she really has no choice."

"I'm sorry, Clark," she answered in dismay. "I really am."

"Yes. So am I." Clark sighed heavily. "Well, I'd better get on over there. She sounds pretty upset, and she shouldn't be alone."

"Thanks," Laurel said. "I'd go myself, but with Julia out for the day, I'm needed here."

"I know. I'll call you if we get any news."

When the others arrived, Laurel plunged into the business of the morning routine, grateful that she was so occupied that it kept her mind off Becky. Today the four-year-olds were excited because Laurel and Pam, one of the staff assistants, were to take them on an outing to a nearby dairy farm and afterward to a picnic lunch in the city park. Carmen would pick up the kindergartners in Laurel's place.

At nine-thirty they set out for the ten-mile drive out of town. The five children, including David, were in high spirits in the back seats of Pam's station wagon, and while she drove Laurel led them in a rousing version of "Old MacDonald's Farm."

The tour was a success as far as the youngsters were concerned. Some of them had never seen a cow before in their lives. They were all wide-eyed with wonder to see the animals lined up in stalls and attached to milking machines while the farmer explained the operation to them in simple terms which they could easily understand.

"Do the brown cows give chocolate milk?" asked David.

Despite her private worries today, Laurel couldn't help but laugh at that, along with Pam and the farmer.

"No, son," the man said after a moment. "That's added later at the milk-processing plant where they put the milk into cartons."

David appeared disappointed at this bit of news, but on the drive back to town he soon forgot it as he and his classmates talked excitedly about the picnic ahead.

The children all carried their paper-bag lunches to a table in the park and chatted happily as they ate. Laurel made a determined effort to smile and laugh with them and to hide her impatience to get back to the center and a telephone so that she could learn whether or not Becky had been found.

Of course the youngsters had to be allowed to play for a little while after their lunch, and Laurel and Pam followed them to the playground. There were a merry-go-round, swings, slides, seesaws, and metal climbing bars. The children sampled them all, gleefully shouting and racing from one lure to the other.

And then it happened. Pam was seesawing with one child while Laurel pushed a girl named Ellie on the merry-go-round. Laurel heard a shriek and glanced up just in time to see David falling from the top of the climbing bars.

A cold terror iced her veins as she raced toward him, her heart thudding madly. She reached David's still form and choked back the scream that rose in her own throat as the other children crowded around, some crying, others too frightened to utter a sound. A pool of blood surrounded David's head, and then Laurel saw the reason. A jagged rock lay nearby, and it, too, was blood-splattered.

Gingerly Laurel felt beneath him, and the open gash that met her fingers sent new fear shivering through her.

"How bad is it?" Pam had joined her now and knelt on the ground beside her.

Laurel became aware of the other children huddling around them, and with supreme effort she managed to smile at them. "Remember the clean tablecloth in the car that we forgot to use on the picnic table? All of you go together and get it for me, will you, so that I can bind it around David's head."

"Is he gonna die?" asked Corey, David's best pal.

"Of course not!" Laurel said sharply. "But we do need to stop the bleeding, so all of you please go do as I ask."

The four children raced toward the station wagon, and as soon as they were out of hearing, Laurel spoke in a low voice to Pam. "It's a bad cut, and as much as he's bleeding, it must be very deep. See the park maintenance man over there pruning bushes? Go ask him where the nearest telephone is and call for an ambulance."

Without a word, Pam got to her feet and ran while Laurel turned her attention back to the unconscious child and checked his pulse. It was erratic, and Laurel caught her lower lip between her teeth in order to steady it.

The children returned with the tablecloth, and Laurel tore it into narrow strips and wrapped several strips around David's blood-matted hair. And then there was nothing more she could do except wait . . . and pray.

Three minutes later the ambulance arrived and David's small body was placed into it. "Need to get him to the hospital in San Antonio, ma'am," one of the men said to Laurel. "You his mother?"

"No. He's in my day-care center. Go ahead and take him to the hospital while I call his father. He'll meet you there."

The ambulance took off, and Laurel and Pam herded the children into the station wagon. As soon as they reached the center, Laurel ran to the office and dialed Julia's number. It was the hardest thing she had ever had to do in her life.

Julia's voice was eager as she answered. "Yes."

"Laurel here. Is Clark there with you?"

"Yes. Why? Have you heard anything about Becky?"

"You haven't found her yet?"

"No." Julia choked on a sob. "I hoped maybe you had."

"Julia." Laurel spoke clearly and precisely. "There's been an accident with David. He's on his way to the hospital in San Antonio."

"My God, no!" Julia exclaimed. "What happened?"

Laurel explained hurriedly. "I don't know how serious it is, but he was losing a lot of blood and he's unconscious. Tell Clark to get there as soon as possible, will you?"

"Certainly," Julia replied. "I'll go with him. I'm not doing anybody any good sitting here, and I'm sure if the sheriff has any news of Becky, he'd call you if he couldn't reach me."

"All right. Call me from the hospital, please, and let me know how David is."

"Right." Julia hung up almost before the word was out of her mouth.

The afternoon was endless. Neither the sheriff nor Julia telephoned, and Laurel was a nervous wreck by the end of the working day. David's accident and Becky's disappearance had cast a pall over everyone, and the staff had had their hands full reassuring the children that their friend David would be all right. In private, it was much more difficult to reassure each other as the telephone remained ominously silent.

When the children were gone for the day at last, Laurel promised the assistants she would telephone each of them when she had any news to pass along. Then she locked the doors behind them and went upstairs on leaden feet. Her chest was heavy with bottled-up emotions. She felt dreadfully responsible about David, and she knew she couldn't bear it if the child was seriously injured. She didn't dare think of the very worst possibility. And Becky . . . where could she be? She had been missing all day and who knew how many hours of last night. It didn't seem possible that a ten-year-old girl could hide herself so effectively.

She called the sheriff's office herself after she reached her apartment, but a bored voice told her there had been no news. Despondently Laurel cradled the receiver and went into the kitchen to make coffee, more for something to do than because she wanted it.

A half hour later, Stephen arrived. "Any word about Becky?" he asked as she let him inside.

"No. I just called the sheriff's office." Her lips trembled and tears stung her eyes.

"Hey," Stephen said softly, "don't give up. We'll find her. Surely one little girl alone can't go off too far."

"It's not just that," Laurel answered dully. "There was an accident today with David, and I feel so dreadful. Clark and Julia are at the hospital with him now. If anything happens to him, it'll be my fault! I should have been watching him more carefully while we were at the park!" The tears began to spill, totally unheeded by Laurel.

Stephen put his arms around her in a comforting gesture. "I can't believe that," he said soothingly. "Come sit down and tell me." He led her to the sofa.

A bit incoherently, Laurel explained. When she had finished, he said, "You can't blame yourself for what was an accident, Laurel. Things just happen sometimes, no matter how carefully you watch a child. If you'd been standing a foot away from him, it's not likely you could have stopped it from happening. Now, let me make you some coffee, and then I'll call the hospital and page Julia. They ought to have some news by now."

"There's coffee already made," Laurel told him, "but I forgot to drink it."

Stephen went into the kitchen and returned shortly, carrying two steaming mugs. "I put a little brandy in yours," he told her. "You need the tranquilizing effect of it."

Laurel obediently sipped at the fiery black liquid and brushed at the tears that kept forming in her eyes. "Julia even broke her engagement to Clark today because of Becky," she said unsteadily. "This has been the most horrid day. There hasn't been a single bright spot in it."

The telephone jangled then, causing Laurel to jump, and she lifted her anxious eyes to Stephen's face.

"I'll get it," he said quietly, getting to his feet.

Laurel listened avidly as he spoke, but she heard little because he spoke in a low tone. But when he returned to her a minute later, a tiny smile lit his face. "You have your one bright spot," he said. "David's doing okay. He has a concussion, lost quite a bit of blood, and had to have a lot of stitches. But he'll be as good as new in a few days."

"Is he conscious?"

"In and out, mostly out because of the painkillers they've given him. Clark is going to stay the night with him, and you and I are going to pick up Julia and bring her home."

Laurel nodded. "Did you tell her there was nothing on Becky?"

Stephen resumed his seat beside her. "Yes," he answered. "She asked if anyone had thought to search along the river. She says Becky likes to go there for walks."

They both looked at each other with a mutual flash of illumination.

"The cabin!" Stephen said.

"Of course!" Laurel exclaimed. "She's always been fascinated with it! It's the perfect place!"

They drove to the ranch, where they exchanged the Buick for Stephen's pickup truck. Then they rode in the waning afternoon light across the rough ranch tracks toward the river.

They entered the dimness of the cabin together, and there they found her. Becky, clad in jeans and a pink T-shirt, was curled up in a little ball on the lower bunk bed, sound asleep. Laurel glanced up at Stephen, and they smiled at each other.

"Seems a shame to wake her," he whispered.

"I know," Laurel agreed in a soft voice. "But we must so we can get to San Antonio and let Julia see that she's safe." She went toward the bed, paused, and noticed the dried tear streaks on her niece's face. A lump rose in her throat before she stooped to kiss the child's forehead. "Becky," she said gently. "Wake up, honey."

Becky stirred and slowly opened her eyes. Then she flipped over onto her back and stared up at them. "What're you doin' here?" she mumbled.

Laurel smiled. "A better question is what are *you* doing here?"

Becky swung her legs off the bed and got to her feet. "I'm not going home," she said defiantly. "That's why you're here, isn't it?"

"Do you have any idea how frightened you've made your mother?" Stephen asked in a stern voice. "Not to mention the rest of us!"

"I don't care," Becky said. She stared at the floor. "I'm not going back."

"You certainly can't stay here," Laurel pointed out.

Becky did not respond, and Laurel sat down on the edge of the bunk bed and pulled the child down beside her. "Do you really hate Clark that much?" she asked softly.

Tears welled in Becky's eyes. "He's taking Mom away from me," she sobbed. "Now she'll leave me just like Daddy did! Laurel"—suddenly she threw herself into her aunt's arms and buried her face against her breasts—"nobody wants me anymore. Nobody loves me anymore!"

In shock, Laurel met Stephen's concerned gaze above her. "That's not true, honey," she said urgently. "Your mother loves you very much and she isn't about to leave you. She'll always want you with her."

Becky drew back slightly and looked at her in surprise. "Are you sure?"

Stephen knelt on one knee beside them and brushed Becky's hair away from her face, tenderly tucking it behind one ear. His smile was warm and held a hint of teasing. "You're about the silliest smart girl I ever met," he told her. "Laurel's right, you know. Your mother loves you more than anyone in the whole world, and she would never want to lose you. But, sweetheart, there are different sorts of love, and your mother loves Clark, too. He wants to love you as well, but, let's be honest . . . you haven't exactly made it easy for him to do that, now, have you?"

Becky shook her head and dashed the tears from her face with the back of her hand. "I guess not," she admitted.

"Your mother and Clark love each other and they want to be happy together," Laurel added. "But part of their happiness is to include you and David in that love as a family."

"You mean David and I will be brother and sister?"

Laurel nodded, seeing by her expression that the idea appealed to Becky.

"Tell me the truth," Stephen said. "Clark's not such a bad guy, is he?"

Becky shook her head. "No. Sometimes he's real nice and kind of fun. But I thought—"

"You thought all wrong, Miss Muddlehead," Stephen interrupted with a smile. "Come on, we've got to go."

On the drive to San Antonio they told Becky about David's accident, and her face went pale. "He's gonna be okay, isn't he?"

Stephen nodded. "They say he'll be fine in a few days. And once he's home from the hospital, I imagine he's going to need a big sister to help keep him entertained until he's completely well again."

"I can do it," Becky said forcefully. "I made this puppet that he likes and I tell him stories about it."

At the hospital, Laurel remained with Becky in

the lobby while Stephen went to fetch Julia. A few minutes later she and Clark both came, and there was a tearful reunion between mother and daughter.

Clark went directly to Laurel, reassuring her again that David would be all right, and then he added, "Stephen told me why Becky ran away. I can't believe she really thought I was taking her mother away from her. Poor baby! No wonder she was so upset." A moment later he walked purposefully toward her, bent, and said something in her ear. Then the two walked outside into the night air.

When they returned about ten minutes later, they were hand in hand and both their faces were wreathed in broad smiles.

"Clark loves me, Mom!" Becky announced with an air of importance. "And he said he's always wanted a daughter just like me!"

"You don't say?" Julia smiled through a haze of fresh tears.

"Yes," Clark agreed, "but one thing I don't want is for my daughter to *ever* play hooky from school or run away from home again. She's promised me faithfully that she won't. Right, Becky?"

Becky nodded. "Right." Suddenly she giggled. "Just wait till I tell all the kids at school that you're going to be my new daddy! They won't believe it!"

Clark laughed indulgently. Then, putting one arm around the child, he put the other around her mother and drew them both close to him. The three of them smiled at one another.

Laurel was glad for them, but when her own gaze happened to meet Stephen's, her heart skipped a beat and she turned quickly away. Without a word he was reminding her of the happiness they might have shared together had she not tossed it away on the altar of suspicion and distrust.

Chapter Fifteen

"Care for another piece of chicken?"

Laurel came out of the reverie she had fallen into and returned her attention to the present. "No, thank you, Clark." She smiled. "Everything was delicious. Julia is going to marry a great cook, I can see that."

The three of them were seated around the picnic table on Clark's patio. It was a Sunday afternoon in late May, and Clark had barbecued their dinner. On the table were the remains of chicken and sausage, a couple of ears of corn wrapped in foil, half a bowl of pinto beans, and a bit of potato salad. The children had finished eating earlier and had already left the table. In the distance, Laurel could see Becky and David inspecting the new barn that was in the first stages of being erected.

Major changes had entered Julia's and Becky's lives this past month. The wedding was set for the end of June, and now Becky was as eager for the big event as she had previously been against it. She was finishing her last few weeks of the school year with top grades, and she enjoyed bragging to her friends that Clark was shortly to become her new father. He, too, seemed to dote on her, now that all their misunderstandings were in the past. He had bought her some ducks and rabbits, all of which were housed on his property, since several acres surrounded his house. From Julia, Laurel had learned that Clark had even approached Stephen about purchasing Becky's favorite mare. Stephen had refused to sell it, but instead he promised it to Becky as her own "special" wedding gift. Hence the need for Clark to finish building the new barn.

David had recovered from his injury with lightning speed and was once again his same sweet self. He followed Becky around as though she were the original Pied Piper, and he seemed pleased to know that they would soon become brother and sister. As far as Julia herself was concerned, Laurel had never seen her happier.

"Oh, Laurel," Julia said suddenly, "I almost forgot." She opened her purse, extracted a check, and offered it to her sister. "In Friday's mail was a large check from Bert covering the past two months of his child support."

"So why are you giving this much to me?" Laurel asked when she glanced at the check.

"I'm paying off my loan from you so from now on I'll only owe Stephen. Besides, things are looking so much better for us at the center that I can easily afford it."

"You just hired two new assistants, I understand," Clark said to Laurel.

She nodded. "Yes. We've had an influx of new children the past few weeks since that new clothing factory opened up and a lot of women went to work. Finally, beginning next month, Julia and I will each be drawing salaries of our own."

"I hope all this additional responsibility won't be too hard on you, what with our wedding coming up and Julia being away on our honeymoon. Not to mention your having Becky to stay with you while we're gone," Clark said with concern. "I have the feeling we might overload your circuits by taking such base advantage of your good nature."

Laurel laughed. "I can cope for those two weeks," she assured him. "I'm certain we'll get along just fine. You know I don't mind having Becky with me in the least. I will admit it might be a little more than I could handle if I were keeping David all that time, too, but since your mother-in-law is going to take care of him, I don't see any problems. Have you decided yet where you'll go?"

Julia nodded and said with animation, "Acapulco. Doesn't that sound romantic?"

"Terrific," Laurel agreed. "You ought to have a wonderful time and come home with gorgeous tans." She got to her feet. "I think I'll walk down to the barn and join the kids. I'll be back in a few minutes to help you carry in the food and clear the table."

Laurel loved her sister very much, and daily she was growing more fond of the man who would soon become her brother-in-law, but, all the same, she could only take so much of their company at a time these days. Their flowing happiness and their total absorption in themselves and their plans for their future were difficult for her to watch. It pointed up so sharply her own abject despair.

As the days passed, her depression grew, and Laurel found it harder and harder to mask her unhappiness. Ordinarily, Julia was a rather observant person. Laurel could only suppose that her present emotions had escaped Julia's notice because she was so engrossed in her own joy that she simply didn't really see anyone else these days.

Laurel had not seen Stephen once in more than two weeks. The last time had been the day they had found Becky hiding away in his cabin. But whenever she was in the town shopping or running errands, unconsciously she looked about, in constant dread that she might see his tall form walking down a sidewalk. She lived in daily fear that she would accidentally bump into him and once again be subjected to the cold, brittle hardness of his gaze.

The nights were the worst. Alone and in bed,

unable to sleep, her traitorous mind remembered the passion of his kisses, the tender way he would smile at her, the feel of his hands expertly stroking her body to a fevered pitch, the pleasure she had taken in running her fingers through his hair or resting her head on his broad, firm chest. The thoughts brought an agonizing sense of loss, and she wondered, for perhaps the thousandth time, whether she had made a dreadful mistake in refusing to marry him. Maybe she had been an idiot and put too much emphasis on love. Maybe it wasn't so important to others as it seemed to her. Maybe there was a chance at happiness in a marriage where all the love was one-sided, so long as the other partner was sexually satisfied. She didn't know. She had no way of knowing, and, anyway, it didn't matter. Very plainly, Stephen had told her that his offer of marriage had been withdrawn. Even if she went to him now and told him she had changed her mind, it wasn't likely that he would change his as well. Stephen could be a hard man, and Laurel knew she would be a real fool to expect him to forgive her and take her back now.

Laurel began to toy with the idea of leaving Tierra Nueva and returning to Boston. She was sure she could easily find a job there, maybe even in the same center where she had worked before. Now that their center here was bringing in a profit, Julia might be interested in buying out her share. She could make the terms stretch over a long period to make it easy for her. Once she was married, Julia wouldn't feel the need for Laurel's presence or support so strongly, and she would hardly be missed. As for herself, she had lost all enthusiasm for small-town living. Staying meant the certainty of seeing Stephen from time to time, and Laurel couldn't envision a time when that prospect would ever be easy.

One afternoon in early June, that certainty was tested and proven for her, had she needed any proof. Laurel was in the office talking on the phone to a plumber about Carmen's clogged kitchen drain when the door opened and Stephen walked inside, accompanied by Becky.

"I'll have someone out there this afternoon, Miss Patterson," the plumber was saying.

Laurel was so shocked at seeing Stephen that for a minute she lost the thread of her conversation.

"Miss Patterson?" The voice on the line sounded puzzled.

"What? Oh, yes, that will be fine. Thank you very much." Her hand went limp as she cradled the receiver and got to her feet, an inquiring expression on her face.

"Hi, Laurel," Becky said in her offhanded manner. "I met Stephen over near the park, and he invited me to go with him to the feed store for supplies, then out to the ranch to ride Daisy. We came to ask Mom."

"I see," Laurel responded slowly. She felt dimwitted, unable to think clearly, while her senses clamored riotously at the sight of the man who stood on the opposite side of the room. "I think your mother is on the sun porch," she told Becky. "Or in the kitchen with Carmen."

"Okay." Becky glanced up at Stephen. "Be back in a minute," she told him before she dashed from the room.

After she was gone, there was a long, awkward silence as Laurel and Stephen gazed at each other. She thought he looked unwell as her searching eyes noted his haggard face. It was thinner than she remembered, and his dark eyes were sunken, appearing like two burning coals set deep in an otherwise colorless face. Concern for him tightened her chest, but she did not dare to let him see.

"How have you been?" he asked finally.

"Oh, fine. Fine." Laurel clasped her trembling hands behind her. "And you?"

He nodded. "The same." Stephen paused, and there was another uncomfortable silence between them before he added, "How are the wedding plans moving along?"

"Very well. It's only two weeks away, you know."

Stephen's brows lowered over the impenetrable depths of his eyes. "How do you feel about it?" he asked. "Your sister's marriage?"

Laurel shrugged and lowered her gaze to the desk that was a massive physical barrier dividing them like the invisible emotional one that separated them. "I'm delighted about it, naturally," she replied.

"Naturally?" Stephen's voice was sardonic. "Coming from a lady whose byword is independence, that's laughable."

"Please," she begged in a suddenly shaken voice, "don't. This is neither the time nor the place for another argument."

"You're absolutely right," Stephen said coolly. "And I have no intention of arguing with you about anything, ever again. I was merely making an observation, that's all." Conversationally he went on, "Is Julia planning to continue running the center after her marriage?"

"Yes, she is. I'm thinking about offering her the chance to buy out my part." The instant she said it, Laurel could have bitten off her tongue. The idea had been much in her mind lately, but so far she had not yet broached the subject with Julia. She could not imagine what had caused her to say it to Stephen.

He picked up on it at once. "You're going to sell out?" he asked. "Why?"

Laurel shrugged her shoulders lightly. "I'm only thinking about it so far. But I'm a bit tired of small-town living. I miss Boston and I'd like to go back. Now that Julia's going to marry, there doesn't seem to be much reason to hold me here."

"I can't imagine any reason whatsoever to hold you here," Stephen commented in a caustic voice. A moment later a carefully bland expression came on his face as Becky returned.

"Mom says I can go as long as I'm home by six," she told him.

Stephen smiled down at her affectionately. "No problem," he said. "We'll get you home in plenty of time." Briefly his eyes went to Laurel's face again and he inclined his head toward her in a nod.

The following Sunday, Laurel felt restless and bored. Julia had called that morning, inviting her to dinner at her house, but she had made an excuse not to go, saying she had mending to do. Her mending involved sewing one button back on one of her blouses, which took exactly five minutes of her time. But the truth was that she was in no mood to be around anybody, least of all the lovebirds who constantly prefaced every sentence to each other with a "darling" or a "sweetheart." Her own glum disposition would not add anything positive to their day, and she felt unequal to the task of pretending to be cheerful and happy for their sakes.

Still, she was suffering from a closed-in feeling today, and finally, by midafternoon, she could not bear to be cooped up in the confines of the apartment a minute longer. Not bothering to change from her white shorts and yellow pullover top, she grabbed her car keys and went downstairs.

The sky was a leaden gray today, the air very still and hot. It was bound to rain soon, and Laurel hoped that when it did, it would cool things off. Already, since leaving the cool air conditioning of her living room, she felt sticky, both from the heavy humidity and from perspiration.

At first she drove aimlessly, going through the emptied, quiet business streets of downtown. She drove past the courthouse square, which was ablaze with bright summer flowers, and past stately old houses with giant pecan trees shading their yards. Here and there a mimosa tree added a bold splash of pink against dark green foliage.

After a time, without even realizing that she was doing it, she headed the car toward the river.

Somehow today she needed the solitude and peacefulness that it offered to a troubled spirit.

She parked the car in her usual spot, rolled up the windows of the car as a precaution against possible rain, then pocketed the keys and set off walking along the bank.

In the strange gray light of the day the leaves of the trees and the grass were a vivid, almost unreal shade of green, but the water itself was dark, an angrier gray than the sky above. It seemed menacing and threatening, not at all the friendly river it had seemed on other days. Still, somehow its mood matched her own, its restless, disturbed disposition a reflection of her own disquiet.

She needed to make her decision about whether to go away or not. Until she had finally made up her own mind, she could not speak to Julia about taking over the center. Laurel knew that if she left here, she would be merely running away from the possibility of seeing Stephen again, but she would never be able to run away from her love for him. That would go with her wherever she went. And though she wanted to get away from his vicinity, in all honesty she had little desire to return to Boston. She still had a few old friends there, of course, but they had naturally drawn apart after she had moved to Texas, and even if the friendships were close, it would mean she would have no family there. Julia and Becky would remain here, and she would miss them dreadfully.

Finally the clouds above broke open and it began to drizzle. Laurel welcomed the cool drops that landed on her, but otherwise she ignored the rain as she plodded onward. Now and then she paused to gaze at the dark water, but mostly she was unaware of her surroundings as she concentrated upon her thoughts.

After a while she became aware that she was now on the opposite side of the river that skirted Stephen's property, and she wondered fleetingly what he was doing on this gloomy Sunday afternoon. But then a rustling in the underbrush caught her attention, and she glanced away from the river in time to see the white powder puff of a rabbit's tail vanishing beneath a bush.

She had gone perhaps another ten yards' distance when a loud, thundering noise violated the heavy silence of the afternoon. Only it had not been thunder. It had sounded like a gunshot!

Laurel froze in sudden fear and her heart leaped to her throat, wildly pounding. Was someone shooting at her or perhaps at some animal? The sound had seemed to come from the opposite bank, on Stephen's land, just beyond the thicket along the fence.

As she stood listening intently, she caught another sound . . . that of a groan, a human groan! *My God*, she thought in panic, *someone's been shot!*

Her first instinct was to run, to get away from this spot, and she even managed to lift one foot and pivot toward the direction from which she had come. But in the next instant she knew that she could not. That groan had meant that someone was hurt, and she could not just turn tail and run away like a yellow coward, even though that was what she ached to do. Whoever had been shot must need help, and out here in this lonely area help was unlikely to come from anyone save herself!

With reluctance and trepidation Laurel turned back, ran the few yards to the stepping-stones in the river, and forced herself to cross them. Then she slipped through the fence and moved through the bushes as quietly and cautiously as she could.

When she cleared them, she remained close enough to duck back if necessary, and then she glanced off to her left, which would be where the shot had been fired. Her eyes widened in shock and dismay as she saw Stephen on the ground, up on one knee, struggling to get to his feet.

All fear of an unknown person brandishing a gun vanished in this new fear for Stephen. Her mouth was dry with terror as she raced toward him and her eyes took in the fact that his shirt was torn and his left shoulder was bleeding.

"Wait," she cried. "Let me help you! You might injure yourself more! Oh, dear God, Stephen . . . who shot you?" By then she had drawn even with him, and she reached out her hands to steady him.

Stephen's head jerked up in surprise and he stared blankly at her. "Where did you come from?" He didn't seem particularly glad to see her, and he pulled his arm from her grasp as he steadied himself on his feet.

"I was walking on the other side of the river and I heard a shot," she gasped. "Stephen, who tried to kill you?" She glanced around as though she might spot the party responsible.

Stephen laughed harshly, and it was not a pleasant sound. "Nobody tried to kill me. I was checking fence lines, and I was carrying my rifle in case I met up with a coyote that's been after some of my animals. I tripped over an exposed root in the ground and fell. When I did, the rifle went off." He bent and reached behind him, pulling the gun from beneath a bush where it had landed.

It took Laurel a moment for his explanation to sink it. Slowly the tension drained from her, leaving her limp and weak with reaction.

"Do you realize you scared me to death?" she snapped. Now she was trembling, completely oblivious to the fact that it had suddenly begun to rain in earnest.

"I apologize," he said in a mocking tone. "I'll try not to have any more accidents when you're nearby. Anyway, who asked you to be concerned about me?"

"And you think I wouldn't be, believing someone was shooting at you?" she asked in a sudden temper.

"I wouldn't have thought you'd be concerned one way or another," he threw back in a nasty tone.

Laurel bit her lower lip in an effort to steady it and to hold back more harsh words. "Really," she said after a minute, "it's ridiculous for us to stand here arguing."

"I agree," he said curtly. "Particularly since we're getting drenched in the process, and my rifle is going to be ruined, as well."

"You need to take care of that shoulder," Laurel said anxiously. "It's still bleeding. Where's your truck so that we can get you home?"

"It's parked about half a mile back, and don't worry about my shoulder," he said unappreciatively. "It'll mend." Lightning flashed across the sky, followed almost immediately by an overhead clap of thunder. "We'd better get to the cabin for shelter," he added as the rumbling died away. "Looks like we're in for a real storm."

Five minutes later they entered the damp darkness of the cabin, and by the time they did, Laurel was shivering with cold.

Stephen knelt in front of the fireplace and, after a little work, coaxed a blaze to the logs. Laurel knelt beside him, holding her hands out to the welcome warmth of the flames, and then she turned to him. "Let me take a good look at that shoulder now."

Miraculously, Stephen didn't argue, but he winced as she pulled the bloody torn cloth from the wound. There was a ragged gouge across his shoulder, but it didn't look deep. Laurel sighed with relief. "It's not deep and the bleeding has almost stopped," she told him. "But it needs an antiseptic."

"Left cupboard above the counter," he said tersely. "Should be some bandages there, too."

Laurel found the supplies, and when she returned, Stephen had pulled off his shirt. His skin gleamed like living gold in the firelight, and the sight of him, partially naked, warmed her senses.

With determination she thrust aside her sharp physical awareness of him as she concentrated on her task. She cleaned the wound with the antiseptic, then covered it with a bandage.

When she had finished taping the last adhesive

strip across the gauze, Laurel stood up, went across
to the cupboard, and stored away the supplies. Her
shivering had begun again, and her wet hair, plas-
tered against her scalp and neck, dripped water
down her shoulders and back.

She lifted a hand to gather her hair into it and
squeeze out the excess moisture. As she did so she
half turned and discovered Stephen's eyes upon
her.

"We really," he said flatly, "should get out of
these wet clothes. Keeping them on is a good way to
catch a chill."

Color flared in Laurel's face, and she turned away
from him so that he could not see.

A mocking laugh came from behind her. "It's a bit
absurd for you to be acting so missish," he grated
out. "After all, I *have* seen your body before."

Hot tears scalded her eyes, and she blinked hard
to keep them from spilling. Stephen was being
deliberately offensive, and there was nothing she
could do to stop him. Stumbling, she went to the
window and gazed out. If the storm had abated even
slightly, she told herself, she would leave.

But even as she reached it, lightning flashed, for a
brief instant lighting up the room, and then thunder
roared. The rain was coming down in sheets and the
wind had picked up so that it was blowing it at a
sideways slant.

She almost jumped when Stephen spoke just
behind her—she had no idea he had left his position
by the fire. "I hope you do leave Tierra Nueva
soon," he said in the bitterest voice she had ever
heard, "because I don't know how much more
torture I can take."

Laurel whirled around and found her face just
inches from his. "Torture?" she gasped. "What
torture?"

"The torture," he said grimly, "of seeing you and
knowing that you don't want me to touch you. Of
being around you and knowing I don't have the right

to possess you, to call you mine. The torture of loving you and wanting to marry you while all you want out of life is to keep your damned independence!"

As abruptly as he had come near her, Stephen turned and put as much space between them as the cabin allowed. He returned to the fireplace and stared down into it.

For a long moment Laurel stood rooted when he had left her. She gazed in awe at his tense back. Very slowly joy spread through her veins, warming her despite the fact that she was still dripping wet. Stephen had said he loved her! Never mind what else he had said. Those precious words remained. He *had* said them! She hadn't imagined it.

Her throat felt tight and she had to swallow hard over the lump that was lodged there before she finally felt capable of speaking. Then she moved slowly across the floor until she stood beside him. Even then, she could not quite bring herself to look into his face, so, following his example, she stared down into the leaping flames of the fire.

"How long?" she finally asked.

She felt, rather than saw, him look at her before he barked, "How long what?"

"How . . . how long have you loved me?"

Stephen made an impatient motion and placed both hands on his hips. "As if you didn't know!"

"I don't," she insisted. "This is the first time I've heard of it. How long, Stephen?"

"Just about since the day I found you walking along the road," he snapped in exasperation. "Does it matter?"

"Yes," she said softly. "Tremendously." She laughed shakily and turned to him. "I haven't wanted my 'damned independence' for a long time now. All I've wanted is you."

"Sure." A bitter twist curled his lips. "That's why you figuratively slapped me in the face when I proposed."

"I love you, Stephen," she said now. "But I didn't think you loved me. That's why I said no."

He withdrew his gaze from the fire and looked at her with disbelief. "That's ridiculous," he said flatly. "You *had* to know. I showed you in every way possible."

"But you never said it," she pointed out gently, "so I didn't know. I knew I loved you, but I didn't believe our marriage could endure if you didn't feel that way, too. And then Annette called and I knew you were promising to go to her later that day and I . . . I knew I couldn't share you like that."

Stephen stared at her long and hard, his dark gaze searching her face. "She called," he said at last, "because her father had suffered another heart attack and she needed an old friend's support. That's all." Suddenly a tiny smile softened his lips, and that was all the encouragement Laurel needed. She flung herself against him, and his uninjured arm curled tightly around her. "You idiot," he whispered hoarsely. "You stupid little idiot! Do you have any idea of the pain you've put me through?"

"I'm sorry," she answered contritely. "But I've suffered, too."

His head bent toward her and his mouth took possession of hers with the rough force of a man who has been starving. Laurel's parted beneath the pressure of his, equally hungry for the nectar of his kiss. One arm went around his shoulder as her other hand rested against the furry hair on his chest. Liquid fire raced through her veins as heady passions once more held her in their sway.

After an endless time, Stephen lifted his head, and the glow of love in his eyes told her in addition to his words that it was true, that she wasn't dreaming.

"Don't ever doubt my love or hurt me again, darling," he said huskily. "I can't bear it if you ever leave me again."

"I promise," she whispered. "Because if I did, I'd only be hurting myself the most." She laughed raggedly. "I . . . all along I thought it was Annette that you really loved, even though you seemed to want me, too. But her things were in your house, and you seemed so fond of her."

Stephen's eyes lit with amusement. "Were you jealous?"

"Desperately."

"Good," he said unfeelingly. "You deserved it for being so silly." He sighed. "Annette and I have been friends all our lives. Our fathers were good friends. She's always been like a sister to me, nothing more. She's currently involved in an affair with a married man, and that, coupled with her father's illness, keeps her unhappy. She comes to me for cheering up, for someone she can talk to about her problems. The reason her things are at my house is that she and her father used to visit me overnight quite frequently before his illness. I'll admit I've never been a saint, Laurel. I'm a man, after all. There have been plenty of women in my life. But I swear to you, since the day I met you, there's been no other."

"I see." Laurel was quiet, trying to digest what he had just told her.

"I, on the other hand," he said in a vibrant, strong voice, "had a lot more reason to be jealous of Dan, not to mention that handsome ex-fiancé of yours. I was sure he had persuaded you to go back to Boston to him."

Laurel laughed and lovingly traced her fingers along his jaw and chin. "Now you're being ridiculous," she informed him. "I was only going to leave here because I didn't think I could stand seeing you and not being with you."

"You'd better make up your mind that from now on you'll always be with me. Forever, darling."

"Forever," she seconded solemnly.

With Stephen's arm still firmly around her waist,

they moved to the window and looked out. The storm had abated. Now there was only a fine silver mist falling.

Stephen smiled down at Laurel. "We met on a misty day, remember? And now it's misting again." He drew her close and kissed her forehead as she leaned against him. "But our future together is going to be golden. No more gloomy days for us."

"Umm," she murmured with contentment. "Golden. I like that."

"Later, we'll go to the house and I'll give you your engagement ring."

Laurel moved so that she could look up into his face. "You already have it?" she asked in astonishment.

Stephen nodded. "I had planned to give it to you for your birthday. I forgot about it that night because of other, more exciting matters." He grinned as she blushed. "But then the next morning you turned me down flat. Very rudely, too."

"I'm sorry," she said again.

If you enjoyed
this book...

...you will enjoy a Special Edition Book Club membership even more.

It will bring you each new title, as soon as it is published every month, delivered right to your door.

15-Day Free Trial Offer

We will send you 6 new Silhouette Special Editions to keep for 15 days absolutely free! If you decide not to keep them, send them back to us, you pay nothing. But if you enjoy them as much as we think you will, keep them and pay the invoice enclosed with your trial shipment. You will then automatically become a member of the Special Edition Book Club and receive 6 more romances every month. There is no minimum number of books to buy and you can cancel at any time.

Coming Next Month

Bitter Victory by Patti Beckman

She had left him years ago, but when Slade
appeared in her office, Veronica still felt the
burning desire and hatred that had driven her to
leave her husband. Could their love
mend their differences?

Eye Of The Hurricane by Sarah Keene

There were two sides to Miranda: the practical
miss, and the daring, wild dreamer. And in Jake
she found a searing passion that would weld the
two together.

Dangerous Magic by Stephanie James

Elissa fought her way up the corporate ladder and
into Wade's arms. Her sultry innocence intrigued
him, and his desire for her was overwhelming.

Silhouette Special Edition

Coming Next Month

Mayan Moon by Eleni Carr

Beneath the Mexican moon, beside the Sacred Well of Souls, Antonio Ferrara, a man of fierce Mayan pride, took Rhea on a journey that encompassed the ages.

So Many Tomorrows by Nancy John

Having been mistaken in her first marriage, Shelley wasn't thinking of love—until Jason found her and taught her the meaning of life, and of a love that would last forever.

A Woman's Place by Lucy Hamilton

Anna's residency under Dr. Lew Coleman was difficult—especially when she saw the answer to all her hidden desires and dreams in his compelling gaze.

Look for More Special Editions from
Janet Dailey and Brooke Hastings,
and a New Novel from
Linda Shaw in Future Months.

Silhouette Special Edition

MORE ROMANCE FOR
A SPECIAL WAY TO RELAX